TAKING STOCK

Also by Monte Dutton

Rebel with a Cause:
A Season with NASCAR Star Tony Stewart

At Speed: *Up Close and Personal with the
People, Places, and Fans of NASCAR*

TAKING STOCK
Life in NASCAR's Fast Lane

Edited by
MONTE DUTTON

Brassey's, Inc.

WASHINGTON, D.C.

Library of Congress Cataloging-in-Publication Data

Taking stock : life in NASCAR's fast lane / edited by Monte Dutton.—
1st ed.
p. cm.
Includes index.
ISBN 1-57488-559-6 (alk. paper)
1. Stock car racing—United States.   2. NASCAR (Association).
I. Dutton, Monte.

GV1029.9.S74 T35 2002
796.72—dc21
2002014690

Printed in the United States of America on acid-free paper that meets the American National Standards Institute Z39-48 Standard.

Brassey's, Inc.
22841 Quicksilver Drive
Dulles, Virginia 20166

First Edition

10   9   8   7   6   5   4   3   2   1

CONTENTS

PHOTOGRAPHS

FOREWORD

I never will forget what my dad told me years ago when I informed him I had taken a job as a sportswriter.

"Do you get paid for that?" he asked.

"Of course," I replied.

"I don't know why," he said. "It doesn't sound very much like work to me."

Those who make their livings painting pictures of games with nouns, pronouns, commas, and the like would strongly disagree.

Theirs is an art form, although arguably not the same as ballet, piano, opera, classical music, or painting.

Nonetheless, it is art, and the stories you will read in this book are some of the best you will read regarding NASCAR racing.

These stories come off the pages at high speed and capture the raw essence of stock car racing today.

Stock car racing is a sport all Americans can relate to, because everyone, at one time or another, drives a car. And racing fans honestly believe they can drive a car just as fast, and just as well, as any of the true NASCAR heroes, drivers like Jeff Gordon, Dale Earnhardt, Richard Petty, Darrell Waltrip, David Pearson, and Cale Yarborough, who are some of the athletes featured on the following pages.

This truly is an awesome collection of stories by some of motorsports' most gifted writers.

Kenny Bruce, Monte Dutton, Mike Hembree, Jim McLaurin, Jeff Owens, David Poole, Thomas Pope, and lastly, Larry Woody, contributed three stories each in this process. (I list them in alphabetical order so there won't be any arguments over who should have been mentioned first. You could probably draw agreement within the group that Woody, a good ol' boy from Nashville, would be considered the reigning Dean of American Motorsports Writers.)

Actually, the mere fact that Larry Woody is still living, not to mention writing, is good news, because Larry had to have been one of the first to say, "If I had known I was going to live this long, I would have taken better care of myself."

Additional good news is that this book is going to read like a fast-moving John Grisham novel—a front-to-back, get-out-of-my-face, leave-me-alone-I'm-reading, one-trip-to-the-bathroom, my-legs-are-asleep-and-so-is-my-ass-but-I-just-can't-put-this-book-down book.

Monte Dutton, for example, writes about Darlington with unabashed and unbridled favoritism because it is his favorite track. Jim McLaurin's grits-and-groceries style is well worth reading, and Woody has been writing NASCAR stories long enough to know a Hudson Hornet was a stock car driven to victory by some of NASCAR's legendary pioneers. (Woody and I also remember Studebakers, Ramblers, Matadors, and other makes that were racing in NASCAR's dinosaur age.)

David Poole, president of the National Motorsports Press Association, always manages to put things in a different perspective, and Mike Hembree, for his writing efforts, has as many trophies in his showcase as Jeff Gordon has in his.

Thomas Pope is a legend in eastern North Carolina circles, almost as famous for his writing as the Wright Brothers are for their flying adventures. Kenny Bruce and Jeff Owens are the youngsters in this eightsome, but their descriptions and opinions on NASCAR Winston Cup activities are read by thousands each week.

If you combined the books and writing awards this talented group has amassed and then compared their achievements to the greatest drivers in history, you'd be talking about Fireball Roberts, Junior Johnson, David Pearson, Bobby Allison, Fred Lorenzen, Richard Petty, the late Dale Earnhardt, and Jeff Gordon.

That's a powerful lineup.

Just like the guys they write about, these writers take it to the next level.

Jim Hunter
NASCAR vice president of
corporate communications
June 12, 2002

AND, NOW, FOR SOMEONE COMPLETELY DIFFERENT

Jeff Gordon was never your typical stock car racer. In his own quiet way, he has changed the sport forever and brought NASCAR to a new generation of fans.

By Monte Dutton

The story of Jeff Gordon has no parallel in stock car racing history. In fact, to find a similarity, one almost has to resort to fiction . . . comic book fiction.

Jeffrey Michael Gordon was born in Vallejo, California, on August 4, 1971. Early in his life, his stepfather, John Bickford, noticed that the boy had a natural aptitude for racing. It didn't matter what: tricycles, bicycles, "Big Wheels," whatever. Bickford dedicated his life to encouraging his stepson to become a racer and providing for his career. The kid proved exceptional in whatever vehicle in which he decided to compete. By age five, he was racing go-karts. Shortly afterward, he began racing quarter-midgets, winning national championships in 1979 (at age eight) and 1981. By his midteens, the family moved to Pittsboro, Indiana, because that state, rich in racing heritage, would allow Gordon to race at an age younger than what was allowed by California regulations.

By age 16, Gordon was a driver of championship caliber in sprint and midget cars. While other kids played jayvee soccer, Gordon found a kind of cult renown on the "Thursday Night Thunder" telecasts of United States Auto Club (USAC) events on ESPN, the cable sports network. He was a sensation, a phenom . . . and all the while he looked like a kid who played jayvee soccer.

While his stepson rode the fast track to open-wheel racing fame, Bickford wisely noticed that stock car racing was becoming America's preeminent form of motorsports. He arranged for Jeff to give it a try. After a visit to the Buck Baker Racing School in Rockingham, North Carolina, Gordon fell in love with the stock cars and decided to leave the open-wheel tracks of the Midwest. When he left, he was a teenaged legend. The legend part, he carried with him.

For a couple of years, Gordon raced in the Busch Series, NASCAR's proving ground. He was named Rookie of the Year in 1991 and, in 1992, established a record that still stands by being the fastest qualifier in 11 events. Ford Motor Company, which, by then, had taken an active interest in Gordon, planned to help Gordon move up to the Winston Cup Series, the country's most popular and competitive circuit, along with the owner of his Busch Series team, Bill Davis.

Enter Rick Hendrick, the already prominent owner who had been impressed—no, wowed—by Gordon in the Busch Series. Hendrick proposed to put Gordon in a Chevrolet and promised him equipment and support that no new team could match. Gordon took the leap, angering Davis and Ford motorsports officials in the process and causing a bit of a scandal in the various racing publications.

Nothing had changed. Everything the Kid touched turned to gold. By the end of 1993, he was the Winston Cup Rookie of the Year. Soon after, he married Miss Winston, Brooke Sealy, with whom he had conducted a secret, but honorable, romance. In 1994 Gordon won his first two races. In 1995 he won his first championship.

Not only did everything Gordon touch turn to gold. Everything I wrote about Gordon turned to gold, too.

Here are the first eight paragraphs from the story I wrote on the occasion of Gordon's first official victory, at Charlotte Motor Speedway, on the night of May 29, 1994:

> The Kid wasn't supposed to win this way. He was supposed to ram his Chevy hard into some fourth turn, risking life and limb, and somehow come out of the smoke and fire in first place.
>
> Instead, Jeff Gordon captured the Coca-Cola 600 stock car race on Sunday night by calmly pulling off a strategic move that would have made all his wily predecessors—David Pearson, Richard Petty, et al.—proud.
>
> The skinny youth—far less imposing than the rainbow-bright Chevy he manhandled—wept in victory lane.
>
> "If there's a feeling any higher than this, I don't know it," he stammered, self-conscious and obviously worried about saying the wrong thing.
>
> Then the governor of North Carolina, Jim Hunt, walked up to bask in the reflection of Gordon's glow.
>
> "Thank you, Governor, this is a memory I'm never going to forget," said Gordon, shedding his caution. "This is the highlight of my life."
>
> "How old are you, son? Twenty-two?" asked His Honor.

"Yeah," said Gordon, "and life is just as great as it could ever be."

That marked the first time I won a writing award for a racing story.

The glory never stopped from that point on, although it slowed a bit in 1999 and 2000. By the time Gordon turned 30, he had won four championships. The significance of that number might be better understood by the fact that only two men in NASCAR's history, which stretched across parts of seven decades, had ever won more. One of them, Richard Petty, had been 35 when he won his fourth championship. The other, Dale Earnhardt, had been 39.

Gordon had won 10 or more races in three consecutive seasons (1996–98), a feat unmatched by anyone in history. He was already seventh on NASCAR's all-time list of winners, behind only the titans Petty, David Pearson, Bobby Allison, Darrell Waltrip, Cale Yarborough, and Earnhardt. Of those, five were retired, and one, Earnhardt, had been tragically killed in a racing accident.

Gordon had become the only man to win the Brickyard 400—NASCAR's annual visit to the racing mecca known as Indianapolis Motor Speedway—three times, and he had been the first to win there when the race was first held in 1994.

It's a Cinderella story, even when told straight.

Here is the revisionist version . . . the fanciful story of Jeff Gordon.

Gordon arrived in Vallejo, California, on a rocket ship launched from the planet Krypton. His natural father, Jor-El, had warned the other elders of the planet's impending destruction. They had scoffed at him, refusing to confront the scientific truths presented by Jor-El. Jor-El knew that he was doomed, but he used his remaining days designing

Jeff Gordon celebrates victory in the first Brick-yard 400 at Indy in 1994. He's won that race a record three times over-all. DMP Archives Photos

and building a capsule for the transport of his infant son to Earth, where he prayed the boy would be accepted.

Jor-El knew it wouldn't hurt that the son would have superhuman powers on Earth.

As fate would have it, the little rocket ship fell in California (the Golden State), and it was an American, John Bickford, who happened upon the boy's capsule. He took the baby home and soon discovered that this, not surprisingly, was no ordinary baby. Bickford's wife, Carol, remarked that this kid was really destined to go places.

Bickford, a big racing fan, murmured to himself, "Or maybe just around and around."

The comic book scenario would explain, for instance, why Gordon is so maddeningly predictable in his public comments. He is trying to draw attention away from abilities that are, obviously, otherworldly. He doesn't want to blow his cover.

Ah, it's an interesting theory, but I have to admit that, deep down, I don't actually buy the notion that Jeff Gordon is an extraterrestrial. I have occasionally caught glimpses of behavior that is damn human in him. There was the 1997 Winston Cup Awards Banquet, when Gordon, upon winning his second championship, wept openly at the lectern. In fact, he just let it all hang loose. "Wept" isn't an appropriate choice of words. Gordon bawled. He boo-hooed. It was embarrassing but, at the same time, astonishingly human.

At Watkins Glen in 2000, Gordon and Tony Stewart engaged in a senseless shoving match, early in the race, that ended up costing Gordon a lot more than it did Stewart. When the race that day was over, the two young drivers nearly came to blows. I watched from a safe distance. Neither distinguished himself that day. Stewart was the more profane of the two, but he also won the debate on points. All Gordon could muster was the rather startling assertion that he would wreck Stewart at the next race. It was a comment he regretted later. But Stewart, unable as always to conquer his own emotions, left the track in a huff. Gordon gathered his thoughts, waited until he had settled down, got back in his "right mind," composed himself, and publicly discussed the matter.

People think Gordon and Stewart are rivals. The fact is that Stewart respects Gordon more than anyone else in the sport.

"He always manages to keep himself under control and behave appropriately," Stewart told me. "I wish I could do that."

In the final race of 2001, Gordon, having already clinched his fourth championship, allowed himself the evil pleasure of a boorish bump delivered by his garish Chevrolet to the rear of another Monte Carlo driven by Robby Gordon, who himself had bumped Gordon from the lead a few moments earlier. This payback, delivered while a yellow flag waved to denote caution, resulted in Gordon being penalized a lap.

"People think I don't get mad," Gordon said. "I can get mad."

On the track, Gordon has always been aggressive. Name one great stock car driver who wasn't at one time or another.

One such aggressor, Bobby Allison, said Gordon is the smartest stock car racer who ever lived.

"Gordon's success proves you can still win races by outsmarting people and by using strategy," said Allison, who compared Gordon favorably with one of Allison's contemporaries, David Pearson.

One of Gordon's contemporaries, the late Dale Earnhardt, once talked about the aggressiveness that lies beneath Gordon's boyish, mild-mannered public demeanor.

"Jeff Gordon is tough," Earnhardt said. "He's a great competitor. He may not look tough, and he may sound like a polite kid, but believe me, on a racetrack, he's as tough as they come.

"He has that competitive nature, and I think, like most champion racers, you can see it in everything he does. I don't care whether it's racing, computer games, or whatever he does, he's competitive. And that's why he's a winner. He goes that extra mile, and he works hard."

Gordon's Daytona 500 victories in 1997 and 1999 demonstrated exactly what Allison and Earnhardt were talking about.

In the former, Gordon and his Hendrick teammates, Terry Labonte and Ricky Craven, deployed their resources with cold-blooded
efficiency on poor Bill Elliott, a great driver in his own right. As the
laps wound down, Elliott, who had dominated the race, found himself
alone at the front, his Ford a sitting duck to the Chevrolet teammates—Gordon, Labonte, and Craven—advancing behind him. Military commanders have a term for what they did: deployment of forces.
At just the right moment, as they entered turn one of the old high-
banked coliseum of speed, Labonte and Craven locked together and
drove to the top of the banking, forcing Elliott to move up to block.
When Elliott's Ford drifted up, Gordon's Chevrolet dove low and
nudged Elliott's car slightly, and by the time the cars reached the backstretch, Gordon, Labonte, and Craven all had passed the hopelessly
outnumbered veteran. Naturally, Gordon went on to win.

"I was dead meat," said Elliott, "and I knew it."

Two years later, it was Rusty Wallace who took the fall, but this
time Gordon was flying solo. Gordon made his pivotal move by driving
low—outrageously low—beneath the line that separates the racing surface from the flat area known as the track's "apron."

One small problem: The dented, previously wrecked Ford of Ricky
Rudd was dawdling along down there, just trying to stay out of harm's
way. It became a high-speed game of "chicken" between Wallace, who
held the lead, and Gordon, who was intent on changing that.

The reflection in Rudd's mirror, meanwhile, must have looked like
the view from a German outpost overlooking Omaha Beach with the
Allied invasion bearing down.

Wallace relented. Gordon got away with it. The great ones always do.

"I just couldn't block him enough," said a dejected Wallace. "I thought I had him blocked off, and he just kept going. I thought he was going to drive right in the back of Rudd on the apron there."

That pass occurred with 11 laps to go. The final 10 laps were spent with Gordon trying to hold off Earnhardt.

And, by the way, succeeding.

"Racing Dale Earnhardt to the finish of the Daytona 500? It doesn't get any better than that," Gordon said.

"I just couldn't get to him," said Earnhardt. "I got beat.

"As we came up through there, we got to racing. The last 10 laps, we were bangin' and slammin.' It was pretty physical. I feel pretty good just to survive those last 10 laps."

Gordon eyed Earnhardt warily. Every trick the wily old master tried, Gordon countered.

"Gordon was backing off in the center of the corner, trying to keep me from getting any momentum," Earnhardt said. "I knew that, but every time I'd back off, he'd back off, too. It probably made it kind of tough for the guys riding behind us."

Two years later, when a last-lap crash claimed Earnhardt's life in the same race, do you think the memorable 1999 battle meant something to Gordon? Do you think recalling Earnhardt's grudging compliments filled him with emotion?

"Dale Earnhardt taught me how to race these cars," Gordon said. "Watching him taught me how to win championships."

The guard doesn't come down often, though.

From the time Gordon began racing stock cars until the season after his third championship, Ray Evernham honed his skills. Evernham was a master mechanic, yes, but he was also a motivator. He had a certain charisma and a leadership style more often associated with a football coach than a mechanic. Evernham merely tempered the Gordon steel, though. He didn't create it.

"I think Jeff would have been successful any time," said Evernham. "I think Rick Hendrick would have been successful any time. I think I would have been successful any time, but I don't think that we could have achieved what we achieved without one another. What we did was pretty special."

Evernham, in Gordon's words, was "a very outspoken leader; he was the cheerleader. The team was kind of looking for something to cling on to."

Enter Robbie Loomis, a pleasant, competent, patient, hardworking crew chief, who joined the team in 2000. Gordon no longer needed a motivator. He had matured and learned the lessons imparted by the motivator Evernham.

"We needed a guy like Robbie Loomis to come in and be the crew chief and work well with me," said Gordon. "I don't feel like I'm on my own here, but I did step up. I lead the team meetings on race day. I don't get to the shop as much as I want to, but when I am there, I feel like I am more part of this team than I ever have been. I can see the guys look at me differently than, maybe, they ever have before.

"I do feel like a much bigger part of this team. I do know more about what's going on behind the scenes. I don't know, I guess I am more intertwined with this team."

Gordon has his detractors. They claim he is too good to be true, too perfect, that he never paid his dues and that it all came too easily. Some call him a sissy. Others insist that his cars are too fast to be legal or that NASCAR is so intent on having Gordon spread the sport's gospel to new fans that it allows him unfair advantages.

"They" said the same things about Earnhardt, Petty, and everyone else who seemed, at one time or another, to be capable of winning races other drivers could not. The alternative, of course, would be to accept that Gordon won his races fair and square. No one in a competitive environment wants to admit that.

Gordon obviously believes the better part of valor is to leave the accusations unanswered. He can be maddeningly adept at taking the high road.

"Jeff amazes me in how he matures to a level and then steps up again," said Rick Hendrick. "I think one of the greatest things, other than just watching him drive a race car and be in awe of his talent, is how he keeps his head up. He doesn't blame the team. You hear drivers out there all of the time saying the car wasn't any good, or this and that. He never blames anybody. He just shoulders all of the responsibility."

"I am not one to take a lot of credit," Gordon said. "I have been part of racing for a long time. Each weekend we race, I know that, when the stuff is right, I feel like the master out there, but I realize that, when it's not right, the same person is driving it, and it's not going to the front.

"I know how important the team is and how important it is to put the right ingredients there."

As a boy, Gordon was much smaller than others his age. His hair was a bit lighter. The early photos appear as though he has strapped himself into some racing monstrosity for the benefit of a few Polaroid shots by Mom, not to take on grown, swarthy, mean-spirited hellions on the Midwest battlegrounds of Salem and DuQuoin.

No, Jeff Gordon's skills are not extraplanetary, not strictly speaking. Maybe his skills are just beyond the ability of less-talented mortals to imagine. Maybe he reveals so little of himself because he is either weary of trying to explain what makes him tick or because he actually doesn't realize himself how remarkable he is.

In the end, what he can do is explanation enough. Gordon's actions do not just speak louder than his words. They obliterate them.

Mere mortals can only imagine what being Jeff Gordon is really like.

HAIL CAESAR, EMPEROR OF TALLADEGA!

Dale Earnhardt outdid even his own legend by winning the 2000 Winston 500 at Talladega Superspeedway, defying belief by rallying from 18th to first place in the final five laps. Earnhardt's 76th–and final–victory would wind up as a lasting memory of the seven-time champion's brilliant career.

By David Poole

Urrrrrrrrrrrrnnnn-haaaaaaaaarrrrrrrt!!!!!!!!
Urrrrrrrrrrrrnnnn–haaaaaaaaarrrrrrrt!!!!!!!

They'd been yelling for nearly an hour. They stood by the hundreds behind the press box at Talladega Superspeedway, a 2.66-mile loop of weathered Alabama asphalt their hero had just reclaimed as his own. Sun-baked, sweat-drenched, adrenaline-hyped fans covered every square inch of the available space. Framed by the fading light of an Indian summer Sunday on October 15, 2000, they were there to pay homage to a man who had just done the impossible.

This must have been what it was like in Rome as Caesar returned from glorious conquests. Instead of tunics, these citizens of NASCAR Nation wore T-shirts bearing the likeness of their mustachioed leader. Instead of laurel wreaths to place across his brow, they waved black caps.

Urrrrrrrrrrrrrnnnn-haaaaaaaaarrrrrrrt!!!!!!!!

The cry went up anew, morphing into the rhythmic mantra of "We want Dale! We want Dale!" He had become Talladega's master, winning there for a 10th time, more than twice as often as any other competitor. His powers went beyond those of mortals. He could, they said, "see" the air.

With five laps left in the Winston 500, the great man had been buried in a seething snake of traffic screaming around the track. With one lap to go, he was leading and on his way to another grand triumph. How? Where did he come from? What magic was this?

As Earnhardt's fans waited to see the man who'd done this remarkable thing, they talked breathlessly about the frantic few minutes in which it had occurred. They couldn't believe it, but yet again they knew their man had it in him. Even if they'd doubted it for a few moments, they never stopped believing he was The Man.

The 2000 Winston 500 weekend at Talladega Superspeedway started in October on Friday the 13th, but in many ways it started long before that.

You could, in fact, go all the way back to 1959, the year that Bill France gave stock car racing its first giant stage—the 2.5-mile Daytona International Speedway in Daytona Beach, Florida, with turns banked at 31 degrees because France couldn't find machines to pour asphalt any steeper.

It was a place where stock cars could go faster than they'd ever gone before and where, several years later, legend has it Junior Johnson discovered the draft. By tucking his car tightly behind one in front of him, a driver could keep up even if his car wasn't nearly as fast running by itself. By the time France opened the Daytona Beach speedway's

Dale Earnhardt in the winner's circle after his amazing come-from-behind victory in the Winston 500 in October 2000. This would end up being the last win of the legend's career. Brian Cleary

sister track in Talladega, Alabama, in 1969, the draft had become dominant in Daytona race strategy. The leader was virtually a sitting duck on the final lap, because a second-place car could wait until the final turn and use the draft to slingshot around the first-place car to grab the win.

The draft would be even more critical at Talladega, which was longer, at 2.66 miles, and steeper, with 33-degree banking in its massive turns. That made it even faster than Daytona, and it was at Talladega in March 1970 that Buddy Baker turned the first lap at better than 200 mph. By 1987 a driver could run a 200-mph lap at Talladega and still be in danger of missing the race.

Bill Elliott won the pole for the track's spring race on April 30 of that year with a lap speed of 212.809 mph, a record that would soon become frozen in time. Three days later, on lap 22, Bobby Allison cut a tire on his Buick as he came off turn four and started down Talladega's 4,300-foot doglegged frontstretch. Allison's car, running at better than 205 mph, yawed and then went airborne, slashing along a cable-reinforced wire fence that provided the only barrier between the track and the thousands in the grandstands.

Allison's car gashed away 150 feet of fencing, snapping nine steel poles and spewing debris. Several pieces swirled into the crowd, but miraculously there were only a few minor injuries. The fencing had done its job, and the race, after a delay of more than two and a half hours, was completed, with Allison's son, Davey, winning.

Had the fence not deflected Allison's car back onto the track, there's no way to tell how many would have died, but it almost certainly would have been a catastrophe. NASCAR knew this. Within 48 hours, it decreed that cars in its top series would begin using smaller carburetors to slow speeds. In December, NASCAR went a step further by introducing carburetor restrictor plates, a square plate with four holes bolted across the opening through which air is brought into the carburetor. Reducing the airflow cuts power and thereby cuts speed.

Dale Earnhardt came to hate restrictor plates. Passionately. He once said anyone afraid of racing at 225 mph or higher, speeds modern cars might attain at Daytona and Talladega without plates, should "tie a kerosene handkerchief around his ankle so the ants wouldn't crawl up and eat his candy ass." Still, no one was better at plate racing than

Earnhardt. In NASCAR's first 51 restrictor-plate races, he won 10 times.

Plate racing took the simple strategy of the last-lap slingshot and made racing at Daytona and Talladega a moving, three-dimensional chess game. Now it was all about positioning, about knowing which line to be in and which one to avoid, when to make a move and when to stay in place. And nobody had the knack for it that Earnhardt did.

By the beginning of the 2000 season, plate racing had almost become an oxymoron. Races at Daytona and Talladega became more a matter of survival than competition. Almost all of the cars in the field had enough power to stay in the draft, but none had enough power in reserve to make a pass by itself.

A driver bold enough to make such a move often found himself being passed by 20, even 30 cars, in a single lap before he could find a place back in the line. So, fewer people made such moves, or made them only out of a desperation that made the already-dangerous matter of racing in tightly bunched packs of 25 or more cars even more perilous.

Instead of waiting for the slingshot pass on the final lap, fans watching races at the two huge tracks spent their days waiting on "The Big One," a grinding, multicar crash that happened often enough to make them seem inevitable.

In February 2000 Dale Jarrett won a Daytona 500 that featured only nine lead changes, with most of them happening on pit road. The race was roundly criticized as boring, and pressure mounted on NASCAR to do something to make restrictor-plate racing more exciting. The 2001 Daytona 500 would be the first race under the sport's new $2.8 billion network television deal, so it needed to be a spectacle and not a daylong game of follow-the-leader.

And so, on Friday, October 13, 2000, Winston Cup teams gathered at Talladega, their cars adorned with new appendages aimed at making the racing "better." The most visible changes were strips of metal running across the roofs of the cars, called deflector blades by most in the garage area, and a small lip protruding backward toward the rear windshield across the top of the cars' rear spoilers, commonly called wickers.

The deflector blades would, in theory, disrupt the air passing over the top of the cars as they ran at speed. That meant the cars would be poking larger holes in the air, bringing back some of the effect of the draft that had been lost over the years as cars became slicker and more aerodynamically sound. The wickers on the spoilers would catch more of the air passing over the cars, creating more aerodynamic drag on the tracks' long straightaways. That would slow the cars, with the important effect being that this reduction of speed would allow NASCAR to open the size of the holes on the restrictor plates from seven-eighths of an inch to one inch. This would increase horsepower and, perhaps, give the drivers that little bit of power in reserve they could use to make passes.

The Winston 500 would be its own event, of course, but it would also be a laboratory to test changes more directly aimed at making the 2001 Daytona 500 an event to remember. That race would, of course, become one no one will ever be able to forget.

On Friday the 13th, Joe Nemechek won the 2000 Winston 500 pole with a lap speed of 190.279 mph. And then he made a prediction.

"Be here early tomorrow," he said. "It could be big."

On Saturday at Talladega, Winston Cup teams had two practices scheduled. One would be in the morning, before a second round of qualifying to fill out the 43-car starting field for Sunday's race. The other, the final practice commonly referred to as "Happy Hour," would follow in the early afternoon.

From the first instants of the morning session, it was clear that Nemechek's prediction from Friday would prove prescient.

On Friday, as the cars practiced for qualifying, they tried to avoid being anywhere near another car on the track. There would be no benefit from the draft during time trials, when one car runs by itself around the track against the clock, so they wanted to see how fast they could go by themselves. It wasn't until the Saturday morning practice, when the cars had been taken out of the qualifying setups and put into racing trim, that they first began to find out just how the rules changes would work.

The effects were staggering.

The cars were blowing larger holes through the air. The draft was back, in spades. Cars were closing in on those in front of them at an alarmingly fast rate; so fast that drivers were forced to make evasive maneuvers just to avoid plowing into them.

At one point in the morning session, Bobby Labonte lifted his foot off the accelerator of his Pontiac and drifted well back behind a large pack of cars drafting their way around the track. Then, Labonte pushed the gas pedal back to the firewall to see how long it took him to catch back up. It didn't take long, and as he caught the pack, he flashed across the timing wire buried in the pavement at the track's start-finish line.

Labonte's lap speed flashed on the scoring monitors in every team's transporter and all around the track. He'd run a lap at an average speed of 198.475 mph—much higher than anyone had expected from the new rules.

Labonte's lap was no fluke. Six other cars topped 196 mph in the session. There were no big wrecks, although Jeff Gordon's Chevrolet did plow through a row of plastic cones set down in turn one to mark an exit lane from pit road, slightly damaging the nose of the No. 24 Monte Carlo.

As the practice was ending, word swept across the garage area that NASCAR had called a drivers-only meeting unlike any such meeting the drivers had attended in years.

NASCAR president Mike Helton informed the 43 drivers who'd earned a spot in Sunday's race that they would be given a new restrictor plate as they left, one with 15/16th-inch openings instead of the one-inch holes they'd used that morning. Drivers took the new plates straight to their cars after the 35-minute meeting and went almost immediately onto the track for the final practice. Speeds were down, with Rusty Wallace topping the charts at 192.703 mph with the smaller plate.

During the meeting, Helton had reminded the drivers that, no matter what rules NASCAR made, the determining factor in what kind of race they would participate in the following day would be the judgment and skill of the men sitting in that room.

Emotions ran high in the meeting. Drivers said things to each other they would never say about each other in public, criticizing some of their peers for making risky, four-wide moves. Ricky Craven, who'd been in a car that flew upside down through turn two during a huge wreck several years earlier, reminded his rivals that their real goal should be to make it through the next day's race and go home to their families at the end of the day.

The point was particularly salient, since the night before in Fort Worth, Texas, Truck series driver Tony Roper had been killed in a crash in a race at Texas Motor Speedway. After the deaths of Adam

Petty and Kenny Irwin in separate crashes at New Hampshire International Speedway earlier in the year, Roper's death only added the specter of what might happen on Sunday if things went wrong.

There had only been two brief cautions in the first 168 laps of the Winston 500, neither of them for big wrecks. Drivers had refrained from making the kind of four-wide moves that had drawn criticism in Saturday's meeting.

The racing had been spectacular. To that point, 19 drivers had led at least one lap, and the lead had changed hands 44 times. Some drivers had held back nearly half of a lap, waiting until the final stages to get into the fray in hopes of dodging "The Big One" that most still expected. But after the day's third yellow flag, caused when Mark Martin and Bobby Hamilton banged into each other near the entrance to pit road on lap 168, it was show time.

Gordon's crew got him off pit road first during the pit stops on the final yellow, but on lap 175, one lap after the green flag, Dale Earnhardt Jr. surged into the lead. At that point, it seemed that the son of the seven-time champion, just five days after his 26th birthday and nearing the end of his rookie season in Cup racing, would be the Earnhardt in victory lane at Talladega that day.

His father, at age 49, had come off pit road so far back in the pack that he, by all appearances, was out of the running for his 76th career victory. Things looked even more bleak after a few laps of the final green-flag run. Earnhardt had tried to make the outside line work for him but had actually lost ground, falling outside the top 20 as the laps counted down.

The feeling in the air was one of remarkable excitement and an equally remarkable foreboding. It was either going to be a great finish or a disastrous one. As Earnhardt Jr. fended off the cars lining up behind him, his father found something. Kenny Wallace, who'd started even deeper in traffic on lap 174 after taking four tires on his final pit stop, was making his way past drivers whose tires were worn. As he picked his way through traffic, Wallace suddenly saw Earnhardt's black No. 3 Chevy pull in front of the nose of his No. 55.

And they were off.

Finding their way into a middle line, a position that would have sent them reeling backward under the old rules, Earnhardt and Wallace began making rapid progress. But time was running out. With five laps to go, Earnhardt was still 18th.

Up front, Earnhardt's teammate Mike Skinner was challenging Earnhardt Jr. for the lead. Earnhardt Jr. went too low in the trioval and got two wheels on the flat apron inside of the racing groove. Earnhardt Jr. had to lift off his throttle almost imperceptibly, but it was enough to jumble things up in the lead pack.

Meanwhile, Earnhardt and Wallace had picked up a third drafting partner in Nemechek, Wallace's teammate. And they were coming fast. As the lead pack sorted itself out after the Earnhardt Jr. bobble, the three fast Chevrolets sped forward and, out of nowhere, split their way through the middle and into the top five.

"Where did he come from?" ESPN analyst Benny Parsons asked on the television broadcast, echoing the thoughts of the 150,000 who were at the track.

John Andretti led lap 185. Skinner led lap 186. On the next-to-last lap, though, Wallace's bump-drafting—the practice of ramming into the rear of Earnhardt's car to provide an extra boost—had finished the job. Earnhardt passed Skinner for the lead just before the white flag. Wallace and Nemechek came right with him.

There was still drama left, of course. With a full lap remaining, Wallace and Nemechek could line up and double-team Earnhardt, sweeping by to take the victory away just like the old days. Earnhardt would have none of that. The 49th lead change of the day, his pass of Skinner, would be the last. Seconds after Earnhardt took the checkered flag, the wreck that everyone had been expecting happened as cars raced for position behind the winner. Several cars were damaged, but nobody was injured.

Later, after Earnhardt had made his way through the crowd behind the press box to sit for the winner's interview, it was time for questions. How can you ask a man to describe the impossible?

Earnhardt talked about being lucky. He said he still hated restrictor-plate racing, getting a laugh when he said he wasn't very good at it. He talked about a lot of things that afternoon, but he couldn't explain what had just happened.

Nobody could.

Nor could anybody explain what happened the next time Winston Cup cars ran under the same set of rules, in the 2001 Daytona 500, on February 18. The wreck didn't look that bad. Everybody kept saying that. Everyone expected Earnhardt to drive the crumpled black No. 3 back to the garage, hop out, and go congratulate Michael Waltrip, driving a Chevy Earnhardt owned, on his emotional victory.

That's not how things turned out, of course.

Urrrrrrrrrrrrnnnn-haaaaaaaaaarrrrrrrt!!!!!!!!

The crowd stayed behind the press box as Earnhardt met the press. They chanted. They hooted. They screamed his name.

They wanted to see him, to remind themselves he was just as human as they were. They wanted to tell him, one more time, how great he was and how proud they were to have been there to see this wondrous feat.

They cheered, you might say, as though it would be the last time they would ever get the chance to.

ALL THAT REMAINS . . .

To many fans, the ill-fated career of J. D. McDuffie is little known, but it was tough, independent men like McDuffie who formed the foundation of what the sport has become.

By Thomas Pope

Lemon Springs, North Carolina, isn't the kind of place that's prone to traffic jams. Most that do occur take place in the summertime. To blame: a John Deere tractor, creeping down the tight two-lane blacktop with a load of freshly cropped tobacco leaves piled high, heavy, and wet.

On a Monday late in October 1995, the tobacco fields stood bare. The leaves that once slouched green and thick on the stalk were now crisp and golden brown, cured to perfection in steamy barns and taken to warehouses in nearby Sanford.

Still, traffic crawled along Willet Road early on this overcast morning, with seemingly every car and pickup headed to the same destination: a nondescript corrugated metal building set in the crook of a curve.

Inside, a crowd of more than 100 people ringed the building's walls, and a few minutes past 10 A.M., Tom McInnis climbed atop a cart and settled onto a bar stool. He slung a microphone around his neck, attached the lanyard, looked out into the crowd and cautioned, "No warranties, expressed or implied." Then, taking a deep breath, he launched into his auctioneer's machine-gun drone.

Only the product for sale wasn't burlap mounds of flue-cured tobacco, but a man's livelihood.

The acre-plus parcel of land, the building and its contents belonged to a hardworking, cigar-loving man named John Delphus McDuffie. The home he shared with his wife, Jean, stood not more than a mile north up the same road, but for better and for worse, this shop full of racing equipment was the centerpiece of his world, and he sustained it with blood, sweat, and tears.

On August 11, 1991, he paid for it with his life.

J. D. McDuffie was like hundreds of drivers who had preceded him into NASCAR's premier Grand National division.

He was a short-track racer of considerable repute, winning Late Model Sportsman events across the Carolinas on dirt and asphalt. On July 7, 1963, yearning for the big time, he tried his hand at Grand National racing for the first time. At the half-mile dirt oval at Myrtle Beach, South Carolina, he came home 12th in the Speedorama 200 against the likes of Ned Jarrett, Buck Baker, Richard Petty, and Bobby Isaac. Afterward, he lit up a Tampa Nugget cigar, loaded up his race car, and headed back up the highway to Sanford with $120 in his pocket.

McDuffie would compete in a dozen more Grand National shows that season, then go back to racing Late Models for two years.

McDuffie returned to the Grand National scene in 1966, but without the money and factory connections of a Petty Enterprises, a Junior Johnson, or the Wood Brothers, his ability to run with the lead pack

J. D. McDuffie (No. 70) runs alongside Ed Negre's No. 8 car at the Western North Carolina 500 in 1969 at the Asheville–Weaverville Speedway. Bryant McMurray

was severely limited. The rich got richer and J. D. McDuffie just kept doing the best he could with whatever funds he could scrape together.

In those days, a driver was lucky if he had two or three cars at his disposal, and any team with more than a handful of employees was definitely considered upper echelon. J. D. McDuffie's race team consisted of J. D. McDuffie and whatever friends might drop by after supper.

"I think if he had gotten the right breaks in the late '60s, he could've won a lot of races," said H. A. "Humpy" Wheeler, the president of Lowe's Motor Speedway near Charlotte. "He didn't get those breaks, and he had to settle for the life of a guy on the road trying to make a living driving a race car."

McDuffie had to run his operation on a shoestring budget, using engine parts far past their prime. To keep his cars running, he simply couldn't tax them. Racing on new tires was a luxury, but the bigger teams would often help McDuffie and other independent owner-drivers in a game of "You scratch my back, I'll scratch yours." At some tracks, "scuffs"—tires with a few laps on them—were actually preferable over the long haul to "stickers"—tires with the manufacturer's label still attached. McDuffie and the others would use those new tires on race day, run them the specified distance—faster than they could go on their own tires that had to last as long as possible—then pit for a new set. The scuffs would be carted over to the high-caliber team and frequently helped lay a foundation to someone else's trip to victory lane.

McDuffie's willingness to accept those assignments gratefully, and his ability to do a lot with a little, earned him the admiration of fellow competitors and fans alike. One by one, the independents began to give up the financial battle, but not J. D. McDuffie.

On occasion, circumstance worked in McDuffie's favor, giving him a chance to show he had the right stuff, just not the right budget.

Fairgrounds Raceway in Nashville, Tennessee, was always kind to McDuffie, rewarding him with a fifth-place finish five times.

In 1971 McDuffie had a race like never before or ever again, finishing third in a 100-mile show at Malta, New York, far from the tobacco fields and brick kilns of Sanford.

And seven years later, in the midst of a battle between tire manufacturers, J. D. McDuffie stole the headlines from the stars.

On a Friday afternoon at Dover, Delaware, McDuffie cashed in on the tire war. The McCreary tires that McDuffie chose, not the more popular Goodyears, proved to be the ticket to ride, and they carried

J. D. McDuffie poses after winning the pole for the 1978 Delaware 500 in Dover. Bryant McMurray

him to a lap time of 135.480 miles an hour, fast enough to win the pole position for the Delaware 500. So surprising was McDuffie's lap that reporters had to search high and low to locate him after it had gone unbeaten. Asked by an Associated Press writer where he could find McDuffie, a crewman answered, "He's probably somewhere fainting."

McDuffie was finally rounded up for the presentation of the pole award. Friendly, but always a man of few words, McDuffie's reaction to the pole was humility: "It's a nice feeling to be running faster than the best in the world."

On race day, McDuffie's moment in the sun was far too short and unsatisfying. He led the first 10 laps of the race before eventual race winner Bobby Allison took command; then he began to fade. He would soon encounter engine trouble, and after completing his 80th lap, he nursed the Bailey Excavating Chevrolet back to the garage area, silent, the victim of a broken valve. His once-in-a-lifetime weekend had ultimately resulted in a 33d-place finish and rewarded him with a mere $1,030.

The good days were far outnumbered by those in which he struggled. At times, J. D. McDuffie was fortunate to escape with his life.

In 1975 a nine-car crash at Talladega, Alabama, left him hospitalized for 15 days with a cracked breastbone and heart and chest bruises. Years later, a wreck in a qualifying race at Daytona ruptured an oil line and that led to a fire that engulfed his car. McDuffie was left with second- and third-degree burns—primarily on his hands—that required plastic surgery.

Still, he wouldn't quit driving, though every day he lost more ground in a sport that was leaving him farther behind. Madison Avenue had discovered a marketing gold mine in NASCAR, and Fortune 500 corporations lined up to get a piece of the action. No one from New York managed to find his way to the metal building hard by the curve in Lemon Springs.

Friends and family tried to convince McDuffie to give up driving, and they ran numerous career options by him. They often cited the route taken by one of his racing contemporaries, Richard Childress. Like McDuffie, Childress never won a Winston Cup race, but he got out when he had the chance to put a talented, aggressive young driver named Dale Earnhardt behind the wheel.

Earnhardt's ability helped bring sponsorship to the team, and in the years to come, he would win six more championships and help make himself and Childress millionaires many times over. "You could do that, J. D.," McDuffie's friends pleaded. "You've got the know-how."

If that didn't pan out, he could cash in on the knowledge he had gained over the years while working for a well-heeled team. "It's time for you to stop struggling to make ends meet," they told him. "It's time for you to get paid what you're worth."

J. D. McDuffie had only deaf ears for their good intentions, even to those closest to him.

"I bring up the subject of him quitting an awful lot, but he loves it," said his wife, Ima Jean. "He just can't bring himself to give it up."

"I ain't got nothing else going," McDuffie said, seeming almost oblivious to the obvious. "Racing is my life. If I don't run, I don't eat. This ain't a weekend hobby to me."

J. D. McDuffie ran 652 races, always returning to the shop on Willet Road to try to figure a way to make his cars fast enough to keep those paychecks, small as they were, coming in.

On his way out the door to race No. 653, at Watkins Glen, New York, McDuffie told his wife he planned to take the car straight from there to Brooklyn, Michigan, for the following week's race. He would never see her again.

On the fifth lap of the 1991 Bud at the Glen, McDuffie zipped down the longest straightaway on the track and prepared to make a quick right-hand turn. Just at that moment, a piece of the suspension behind the left front tire broke.

"If you lose your brakes or have any kind of problem (in turn five), you're running too fast," said Jimmy Means, who had been racing alongside McDuffie. "The track's flat, and you go with the momentum of the car wherever it's going to take you."

The car barreled off the course, picked up speed as it slid across the grass and skidded sideways into a pile of tires and guardrail. McDuffie's red No. 70 Pontiac flipped and landed on its roof alongside the crashed car driven by Means.

Racer Jim Derhaag watched the entire sequence as he followed the two drivers into the turn. He said, "Just about the time J. D. got to the braking area, I saw some smoke. It was maybe like from a brake line, like brake fluid was hitting the (exhaust pipes), but it looked like he never slowed down.

"He went charging right to the inside and hit Jimmy and took both of them right off the track."

Two-time NASCAR champion Ned Jarrett was at the track reporting for ESPN. He was standing on a tower about 75 feet from the crash and instantly had a sense that something horrible had occurred. He had seen those kinds of incidents before in his days as a driver, most notably in the fiery Charlotte Motor Speedway crash that would lead to the death of Glenn "Fireball" Roberts.

The McDuffie-Means crash happened so quickly and ended with such violence that Jarrett, at first, didn't know whose cars were involved. He clambered down from the tower and was able to interview Means, who escaped with only a cut on his chin. But after chatting off camera with Means and watching rescue workers swarm over McDuffie's car, Jarrett was certain that the worst had happened.

"You always hope for the best and pray that everything will be OK, but after I had done the interview with Jimmy . . . I told our producer,

Neil Goldberg, that I was going back up to my position because there was nothing else I could do (at the crash site)," Jarrett said. "One of the workers on the scene overheard me and said, 'No, there's nothing else you can do here,' and that's when I had a feeling J. D. was dead."

He was right. Before J. D. McDuffie's car came to rest in a cloud of dust and steam, he was dead at age 52.

Jean McDuffie, watching her TV at home, screamed, then collapsed on the floor.

Four days later, John Delphus McDuffie was laid to rest. Many of the sport's biggest names—Richard Petty, Richard Childress, Junior Johnson, Rick Hendrick—came to his funeral. More than 700 mourners filled Grace Chapel Christian Church, and more than 3,000 had come to pay their respects two nights earlier at a funeral home not far from the McDuffies' home.

It would be more than four years later before Ima Jean McDuffie could summon the will to sell off her husband's shop and equipment. "I just can't hold on to it forever," she said, dabbing at the tears with a tissue.

The day following a race at Rockingham, North Carolina, the Winston Cup track closest to home, she turned that duty over to Tom McInnis and his company, Iron Horse Auction.

The crowd wandered through the building that had been J. D.'s pride and joy. It was cramped and sparse compared to the gleaming facilities under construction in the Charlotte area, where most of the teams are headquartered. But it was big enough to provide J. D. McDuffie with an engine shop, a spray booth for painting the cars, and room enough for several cars in various stages of construction and reconstruction.

The buyers and the simply curious in the crowd inspected the merchandise piled on tables and shelves. Acquaintances exchanged small talk. Coffee from a makeshift concession stand helped blunt the morning's chill.

The tables and shelves in the shop were crammed with everything necessary to outfit and maintain a race team. Boxes of unused spark plugs and air filters were stacked high. A dashboard panel still had all the telltale gauges in place, just as J. D. McDuffie had left it four years earlier when he locked the door behind him and began the northward trek to Watkins Glen.

Yellow suspension springs were arranged neatly here, and a row of white driveshafts lay in neat alignment there. Boxes of nuts, bolts, and washers were within arm's reach in all directions. Atop a cabinet in the engine shop was an eclectic collection of eight-track tapes: What's your pleasure; Conway Twitty or Sly and The Family Stone?

Once-mighty teams that had fallen on hard times had been dismembered by Iron Horse Auction. J. D. McDuffie had been present when Blue Max, Holman-Moody, DiGard, and others were sold off. McDuffie didn't buy new parts often, and the auction of those championship teams and their high-quality used materials were a godsend to him. Now, the roles were reversed, and when Tom McInnis scanned the faces in the room, the familiar one with the mustache and the glowing Tampa Nugget was missing.

McDuffie's equipment was of little use to Winston Cup teams, who routinely spent more in a matter of months than the $1.4 million J. D. McDuffie made in 28 years in NASCAR's premier division. Some of the equipment would be useful at lower levels of competition such as ARCA or NASCAR's Late Model Stock class. Some would have nostalgic value and little more.

Winston Cup driver Ken Schrader and noted engine builder Keith

Simmons had friends in the crowd to place bids on the 1970 Chevy ramp truck that McDuffie affectionately dubbed "Ol' Blue." It took Ima Jean McDuffie 17 months and the help of one of her husband's competitors, Dave Marcis, to get the truck back from a sponsor in New Jersey. The August 9, 1991, issue of *Winston Cup Scene* still lay on the backseat, and its companion was a worn road atlas, its pages yellowed and curled.

McInnis worked the crowd hard for several minutes before Schrader's buyer nodded the winning bid of $7,750 for "Ol' Blue." The land and the 5,000-square-foot shop sold for $72,500 to Ellis Ragan, who fielded a car in NASCAR's Goody's Dash series for compacts. "I'll probably resell it," said a smiling Ragan, whose overalls and gray camouflage cap belied his wealth. "It's worth at least as much as I paid for it."

The two race cars on hand—one wrecked and the other having been mended—were bought for $6,900 by Richard Pugh. He had come all the way from Auburn, Alabama, to add them to a collection that included cars raced by Kyle and Richard Petty, Darrell Waltrip, and Brett Bodine.

At 5:15 P.M. the Iron Horse crew had finished its job. Everything that J. D. McDuffie had sunk his life into was gone: all of it—the shop, the cars, the seemingly bottomless pit of parts. Every single item in that shop had passed through the rough hands of J. D. McDuffie, and he squeezed everything out of them that he could. Now it all was in the hands of others, forever.

Once, following a good showing at Martinsville Speedway in the late 1980s, McDuffie had stopped at a Greensboro, North Carolina, restaurant to treat himself and Ima Jean to a steak dinner. One and two at a time, the numerous race fans in the room turned their heads to note the McDuffies' presence.

On their way out, one group of fans stopped by to speak to J. D. McDuffie and congratulate him on his efforts against the growing tide of drivers with Madison Avenue backing and their cadre of crewmen. As they began to leave, one of the group left behind on the table more than enough money to cover the cost of the McDuffies' meal. The smile already on J. D. McDuffie's face grew even larger, and he thanked them for their generosity in his typical understated fashion: "'Preciate it. That's mighty kind of you."

Money passed hands again on the evening when Iron Horse had finished selling off the assets of J. D. McDuffie Racing. Eastern standard time had quickly pulled a curtain of darkness across the horizon, and the cars and trucks that lined the roadside began to pull away, their red taillights glowing smaller in the distance.

For the most part, the shop hard by the curve on Willet Road had been emptied of its stockpile of parts and pieces. All that remained of J. D. McDuffie in that place were the memories.

AN AMERICAN ICON

He was a living legend and a larger-than-life folk hero,
but no one knew how big Dale Earnhardt really was until
he was gone.

By Jeff Owens

Mike Helton is a mountain of a man, an intimidating figure with a menacing glare that could make hardened criminals tremble.

When he crosses his bulky arms and trains his steely eyes on a subject, his bushy, black-gray mustache looking like a perpetual frown, you can feel his calculating intensity.

Though gentle and warm at heart, it is Helton's mafia-like look and demeanor that make him a perfect fit as the president of NASCAR, a sanctioning body that rules its benevolent dictatorship with an iron fist.

Few can put Helton on the defensive, not fearless race car drivers, not wealthy, greedy team owners, and certainly not aggressive, opportunistic reporters. Helton, as most in the NASCAR world has learned, can stand his ground against anyone.

There is only one man in racing who has ever intimidated Mike Helton, and for that, Helton admits no shame. For it was that man,

Dale Earnhardt shows the look that helped earn him the nickname "The Intimidator." DMP Archives Photos

"The Intimidator" himself, who unnerved nearly everyone he encountered during his 21-year NASCAR career.

As Helton leaned on the back of his rental car during the summer of 1979, he couldn't help but feel a bit apprehensive when the confident 28-year-old race car driver swaggered up to him.

Still a wet-behind-the-ears rookie at major league stock car racing, Dale Earnhardt was already making a name for himself, winning his first Winston Cup race in just his 16th start, and at Bristol Motor Speedway, one of NASCAR's toughest tracks, to boot.

As a young Bristol (Tennessee) radio personality, Helton had to interview Earnhardt during his return trip to the track he had tamed four months earlier. Despite his own intimidating nature, he felt a bit like a dime store novelist approaching Wyatt Earp upon his return to the OK Corral.

Though a rookie, Earnhardt's cowboy good looks were already inspiring an image that would prompt Wrangler Jeans to dub him "One Tough Customer." He was as shaggy and rugged as a young Clint Eastwood, but as confident and intimidating as John Wayne. Yet his engaging smile and boyish charm gave him an aura that attracted aspiring young journalists, not to mention a host of courting sponsors and a legion of race fans.

As Helton first met Earnhardt on that bright summer day, he knew instantly that he was in the presence of greatness.

"The energy around Earnhardt was pretty quick in '79," Helton recalled. "Even his introduction to the sport came in a big way, and a lot of it had to do with the magnetism he had. He was just different.

"Even then, when nobody really knew who he was, everybody knew he had a lot of charisma. That same bigness that introduced him to the sport, you felt when you were there with him one on one. He had the uncanny ability to catch your eye. When he would walk into a room, everybody paid attention. It was just a chemistry that few people had."

As Helton, NASCAR's venerable leader, sat in the back of NASCAR's big red trailer 21 years later, a week after Earnhardt's death, he was as humble and vulnerable as he's ever been.

He swallowed his pride and choked back emotion as he shared his feelings about the man a whole nation suddenly mourned. Helton's mind was flooded with memories as he shared his unique relationship with the man who was his friend and confidant, the man who was as much a part of NASCAR as "King Richard Petty" and Big Bill France himself.

"From catching my first blue marlin on the back of his boat to just having dinner with him, they were all great," Helton said. "Every time you were with him was great."

Helton, whose climb to the top of the NASCAR hierarchy paralleled Earnhardt's rise to stardom, knew on this sad day that those memories will follow him the rest of his life. When the sun sets over the ocean in Daytona Beach, Florida, he will think of Earnhardt fishing on the back of his boat, the one he appropriately named "Sunday Money."

When he watches a deer run through a field or an elk standing on the side of a Colorado mountain, he will think of Earnhardt, whose affection for his family and racing were the only things that surpassed his love of the great outdoors.

Every time he sees Dale Earnhardt Jr., NASCAR's newest star, holding court with fans or the media, he will see the young man's father flashing that trademark grin and radiating enough charisma to charm a snake.

And when he sits in NASCAR's control booth high above its fast superspeedways, he will envision Earnhardt steering his famous black Chevrolet through traffic like no one who has ever handled a stock car.

Like many in America's most popular motorsport, Helton will forever be comforted and haunted by Earnhardt's tragic death in the 2001 Daytona 500.

"That's the difficulty of someone with Dale's personality and character and stature," Helton said, his voice quivering, his heart struggling to contain a floodgate of tears. "There are going to be a lot of moments when you think about him. There are an unlimited number of opportunities to feel that connection to Dale, and it's an ongoing process that will go on for a long, long time. The memories of him will last forever."

Ah, the memories. They are stories so incredible they seem as much folklore as history. That's the way it is with larger-than-life characters, and Earnhardt was one of the largest in the sport's history, a modern-day Babe Ruth who created his legend with a race car instead of a baseball bat.

"Dale was the Michael Jordan of our sport," said H. A. "Humpy" Wheeler, the Charlotte, North Carolina, track promoter who watched Earnhardt grow from.

Earnhardt was arguably the greatest race car driver who ever lived, but he was much more than that. He was the idol of millions of middle-class, blue-collar workers who reveled in his rise to fame. His was a rags-to-riches story they could relate to, making him a cultural icon in an age short on cult heroes. It was his stature not only as a famous athlete, but as a folk hero, that caused a nation to mourn his shocking death.

"He was our Elvis," driver Kenny Wallace said.

As NASCAR struggled in the late 1970s to shed its Southern roots and carve a niche on the national sports landscape, it was Earnhardt who supplanted "King Richard" as its biggest star. It was Earnhardt whose popularity and star power first took NASCAR to Wall Street and into living rooms across America.

It is one of sport's great ironies that a mild-mannered, self-educated country boy from the mill village of Kannapolis, North Carolina, could put NASCAR, a backwoods, redneck sport, on the map.

But it was his deep-rooted, Southern heritage that attracted a legion of race fans, giving them someone to pull for in an age when mainstream America was still lured by Hollywood's glitz and glamour.

Ralph Dale Earnhardt grew up tugging at the greasy pants legs of his father Ralph, who built his own race cars and raced them on bullrings throughout the Carolinas. While Ralph made a name for himself as one of the best dirt track racers around, Dale watched his every move, learning to build race cars from the ground up and sling them around short tracks like his father and legendary drivers like Junior Johnson and Curtis Turner.

By the time he was a teenager, Earnhardt knew his destiny. It was his dream to follow in his father's footsteps that prompted him to drop out of school in the eighth grade, a move he later called "a damn fool thing to do."

Though his talent as a driver was immediately evident, it was a rough life he chose. Married and living in a trailer at age 18, he struggled just to make ends meet, working in a mill during the day and racing at night.

After his father's death at age 44, Earnhardt started racing full-time, chasing his dream but struggling to make a living in a small textile town with few prospects beyond years of hard manual labor.

"I started racing full time, and that's when I started starving to death," he said. "It was tough. Money was tight; racing was hard. All the time, you had to keep going after it."

With a family to feed, Earnhardt moved into a mobile home behind his mother's house in Kannapolis, where he kept his race cars. Still, it was a meager existence, with little money and even less time for his family. By 1977 he was divorced from his second wife and the father of three children.

"I don't recommend it," he said of marrying so young.

But by working odd jobs and borrowing car parts, equipment, and even money, Earnhardt persevered, eventually drawing the attention of wealthy car owners who made a living racing fast stock cars.

By 1979, when Helton first met him, Earnhardt was a hotshot

rookie at NASCAR's highest level, and there was little doubt that he would become one of the sport's biggest stars.

At 28 he won his first race and Rookie of the Year honors. A year later he stunned the NASCAR world by winning five times and capturing the coveted Winston Cup championship, becoming the only driver ever to win Rookie of the Year and the series title in consecutive seasons.

Perhaps more important, he began developing an image that would make him a marketing miracle and a role model to working-class race fans all across America. Rugged and rough around the edges, he was indeed "One Tough Customer," both on the track and off.

But after his instant success, Earnhardt struggled for several years, winning races but failing to win another championship while bouncing from team to team. It wasn't until he hooked up with former driver Richard Childress in 1984 that the groundwork was laid for one of the greatest careers in racing history.

Two years later Earnhardt captured his second series title, outdueling three-time champion Darrell Waltrip. It was that year, however, that Earnhardt enhanced his reputation as an aggressive, intimidating force.

During a close, fender-banging battle at Richmond International Raceway, Earnhardt hit Waltrip's car in the rear, sending them both spinning into the wall and drawing the wrath of both NASCAR and his biggest rival.

It was Waltrip's quick wit and clever rhetoric—"He meant to kill me," he charged—that saddled Earnhardt with the reputation for being a reckless, overaggressive driver.

Ironically, his feuds with Waltrip, Bill Elliott, Geoffrey Bodine, and others only added to his growing legend. The more he was accused of being reckless, the more fans responded. Many loved him, others hated him, but in all, he stirred spirited emotions, becoming both NASCAR's most popular driver and its biggest villain.

What no one disagreed with was that Earnhardt had quickly emerged as NASCAR's most talented driver. He won 11 races in 1987 and nine in 1990, both championship years. From 1986 to 1994, he won back-to-back titles three times. The sixth tied him with Petty for the all-time record.

Equally as impressive was his flare for the dramatic and his knack for doing things no one else could do, spinning out in traffic only to recover without losing track position, or nudging a car just enough to get by, often sending someone else spinning, but never himself.

"He was the greatest race car driver who ever lived," two-time champion Ned Jarrett declared the day Earnhardt died. "He could do things with a race car that no one else could."

He was at his best on NASCAR's fastest, most dangerous tracks, manipulating the tricky aerodynamic draft like magic. He was so good at Daytona and Talladega that drivers swore he could see air. Perhaps his most spectacular move came at age 40, just four months before his death, when he dashed from 15th to the lead in the final five laps of the Winston 500, collecting his record 10th win at Talladega and a $1 million bonus in the process.

Yet he was often just as breathtaking on short tracks, driving his ominous black Chevrolet where most drivers didn't dare go. He once split the middle of two cars racing side-by-side at Bristol, a track where racing two-wide is treacherous. Wheeler often claimed that Earnhardt could drive a stock car "where angels fear to tread."

It was Wheeler, the brilliant race promoter, who dubbed one of Earnhardt's most memorable moves "the Pass in the Grass," when, in fact, he actually sped through the grass at Charlotte to protect his lead and keep from wrecking.

"It was never a pass in the grass," Earnhardt once barked. "I was bumped into the grass." Yet he was so good that many of his feats took on mythical proportions, only adding to his legend.

Exaggerated or not, Earnhardt had a habit of getting into and out of situations that other drivers typically could not escape. It was his penchant for controversy and drama and his ability to intimidate other drivers that marked his historic career and added as much to his mystique as his seventy-six career wins and seven championships.

"That [No.] 3 car scared every driver because they knew what was coming," said driver Jimmy Spencer, who had his share of scrapes with Earnhardt.

Hell-bent on chasing down leader Terry Labonte on an August 1995 night at Bristol, a night when NASCAR repeatedly sent him to the rear of the field for rough driving, Earnhardt finally caught his prey on the last lap. As they entered the final turn, he slammed into Labonte, knocking him across the finish line and under the checkered flag.

Win or wreck trying. That seemed to be his motto at times.

But to his critics it was more along the lines of "If you can't beat 'em, wreck 'em." Other drivers never hesitated to publicize their wrath when winding up on the wrong end of Earnhardt's bumper.

Rusty Wallace once thumped his friend in the head with a water bottle after going for an Earnhardt-induced spin at Bristol. Told once that Earnhardt had apologized for hitting him at Pocono, Ken Schrader quipped, "That's what he said the last time he wrecked me."

"You've got to look at who you're dealing with," Ricky Rudd once said. "He's been wrecking people his whole career."

Four years after punting Labonte to victory at Bristol, the two tangled again on the rough short track, producing one of the most infamous moments of Earnhardt's career. Once again he chased down Labonte on the final lap, but this time he caught him before the final turn, wrecking him on the backstretch and speeding away to take the checkered flag, leaving a mess of mangled race cars in his wake.

It was such dramatic moments that stirred the emotions of his rivals and fans. When Earnhardt pulled into victory lane that night, a chorus of boos descended upon him. Embarrassed and ashamed of his roughhousing, his own fans ripped their black T-shirts off their backs and tossed their coolers, complete with the famous No. 3 decal, over the fence.

Afterward, Earnhardt claimed he didn't mean to wreck Labonte, saying, "I was only trying to rattle his cage," to which Labonte replied, "He better tighten his belts."

Though he appeared to be spooked by the outrage of rivals and fans, Earnhardt actually reveled in such moments, knowing full well that they only sold more T-shirts and helped his legend grow.

As he made his way to the press box that night, he was confronted by a mob of angry fans, many booing and spewing obscenities. When the elevator doors closed behind him, securing him from a virtual lynch mob, he grinned and said, "Man, I love this shit."

True to form, his legion of fans were back in his corner the following week, greeting him with a thunderous ovation when he was introduced at Darlington. Despite his misdeeds, all was quickly forgiven. He even seemed to have added two fans for every one he had lost.

Perhaps no other moment summed up Earnhardt's hard-nosed, tough-as-nails nature than the 1997 Daytona 500. Eighteen times he had raced in the "Great American Race," and 18 times victory had eluded him. He had won nearly every race in the Winston Cup Series, all but the one that meant the most. And he had lost it nearly every way imaginable—a flat tire, a dry fuel tank, a bad pit stop, and wrecks galore. This time he fell victim to NASCAR's brightest young star.

As "Wonder Boy" Jeff Gordon sped past him in the closing laps of the 1997 race, Earnhardt lost control of his car, tagged the outside wall, and went flipping down the backstretch in a horrifying crash. As the hushed crowd held its collective breath, just as it would do again four years later, Earnhardt climbed from his car unscathed. That in itself was dramatic enough, but what he did next will forever be etched in racing lore.

Earnhardt was taking the mandatory walk to the ambulance when he noticed that his car was still sitting upright, on all four wheels and with most of its parts and pieces still intact. Instead of climbing into the ambulance and making the mandatory ride to the infield care center, he walked over to his battered race car, fired it up, and climbed back in, completing the final six laps in a car that would barely run.

"I looked back over there and said, 'Man, the wheels ain't knocked off the car yet.' So I went back over and told the guy in the car to fire it up," Earnhardt said proudly as he stood on a tool chest after the race. "He hit the switch and it fired, and I said, 'Give me my car back.' I just wanted to get back in the race and try to make laps. We were running for a championship."

Afterward, car owner Richard Childress fought back tears as he swallowed another bitter Daytona defeat and watched an undeterred Earnhardt take it in stride.

"That's the toughest man alive right there," an emotional Childress said. "He deserves to win this race more than anybody ever has."

A year later, Earnhardt would finally win the big one, choking back his own tears as he took the checkered flag in the 1998 Daytona 500. Afterward, he was the focus of one of the most fitting tributes in NASCAR history as every pit crew at the track lined pit road to congratulate him.

His Daytona triumph was not the first time Earnhardt had bounced back from adversity. He did it, in fact, right up to the very end, winning races despite numerous injuries and when many thought he was nearing the end of his career. In April 1996 he flipped upside down during a tumbling crash with Bill Elliott at Talladega. When Elliott's car burst into flames, it singed the hair off Earnhardt's neck and face, a frightening injury he shrugged off as a minor inconvenience.

"I'll have to grow some new ones, but I'll be all right," he said as he emerged from the infield care center.

Later that summer he was involved in another spectacular crash, again tumbling down the straightaway at Talladega, this time breaking his collarbone and cracking his sternum.

Beaten and battered, he refused to back down. In the middle of a championship race, he was determined to return for the next race. Despite intense pain that would have crippled most men, he ran six green-flag laps in the Brickyard 400, a race he had won the year before, before reluctantly turning his car over to a relief driver.

When he climbed from his car, the disappointment on his face far surpassed the pain in his throbbing chest. It was the first time anyone in racing could ever remember Dale Earnhardt choking back tears.

"Dadgum, it was hard to get out of that car," he said, his voice cracking on national television. "I mean, you know, that's my life right there. I just hate to get out of that race car."

The following week, he turned in one of the most courageous performances in Winston Cup history, enduring incredible pain to win the pole on the winding road course at Watkins Glen. Two days later, he ran the whole race with a broken sternum, finishing sixth.

"It hurts, but it's a good hurt," he said.

"Just tell him he can't do something," former crew chief Larry McReynolds boasted. "Tell him he can't go to Watkins Glen and race with a broken sternum, or tell him he can't outrun you. That's all he needs to hear."

That was Earnhardt, as tough as a middle linebacker, as fearless as a front-line Marine. That's why his death on the last lap of the Daytona 500 was such a shock. Though NASCAR had suffered three on-track deaths in the past nine months, Earnhardt, "The Intimidator," was the last driver anyone expected to die in a race car.

"We always thought of Dale as being invincible, so when he didn't climb out of that car after the wreck, we all knew it was bad," Wheeler said.

"Everybody believed that when he was in an accident, he would get out of that car," Spencer said. "He was John Wayne; he was Clint Eastwood. He wasn't supposed to die."

As invincible and as larger-than-life as he seemed to be, no one really knew the full extent of Earnhardt's impact on NASCAR or the sports world in general until he died. With his death came the end of an era. It marked the loss of a true American hero, one so popular his funeral was broadcast nationwide.

His death struck a devastating blow to a sport and a generation that will be felt for years. To many, there will never be a race car driver, nor a man, quite like Dale Earnhardt.

"For a lot of people, Dale Earnhardt was what they thought about when they thought about NASCAR racing," said Kyle Petty, the son of "The King." "He was the last cowboy."

"We lost a legend," driver Jeff Burton said. "A living legend."

DIGGIN' IN THE DIRT

Not all racing takes place in front of national television audiences and crowded, double-decked grandstands. Racing clings to its roots on the short tracks, particularly those whose surface is dirt.

By Jim McLaurin

Monday to Friday, Vic Evans is a mechanic at Spring Valley Tire, near Columbia, South Carolina, and a damn good one. He can change your oil, realign your front end, or slap you on a new set of brake pads before you're halfway through the sports section of the day-old newspaper someone left in the lobby.

Saturday is a different story. On Saturdays, Evans is there doing his chores, but his head is elsewhere. He's thinking about the one thing that consumes him.

At 4:30 P.M., it is hot in the bays. A huge shop fan churns manfully, but the place is heady with the smell of grease and rubber and sweat. The best the big fan can manage is to swirl it around. It will be hot long after the doors are closed for the night.

Evans has escaped a few minutes early and is outside, loading Gatorade, water, and soft drinks into a cooler on the back of his pickup truck. Hooked to the truck is an open-air trailer on which sits a Ford

Pinto of indeterminate vintage. On the side of the car is painted "07," and several hand-printed logos: "Spring Valley Tire. Muffler Works on Two Notch Rd. Garrett's Grill and Grog. Brenson Towing. Jimmy's Mart—Home of the Big Biscuit." There are dents, but not so many.

On the side of the rack where the spare tires are stored is another hand-painted sign. It reads, "Fat Boy Motorsports."

In 15-inch letters, the placard on the highway side of the building that serves as the scorer's stand at I-20 Speedway says it all: Dirt Racing.

For half an hour, the haulers have been making their way up to the crossover gate at the five-eighths-mile oval scraped out of the piney woods north of the Batesburg exit, between Columbia and Augusta.

On a given summer Saturday, the scene at 6 P.M. is being repeated at little bullrings stretched all across the land. It has been going on for generations all over the United States, but below the Mason-Dixon line, it has a certain feel, a certain smell, unlike anywhere else.

Country music blares over the track's public address system, interrupted occasionally by the announcer's calls to stop by the souvenir and concession stands. The smell of onions and simmering hot dog-chili will soon mingle with the incense of burning motor oil in an aroma so pagan that you half expect the next logical step to be human sacrifice.

The early arriving fans grab a hot dog and a cool drink and browse among the souvenir tables. Tonight they include, among the usual array of racing posters and Jeff Gordon T-shirts, a framed photo of wrestler "Stone Cold" Steve Austin and Sable. Sable, Stone's main squeeze, is so scantily clad that one mother shoos a couple of grinning youngsters away before they can get a good look.

Some fans have disdained the grandstands in favor of backing their cars and trucks up to the fence outside the third and fourth turns. They are pulling out lawn chairs, shifting coolers about and firing up charcoal grills in order to minimize their wanderings later on. They are hunkering down.

The haulers at the sign-in gate run the gamut from a fancy one that encloses one of the slick-looking Late Models right on down to home-welded versions like the one Evans hauls behind his truck. The drivers and "crewmen"—most of whom, like Evans, have just gotten off work—visit back and forth as they inch their way up to the booth, trading gossip and lies about what they've got under the hood for the others this week.

When they reach the gate, everybody signs the obligatory release form and a modest amount of money changes hands. The trailers squeak in protest as they clunk and bang over the hump created by the banking of the first turn, then roll down into the infield. The night's work begins.

A few minutes after 6 P.M., Evans pulls his truck into an unmarked slot inside the first turn. He gets down from the cab and places a spare tire on either side of his trailer. It's to mark a spot for his pals, but it isn't necessary. Most everybody has his favorite spot and generally one doesn't claim another man's land.

A few minutes later, Evans is winding his little Pinto loose from the come-along and backs it down the landing-mat ramps onto the gritty clay.

Someone asks, where's his help? He grins.

"They'll be here when it's time to watch," he says.

Evans is one of several thousands of normally sane working men who spend weeknights with their heads under the hoods of race cars, either in modest shops behind usually modest homes or—it still happens—under the biggest tree in the back yard, where the chain hoist hangs.

They work without pay, and sometimes without supper, and the best they can hope for is to break even. The ones with sense don't take food off the table to feed their habit, but it happens. At any rate, every spare nickel and every spare minute seems to find its way onto the race car.

"My wife is very understanding, because she has to put up with a lot for me to be here," Evans says. "If you're lucky, you don't have to spend but two or three days a week getting it ready, but that's a lot of time that she has to put up with watching the kids and put up with you complaining because the car didn't do this and didn't do that."

Evans is still new to the game, drawn into it by one of the guys who'll park beside him tonight.

"Bill Medlin, from Columbia," Evans says, grinning. "I call him 'Elvis, the Fat Years.'

"Bill was racing before I was and one night he let me drive his car during the warmup. It wasn't long before I had one of my own, and I've been at it ever since."

A few minutes later Medlin and his brother-in-law/crew chief, Tommy Case, roll in on one side of Evans's pit, and their buddy Rusty Covan pulls in on the other. They've been parking in the three-wide arrangement since they began racing at I-20.

Medlin does bear a resemblance to Elvis Presley, but it's his attitude more than anything else. He has a bit of the King's swagger in him, and indeed does pick up a few bucks as an Elvis impersonator. ("I just lip-sync," he says. "I let Elvis do the singing and I take care of the dancing.")

Covan's car is a newer, shinier version of a Pinto than Evans's, which he runs in the Mini Stock division, and Medlin's is an old Chevrolet Monte Carlo, a mainstay of the Stock 8 class.

Medlin's old Chevy is the worse for wear of the three, but he doesn't seem to mind. He and his brother-in-law pay the bills, so it doesn't have to be a show car for the sake of some sponsor. The dents of last week might get beaten out or they might not, depending on their mood.

"I don't think too many sponsors would take us on," Medlin says,

Dirt-track racer Vic Evans climbs out of his car after readying it for the night's races. The State

laughing. "But I love 'em. I bet half the Stock 8s in the country are old Monte Carlos. They're tough. You can't tear 'em up. They can have those little old cars. If I hit the wall, I want something between me and that wall. 'Course, they're so heavy that it takes a heap of motor to pull them around a racetrack."

Then he adds: "I'd hate to have to build one from scratch, though. I'll bet there ain't a dozen left in junkyards all over this country."

Since most of the tinkering has already been done, the downtime before the qualifying heats begin is spent visiting and being visited. Evans wanders off to see some friends, and Medlin explains how the two met.

"Me and Vic's been buddies for about 13 years, I guess. Me and him met one night when I helped push his car off. He had a Pinto then, too," raising his voice just in case Evans is still within earshot. "We started hanging out after that and I hooked him up with Cheryl. Cheryl grew up right down the road—rock slingin' distance—from where I lived. He started hanging out with me, and they met at a party.

"Our lives have changed quite a lot. Me and him were running the streets wide-open, teen-age boys, just raising sand and getting in trouble. He got married and I got married and we got settled down.

"He came to the track at Columbia (Speedway) and I was driving not that car, but one just like it, two and a half years ago. I let him warm it up, and he enjoyed it and went and bought a car."

At 7:30, give or take, the country crooner is interrupted by the track announcer to let everyone know the drivers' meeting is going to start in five minutes, asking the drivers and crews to gather at the usual place. But it is unlike any drivers' meeting ever held in Winston Cup.

One of the officials begins by explaining that, even though

tonight's main feature is an "All-Pro" race—meaning that a little extra money has been added to the purse by the auto parts company of the same name—it will remain at 25 laps, not the 35 set for the special event. The reason, he says, is that it gets pretty dusty for the late-running classes. Two old boys from Georgia who are running the Late Models, which stand to get the All-Pro money, want to go 35.

And this is why the meeting will never take place in Winston Cup:

"Let's take a vote on it," the official says. "Late Models, everybody that wants to run thirty-five laps, raise their hands."

Two hands go up.

"I've got an idea," says Nicky Smoak, a Late Model driver from Gaston. "Why don't the rest of us run 25 and then let them run 10 more? Twenty-five laps is enough."

The two Georgians take their medicine good-naturedly, and the meeting goes on.

The official who works the infield says, "First three in the heat races to the scales. Remember that. And if you win, come in down there," pointing to the pit entrance. "Don't make nary 'nother lap. If you make that other lap, I'm gonna disappoint you when you get here, I can promise you that."

The heat races are scheduled to begin at eight, but at about 7:45, the dark clouds that have been gathering since late afternoon are pushing hard for the speedway. The wind kicks up and is sand-blasting everything with a stinging grit. Almost at the chime of 8 P.M., the rain comes down in buckets.

In five minutes, the infield is a swamp. In ten, the track, which has already been watered down for the racing, is running rivulets.

At 8:15, I-20 Speedway has its first rainout of the season. The

P.A. announcer reminds everyone to hold onto their tickets—they're good for the next two weeks, he says—and to be careful driving home.

Twenty minutes later, Evans is still tightening down the straps that hold his car on the trailer. Covan has loaded and gone. Medlin's big Monte Carlo is already on board his trailer, and he and Case are in the long line to get out.

Evans, drenched, looks up from his chore.

"This was for practice," he says.

The next week, Evans has some company. Cheryl, nine-year-old Christopher, and the four-year-old twins, Mathew and Nikki, pile out of the truck. He doesn't have any illusions, however, that the kids are there to watch Daddy race. If things go well, the Stock 4 feature may begin by midnight.

"They'll probably last through the heats," Evans says. "They won't see the main."

Then, like every racer who has ever lived, he knows a better way to do it.

"If I ran this track, I'd let my smaller divisions run first. A lot of people come to see the big cars, and once they're through racing, they start leaving before we race," he says.

His boss, Chuck Crapps, is supposed to be among his rooters this week, and some of the guys from Spring Valley Tire usually show up, too. It is a small, but strong support group.

"Chuck is as good a man to work for as you could ever ask for," Evans says. "I've been working for him about 10 years, and you couldn't have a better boss. If I need to be off, he lets me off. He helps with the car, too."

Evans's job is hot, dirty work, but he never minded getting dirty.

He began as an oil changer at Spring Valley shortly after he and Cheryl were married and has worked his way up to full mechanic.

"I do front-end alignments, engine diagnostics, whatever the car needs," he says. "That's what's pretty neat about working somewhere like that instead of a dealer. You don't have a set job, so it don't get boring. Everything's different."

Evans goes over to draw for a starting spot and comes back looking glum.

At I-20 the cars don't qualify for the heat races. They draw a pill and then are lined up by class, according to the number they've drawn. They qualify for their main events by where they finish in the heat races. There are 100 pills, and Evans drew 85.

"Last week, when it didn't count, I drew 15," he says. "I start dead last. Bill's starting last in his heat, too. We didn't have a good night of drawing."

Then he smiles. "Makes you work harder for it."

The drivers' meeting is the same drill, but this week the official mentions, "Pure Stock and Stock 4s: Y'all remember, no mirrors," he says. "If you get to the scales and you've got a mirror in the car, you can park the car."

A guy in the back pipes up: "I haven't been here lately. What happened with the mirror deal?"

"Got too many people using 'em," the official says, to hoots of laughter. "You need to be worried about what's in front of you, not what's behind you. What's behind you will take care of itself.

"The running order's the same as it has always been. Hobby cars, just as soon as you can help us out, I'd appreciate you on the track."

*   *   *

Evans is fidgety, but it's not all prerace jitters. He has a new motor that was built by Richard Johnson, from Hardin. He ran the motor once, untuned, but took it back to Johnson a couple of weeks ago, and it hasn't been cranked since.

"We got it in and were supposed to take it back to him to get it set, but we got it in so late that we wanted to come run," Evans says. "It just wasn't right, so we took it back to him and got the timing right. He told me to not even pull the hood pins. Maybe it'll make a big difference tonight."

Despite the name, the Hobby cars are one of the higher classes, right below the Late Models. The dents are repaired and the paint jobs—sporting bigger logos for their sponsors—are polished to a high gleam.

That lasts about one lap.

On a dirt track, you don't drive the car straight into the turn, you power-slide it. That entails "crossing it up," cocking the right rear toward the outside wall while you're still barreling down the straight-away, then gunning it through the corners in a controlled slide. As the car straightens out, you ease out of the throttle just enough to let the rear wheels grab, then punch it again. In two laps, the fine paint jobs are covered with mud.

It will be almost an hour and a half before either Medlin or Evans run in their heats, so Evans goes off in search of corndogs for his kids, and Medlin tries to explain how racing gets you by the throat.

"It's a power . . . ," he says, pausing to get the right words. "It's an adrenaline rush. When you buckle up . . . I don't care how many times you get in the car, when you buckle up, the adrenaline starts pumping, your heart starts pumping. There's butterflies in your gut. You don't know who's gonna take you out or who's gonna win or if you're gonna be able to finish the race.

"It's an adrenaline thing, I guess. You get like a junkie. You've got to have that fix every week."

Evans returns from the concession stand, not only with food but with a glow-in-the-dark necklace for each of his kids.

"Makes 'em easier to keep up with," he says.

The heat races in each of the classes are roaring on. At the low end of the totem pole are the Stock 8s and the Stock 4s, so they'll go last.

Covan, who has been pretty quiet all night, has drawn a good number, and his car is near perfect. When he goes out for the first Mini Stock heat, he starts on the outside of the second row, turns it up a notch with five laps to go, and wins going away.

After Medlin roars out for his heat, Evans sits quietly for a few minutes, putting on his game face.

"I played football, but it's nothing like this," he says. "In football, the butterflies left after the kickoff. Here, they stay with you past the checkered flag. I'm wound up so tight that it's two or three hours after I get home before I go to sleep."

Medlin moves up quickly, getting to third place in a couple of laps. Then he gets a nudge coming out of the first turn and slaps the inside wall down the backstretch. The next time around, his steering almost gone, he slips into the outside wall.

He pits, smoke pouring from under his hood, and the first thing his crew chief/brother-in-law does is give the car a swift kick on the right front fender. Whether it's frustration or body work, no one knows.

Evans also starts off like a house afire in his heat. Starting on the back row, he clips off a couple of cars, then slows going down the backstretch. He putters around to the flag and limps home in seventh, right where he started.

"It started running hot," he says, perplexed. "Got up to 225."

A small knot of would-be mechanics have gathered around the car, and nobody can figure out the overheating problem. The first suspect is the radiator fan. Evans swapped the old fan, which was run by belts, for an electrical fan so that it may draw cool air even if the engine's shut off.

"It's blowing the wrong way," Covan says. "Cut the wires and splice them back together backwards."

Rob Butler, who runs ABC Radiators in West Columbia, wanders by. He reaches down, feels the hose connecting the bottom of the radiator to the engine. It is cold. He and Evans pull the hose off and make a makeshift repair.

"The hose probably collapsed," Butler says. "It wasn't drawing enough water to the engine."

Such unsolicited and unpaid help isn't unusual. Nearly every car at the track is, to some degree, a community project. Butler's son Mike, in fact, found Evans's car in a junkyard and helped him turn it into a race car.

"All the neighborhood," Evans says, by way of explanation, "when they hear the car crank up, hangs out at the house. They'll drink a beer and help us work on the car."

Somebody comes back from the parts trailer parked beside the concession stand and offers, "The fellow up there said we ought to put some Pro Blend in it."

Pro Blend is sort of a super antifreeze that costs $23 a can. Crapps, who's been watching, doesn't make a big show of it, but reaches in his wallet, pulls out a bill and slips it to Evans.

"That man turned $7,200 by himself last week," Crapps says a few minutes later. "A few bucks every now and then won't hurt."

Covan is again on the ball. In his main, he bores in on the leader, but can't make the pass. Second-place money isn't bad.

The congratulations are brief. Medlin is already headed out for his race, and Evans is praying the Pro Blend will hold.

The fates have it in for Medlin. He gets whacked pretty hard and crashes into the outside wall on the backstretch. He comes into his pit, steaming. Evans grabs a four-way lug wrench and furiously works to get the mangled right front wheel off while Case is checking out the smoke. Medlin doesn't have a prayer of winning, but you have to be running at the checkered flag to draw a check.

"I don't know why I bothered to take a shower," Medlin says. "I sweat like a sow every time I come out here."

Then he's back out on the track, smoking around to the finish. Evans explains that, just like the Big Boys in Winston Cup, points count. Then he adds, "There's a lot of pride in just being able to finish a race, too."

Medlin herds his mangled car in after the checkered flag, his right front wheel turned out at about a 30-degree angle. He gets out and goes looking for the fellow he figures is responsible. Somewhere between his car and the scales, he has a change of heart. He says a few words into the window of the guy's car and comes back.

"I told him, 'Thanks for the lift,'" he says. "I don't need to go to jail tonight. I'm going to the beach."

It is a quarter to midnight before Evans goes out for his main, and, true to his prediction, his three kids are fast asleep in the cab. The problem with his car hasn't been fixed, either. Almost at the drop of the green flag, he slows. He's off the pace the rest of the way and comes in smoking at the checkered flag, dead last.

"I'm disappointed," he says, that sentiment etched all over his face. "All these people. Chuck, my family. I just wanted to run better. I'm sorry. I tried to give y'all a better show.

"I've just got too much money in the motor to risk blowing it up running it hot. Last year we didn't have a strong motor, but it didn't run hot. Now we've got a strong motor, but we can't keep it cool."

Covan is loaded up, but comes over to say good-bye. He gives Cheryl a hug, and, because John Boy Isley—he of "The Big Show" fame—has made it okay, he exchanges a tired high five with Evans and says, "Love ya, man."

If it weren't so late, it would be funny. Neither Medlin's nor Evans's cars will crank. The batteries are stone-cold dead, and Covan has left with the only booster cable. It's push or walk.

Evans's little Pinto is no problem. A couple of guys help him get it on the trailer. Medlin's monstrous Monte Carlo, however, is a different story. It takes six guys, five pushing and one hanging on the cockeyed front wheel to keep it straight, to get it aboard his trailer.

"See you tomorrow, buddy," Medlin says, as he fires up his truck and pulls away.

At five after one, the lights go off. Evans has nearly completed the tiedowns and, in spite of a bone-weariness that has settled in, manages a smile.

"You're not in it for the money," he says. "Anybody that thinks they're gonna come out on a dirt track and make a living at it, they're wrong. You're lucky if you make enough when you leave here to cover your gas and eating.

"It's all about fun and the friends you make. It's a rush. If you didn't make a dime, at the end of the night to have people walk up and say they enjoyed watching you, that's something."

REFLECTIONS OF A RACING REBEL

For much of a spectacular three-decade career, Darrell
Waltrip ran his mouth as hard as his race car. He teased
and tormented his rivals and jabbed at NASCAR's haughty
hierarchy. Silence finally descended with Waltrip's
retirement, and the sport hasn't been nearly so lively
since.

By Larry Woody

The line crackled as a "fed up and madder'n hell" Darrell Waltrip
sputtered on the other end.

Waltrip had crashed hard the day before in a race at Charlotte
(now Lowe's Motor Speedway), and the Carolina crowd had cheered
insanely. Dazed and semiconscious as rescue workers helped him from
the wreckage, Waltrip could hear the cascade of catcalls, whistles, and
derisive hoots from thousands of fervent Darrell-haters.

The barbs dug deep. For the first time in his career, the Driver
Fans Most Loved to Loathe admitted it hurt, and he fired back.

"Did you hear that crowd?" Waltrip said, speaking to a reporter
from his home in Franklin, Tennessee, where he was nursing his not-
too-serious bumps and scrapes, along with a considerably more bruised
ego and wounded feelings.

"That was a hard crash, they didn't know if I was dead or alive,
and there they were, cheering! *Cheering!* What kind of sick mentality

is that? It makes me ashamed of our sport, of the fans who go to races. I wouldn't let my children sit in the stands with people like that."

Waltrip, who for years had seemed to relish his carefully crafted role as NASCAR's resident villain, paused for breath, then continued: "I'm fed up with people like that. There's times that I feel like posting a notice on light poles around the track: Anybody who doesn't like me can meet me at the Big K parking lot the next morning and we'll duke it out. I mean it. I'm tired of these so-called fans."

Gradually Waltrip cooled down, and shortly thereafter he began to mend the fences he had spent so many years gleefully destroying. He had earned a reputation as a brash, cocky, outspoken, flamboyant, know-it-all, taunting loudmouth: a motorized Muhammad Ali.

Waltrip broadsided the sport at a time when most of the drivers

Darrell Waltrip roughhouses with Dale Earnhardt (left) and Buddy Baker (right).
Darrell Waltrip

were the strong, silent type. They raced hard, kept their mouths shut, toed the company line. No other driver, for example, ever dared to refer to venerable NASCAR founder and president Bill France Sr. as "Our Great White Father in Daytona." But Darrell did. (NASCAR would get the last word: In 1973, it doled out its then-arbitrary Rookie of the Year award to mild-mannered journeyman driver Lennie Pond over the pesky gadfly Waltrip.)

What other driver mimicked a prominent team owner by pretending to talk with a large chaw of tobacco in his jaw during a rain-delay TV interview? ("Dad-gummed car's slower'n goober-slobber-botter!" drawled Waltrip—or words to that effect—as he clowned with his cap turned sideways, Goober-style.

Or was brave/reckless enough to call the great Dale Earnhardt "Ironhead," and suggest that any driver who took him out of a race should receive bonus points? (Waltrip and Earnhardt, archenemies on the track, would eventually become close friends, and Waltrip briefly drove one of Earnhardt's cars.)

Waltrip, a native of Owensboro, Kentucky, moved to Nashville in the late 1960s to pursue a racing career that had outgrown its rural Kentucky boundaries. In the early 1970s, he hit NASCAR with the impact of a runaway locomotive.

He gouged at the Establishment. He thumbed his nose at beloved old legends, like Richard Petty. He made outlandish statements ("Earnhardt's not *smart* enough to win a championship!") Nothing was sacred for Waltrip. Nobody could match his wicked wit, and he took no prisoners.

One season, locked in a tight championship battle with Bill Elliott, Waltrip psychologically tormented the Dawsonville, Georgia, driver into near-shell shock. While Waltrip played the media like a violin,

Elliott fled from it. "Gawleeeeeee!" Waltrip told reporters, mimicking Elliott's grits-curdling Georgia drawl, "Yew fellers git on away from me now, y'hear!"

By the time it was over, Waltrip had almost reduced Elliott—a shy, retiring country boy—into a twitching basket case.

Waltrip would go out of his way—swerve across the lawn, knock down a light post, and bounce up on the sidewalk—to run down trouble and swideswipe controversy.

"I like to stir the pot a little bit now and then," Waltrip said. "Keeps things interesting."

Waltrip craved attention, a craving to which he freely confessed, yet maintained that it was not entirely ego driven. He said there was method to his madness.

"When I came into NASCAR, I was just another good ol' boy rolling in from the hills," he explained. "Nobody outside of Owensboro or Nashville had heard of Darrell Waltrip. Nobody knew who I was. Well, I was determined to change that. I realized that if I was going to make a name for myself, I needed to get the media's attention. I learned that if I said something or did something fairly outrageous, I'd be on the front page the next morning. They say the squeaky wheel gets the grease, and I learned how to grease that wheel like nobody had ever greased it."

And so, over the years, Waltrip would become the greasiest wheel in NASCAR. But he found there was a price to be paid. In the process of attracting reams of publicity, he also became reviled by fans and fellow drivers. No driver in the sport was met with more seething hostility, greeted with more animosity, than was Waltrip when he took the stage for prerace driver introductions.

Fans hissed and booed and wore "Anybody But Waltrip" T-shirts.

More and more, drivers let it be known that they didn't find Waltrip's acts and antics amusing. Cale Yarborough, one of Waltrip's early antagonists, nicknamed him "Jaws" after the shark in the blockbuster movie of the time.

"There were a couple of reasons," Yarborough explained. "One, Darrell liked to run his mouth and flap his jaws all the time. Second, he was so wild and reckless on the track that he was always chewing up everybody's cars, just like old Jaws chewed up everything that got in [its] path."

People who knew Waltrip realized that it was essentially all an act: His barbs were more mischievous than malicious. But some stung. He openly criticized the folk-hero Petty for, "hanging on past his prime." As Petty floundered through the twilight of a once-great career, Waltrip told reporters: "It's sad to watch. Somebody ought to take Richard aside and explain that it's over. He needs to stop embarrassing himself like that." (Years later, in sad irony, Darrell would stubbornly refuse to heed his own advice as he wobbled through seven final, winless, noncompetitive seasons.)

One rivalry festered and turned especially ugly. Bobby Allison came to detest Waltrip. If Waltrip was only kidding during many of his hijinks, Allison didn't think it was funny, and even less so when his son Davey began to race and found himself caught up in some tangles with Waltrip.

After his career was over, ended by a near-fatal crash at Pocono in 1988 and followed by the heart-wrenching deaths of his two bright young sons, Clifford and Davey, the devout-Catholic Allison told a friend, "I may burn in Hell for it, but I can't bring myself to forgive Darrell Waltrip."

Waltrip defended his driving style. He said he was no more rough and reckless on a racetrack than most of the other top drivers. "I won't move over for them, and they don't like it," he would say. "They want to dish it out, but they can't take it."

As for the hostile fan response: "It's like when Jack Nicklaus came along and started beating Arnold Palmer," Waltrip said. "Palmer had a lot of fans, and they resented Nicklaus for beating their hero, just like a lot of race fans don't like to see their favorite old drivers get beat. I'm NASCAR's Nicklaus."

And about challenging NASCAR's largely unchallenged authority: "I speak my mind. I say what I believe. If I see something that I consider to be wrong or unfair, I'm not afraid to speak out about it. I don't apologize for that."

But gradually, Waltrip began to realize that he was taking the game too far, pushing too hard. The boos and the barbs began to take their toll.

"Nobody likes to be booed every time he steps onto the stage," Waltrip confided to a friend. "I'm like any entertainer or professional athlete: I want the fans to like me. I may be wisecracking and laughing on the outside, but I'm hurting on the inside."

"It broke my heart to see how Darrell was treated by the fans," said Waltrip's wife, Stevie. "I can't tell you how many times I left the tracks in tears."

"I had created a monster," Waltrip said, "and that monster got out of control. One day it hit me: People actually hated me. I never wanted that. That's not how I wanted to be remembered in this sport. I decided I had to stop it. I had to change my image."

It wasn't easy, and it didn't come quickly. Waltrip had planted the seeds of resentment deeply. But, eventually, the change began to come. Waltrip buttoned his lip and began to mind his manners. He could still be outspoken on issues, but without the former sharp edge. Always eloquent and glib, Waltrip became a positive spokesman for the sport. His on-track feuds became fewer and less fierce, the cascade of boos from the stands less vicious. Age and maturity had mellowed the one-time firebrand, and eventually the kinder, gentler Waltrip began to win the fans over. His personality makeover was completed when, in 1989 and 1990, he was voted NASCAR's Most Popular Driver.

Try as he might, however, Waltrip was unable to mend all the rifts. In the spring of 2000, during his final season on the circuit, Waltrip was feted with a retirement dinner in Bristol, Tennessee. Many of the top drivers, past and present, were on hand and took turns giving Waltrip good-natured digs and gouges, accompanied by laughter from the audience.

Then Allison, Waltrip's old nemesis, took the podium, and a perceptible chill descended over the banquet hall. Allison began by talking about "what a nice family Darrell has," but added, "I'd like to say something nice about Darrell Waltrip . . . but I just can't think of anything."

A few nervous chuckles rippled through the audience, but the tension hung thick as Allison made a few more remarks, then took his seat.

Waltrip stepped to the dais and, knowing that everyone was aware of Allison's bouts with amnesia caused by his terrible crash years earlier, said with a grin, "Bobby's sitting back there now thinking how much he hates me . . . and trying to remember why!"

Laughter erupted, and even Allison managed to smile.

But it was clear that Allison's comments had cut deep and wounded NASCAR's Clown Prince. Despite all the brashness and bravado, Waltrip is a highly sensitive individual. He is a good man, a moral person, and his feelings run deep. Today, in retirement, he is

pained by the knowlege that Allison, unlike most fans and other drivers, can't bring himself to forgive and forget. The shadow of the monster he created so many years ago still lurks in at least one corner.

That aside, NASCAR's one-time bad boy and resident rebel looks
back with few regrets. In fact, his Howard Cosellian, tell-it-like-it-is
ways seemed to appeal to NASCAR's growing TV audience. His
frank, candid style was especially favored by Fox network officials.
When they signed to begin telecasting NASCAR races in 2001, they
quickly scooped up Waltrip as a color commentator. Today he still
occasionally shoots from the lip, but he no longer fires steel-jacketed
bullets and aims for the heart. The sting is gone, his humor more
gentle.

"For the most part I was just trying to have a little fun, stir things
up a bit, get a little attention," Waltrip said, reflecting on his old ways
in the old days. "I thought it was good not just for me, but for our
sport. I tried to make things interesting and give you guys (media)
something to write about."

That he did. For three decades Waltrip joked and laughed and
jibed and jived and invited controversy to trot at his heels like a faithful
old dog. It was common knowledge among the motorsports press:
Things a little dull? Need a good story? Where's Darrell? Toss out an
issue—any issue—and he was Mr. Instant Copy. Ask Waltrip if he
thought it might rain, and an hour later you'd filled up two notebooks.

"Y'all gonna miss me when I'm gone," Waltrip told the media,
only half-jokingly, in his final press conference as a driver, at Atlanta
Motor Speedway in the fall of 2000.

He was right. We do miss him. The sport misses him.

Sure, he talked big, but he backed it up with 84 wins and three
championships. ("Boys, it ain't braggin' if you do it," he used to pro-

claim.) Yes, at times he came across as a brash motormouth, an obnoxious troublemaker. But most of us knew that he didn't intend to be malicious and hurtful.

We knew he was just kidding, joking around, having a little fun. "Just stirring the pot a little."

He was determined to be the life of the NASCAR party, and he succeeded . . . sometimes almost too well. But even his critics had to give him credit: Life with D. W. anywhere in the vicinity was never dull.

A YEAR OF TRAGEDY FOR NASCAR'S ROYAL FAMILY

Four generations of the Petty family have competed in NASCAR and, along the way, influenced the entire history of the sport. Lee, Richard, Kyle, and Adam Petty combined for 10 championships and 264 victories. Within a few weeks in 2000, however, the family's patriarch, Lee, died from complications following surgery, and its hope for the future, 19-year-old Adam, was killed during practice at New Hampshire International Speedway.

By Kenny Bruce

P hysically spent and emotionally exhausted, Kyle Petty climbed from behind the wheel of the No. 44 Hot Wheels Pontiac, his car looking every bit as drained as Petty himself.

Petty's night was done, and he was drenched in sweat. A 22d-place finish on the rugged high banks of Bristol (Tennessee) Motor Speedway was in the books. Petty had finished one lap down to the race winner, but it was his team's third-best effort of the season.

Meanwhile, over between turns three and four, amid a shower of postrace fireworks, Rusty Wallace was celebrating another victory at BMS. Nearly 150,000 fans had turned out for the evening's festivities, and now they began making their way toward the parking lots to begin the long journey home.

For Petty, however, this particular journey was coming to an end. The Bristol event would mark Petty's final start in the team's No. 44 Pontiac. Eleven events remained on the 2000 NASCAR Winston Cup

Series schedule, but Petty would not be a part of the series' stretch drive.

For the remainder of the year, Petty would turn his attention to another entry, the No. 45 Busch ride that had been driven by his son, 19-year-old Adam Petty.

"We might could have been farmers and been better off," said Richard Petty, "I don't know. We might could have owned a grocery store and owned a big chain by now. We might have been a whole lot better off."

The idea that a Petty, any Petty, would come along and find himself involved in anything other than racing seems ridiculous to today's race fan. But that's because the familiar moniker and NASCAR racing have been intertwined ever since the sport's founder, Big Bill France,

Left to right, Kyle, Richard, and Lee Petty chat together in Daytona in 1985. DMP Archives Photos

cinched up his belt, rolled up his sleeves, and said, "Boys, this here's how we're gonna get this thing off the ground."

Lee Petty, father of Richard, grandfather of Kyle, and great-grandfather of Adam, was 35 years old when he and a host of other daredevils descended on a three-quarter-mile dirt track in the outskirts of Charlotte, North Carolina. The date was June 19, 1949. The occasion was NASCAR's very first "Strictly Stock" race.

Thirty-three drivers took part in the event. Petty didn't win, but did distinguish himself. He was the only driver to crash during the 197-lap event.

It didn't take Petty, a truck driver by trade, long to get his bearings. That same year, on October 2 at Heidelberg Raceway in Pittsburgh, Pennsylvania, Lee scored the very first NASCAR-sanctioned win for Petty Enterprises.

By 1954 NASCAR's original eight-race schedule had expanded to include 37 events, stretching all the way from the beaches of Daytona Beach, Florida, to the coast of California. Petty, by now a full-time racer, captured seven events en route to his first series championship. Driving against the likes of Buck Baker, Tim Flock, and other early legends in the sport, Petty did more than just leave his mark. He began a tradition of winning that continued through the next three generations. And along the way, he made the Petty name a household word.

His days as one of the sport's premier competitors came to an end, however, at Daytona in 1961. On the final lap of the first of two qualifying races, Petty was involved in a crash while racing with Johnny Beauchamp, the same driver Petty had edged out for the win in the very first Daytona 500. Beauchamp hit the No. 42 entry square in the driver's side door, and both cars went over the track's retaining wall.

Lee suffered a punctured lung, leg injury, and numerous lacerations. While he continued to race for three more seasons before finally stepping aside in 1964, Lee Petty never regained the steely, hard-edged driving style that had catapulted him to three championships and 55 victories—literally the top of the sport.

It wasn't, however, the end of the Petty dynasty. Only the first few chapters. For as soon as one Petty began to fade, another was already making his way into the spotlight.

May 13, 1967. The Rebel 400 at Darlington (South Carolina) Raceway. Richard Petty finished a lap ahead of runner-up David Pearson to score his seventh victory of the season. It was notable at the time because it was also career win No. 55, tying the series record held by his father.

A week later, at a dirt track known as Langley Field Speedway in Hampton, Virginia, Richard eclipsed his father's mark, edging Bobby Allison in a Cotton Owens–owned Dodge for win No. 56 and the record.

Few doubted that Richard would own the mark before the season ever got under way. After all, at the relatively young age of 30, he already had one series championship to his credit, and was coming off what could only be termed as an "off year" by his team's standards. The previous season he had won eight races and scored nine seconds but failed to captured the series title. In 1967, however, there was no stopping the No. 43 entry. Petty collected a record 27 victories, including one stretch when he strung together 10 consecutive wins.

It's the stuff of legends, but that's one title that Richard Petty isn't comfortable wearing.

"We're just a family, just doing our thing," he said. "We just happened to be in the business and happened to have had fairly good success at it, made a good living out of it. The big thing was, all the family enjoyed what we were doing. The family's always been involved and prospered from it."

It's more than that. Yes, without a doubt the Petty family prospered from its involvement in NASCAR racing. But by the same token, the sport flourished over the years in large part because of the Pettys' participation. By the time he stepped out of the car in 1992, Richard Petty had become an icon, and not just in the world of auto racing. To this day he remains as widely recognized as a Muhammad Ali or a Michael Jordan, a Mark McGwire or a Joe Montana. Just like those bigger-than-life athletes, Petty transcended the sport, whether he realized it or not.

If it only seemed natural for Richard to follow in his father's footsteps, then how much more natural must it have seemed for Kyle to continue the tradition, only to be trailed by his own son, Adam? Lynda Petty, Richard's wife, had other hopes for her only son, hopes that only a college education would keep alive.

The Pettys had not lost a family member to the sport throughout the years. But there had been too many times when horrendous accidents on the racetrack had threatened to end that string of good fortune. Lee and Richard had survived their share of life-threatening encounters, but the Pettys were close to several other racing families that were not as fortunate.

But Kyle, just like his father, knew he had to give racing a shot. And when he won the very first event he entered, an ARCA race at Daytona International Speedway, the newest Petty racer was officially hooked.

Unlike his father, Kyle enjoyed only marginal success while racing for Petty Enterprises from 1979 through 1984. His father earned his seventh, and final, championship in '79, but the First Family of Racing was finding it harder and harder to keep up with the sport as it burst upon the American scene. As a result, Kyle looked elsewhere to satisfy his competitive yearnings. In 1985 he joined another veteran team, Wood Brothers Racing out of Stuart, Virginia, and scored his first career victory a year later in Richmond, Virginia.

By the time he finally returned home, in 1997, to the team's shop in Level Cross, North Carolina, Kyle had carved out a fairly respectable career. He had eight victories, had finished as high as fifth in the points battle (twice) and was generally regarded as one of the most well-spoken competitors in the garage. He could be funny or colorful or brutally honest. He may not have had the success of others who went before him, but he had grown up with the sport firsthand, and his views on the goings-on in the sport were much valued.

While several of his fellow competitors were able to concentrate solely on driving, Kyle's racing agenda had become much more complicated. Hoisted upon his shoulders was the task of bringing the once-proud Petty Enterprises back to respectability. A multicar operation, Petty Enterprises had fielded entries for Petty and John Andretti in 1999. The 2000 season was to be a special one for the organization. Adam, 19, would be competing in a handful of Winston Cup events while also competing full-time in the Busch Series.

With his easygoing manner and quick smile, Adam Petty was already becoming a well-known and much-liked personality in the garage area. The lanky teenager, many noticed, had his father's aura, his easygoing attitude, and his humorous outlook on life. As well as his grandfather's talent. If true, it would surely be a powerful combination.

* * *

It was supposed to be a momentous occasion, father and son competing for the first time in the same race. Much like Richard and Kyle had done, just as Lee and Richard had as well.

Adam Petty made his Winston Cup debut on April 2, 2000, qualifying 33d for the DirecTV 500 at Texas Motor Speedway. But in a twist of fate, Kyle failed to qualify for the series' seventh race of the season, his No. 44 Pontiac failing to post adequate speed during qualifying on the 1.5-mile track. Instead of racing with his son, the father was reduced to serving in an advisory role from the pits.

Kyle eventually did make it out onto the racetrack, stepping in to relieve Elliott Sadler after the Wood Brothers driver was injured in an accident. Unfortunately, it was too late to put father and son together: Adam had fallen out of the event just 14 laps earlier, victimized by engine failure.

Still, the 19-year-old Petty was upbeat afterward, telling reporters he thought the dream of racing alongside his father "was going to come true there for a minute. It would have been fun to be out there with him."

That he made it through the event unscathed was another good sign, he said, noting that just being able to compete against the best drivers in the sport teaches younger drivers so much.

"I became a 10-times better driver than before I started the race," he said. "Those guys out there are the best in the business, and whenever they get to you, they teach you something."

Missing from the weekend's festivities was Richard Petty, who had remained in North Carolina to be with his father. Lee, now 86, had been hospitalized after problems developed following surgery for a stomach aneurysm.

All in all, the Petty family remained confident. There were to be other Winston Cup events in 2000, four to be precise, where the youngest of the Petty clan would attempt to qualify. If racing alongside his father for Petty Enterprises didn't happen in Texas, then surely it would take place somewhere else during the season.

Three days after Adam Petty's Winston Cup debut, the Petty family was dealt a jarring blow. Lee, the hard-nosed patriarch of NASCAR's most successful racing family, passed away while in Cone Hospital in Greensboro, North Carolina.

The elder Petty had distanced himself from the sport since turning over the reins of the team to son Richard. In later years, he busied himself around his home, often making the short walk over to the team's shops to "tell 'em what they were doing wrong," recalled Kyle.

Unlike his son, who became the sport's most popular figure, Lee didn't have an abundance of friends throughout the NASCAR community. But that never bothered the three-time champion, who would tell anyone that winning was more important than being popular. Winning, after all, had helped him put food on the table in the early years, and if that cost him a friendship or two along the way, he could live with that.

Bill France, president of NASCAR, noted Lee's impact in a statement released by the sanctioning body following the news of Petty's death.

"Lee raced in our first Winston Cup event in Charlotte, won the inaugural Daytona 500 and played a leadership role in the early growth of our sport. He began the great Petty family tradition in NASCAR and, of course, was the father of one of the sport's superstars in Richard. . . . All of us at NASCAR are saddened to hear of Lee's passing and extend our deepest sympathy to his family."

"He had a lot of influence, a lot of suggestions and stuff," Richard said of his father. That the two often found themselves competing for the same trophy and, more important, prize money made little difference. Both, he noted, were racing for Petty Enterprises. For the family. And in the end, that was all that mattered.

"I guess it was just the way of doing things," he said. "We never thought that much about it. It was never any challenge to race with my dad. We were all working out of the same pot. . . . It wasn't that we were in competition with each other; we were trying to do the best we could for each other."

Thirty-seven days. Hardly enough time to mourn the loss of a loved one. Time to pay one's respects and move on, perhaps. Lee Petty was gone, but his memory, and the organization he built, would live on, hopefully to thrive once again.

Richard was no longer driving, and Kyle, who had only recently taken over the day-to-day operations at Petty Enterprises, was already laying the groundwork for Adam's pending arrival as a full-time Winston Cup competitor.

With many of the Busch and Winston Cup events being held in conjunction with each other, Kyle and Adam were able to spend plenty of time together as the youngest racing Petty began his career in earnest. Even when the two series weren't headed for the same venue, the father and son stayed in contact via telephone, Kyle offering support and advice to a son still so full of questions.

Competing on a 34-race schedule while attempting to rebuild a failing racing operation didn't leave Kyle with an abundance of free time. It was a schedule his wife, Patti, and younger children, Austin and Montgomery Lee, had long grown accustomed to.

Breaks in the racing schedule didn't come often, and when they did, Petty liked to use them to spend time with his family away from the sport. So when the opportunity to travel with Montgomery Lee to London arose, Kyle didn't hesitate. The Winston Cup Series was on a brief break, having just completed an event at Richmond, Virginia, on May 6. It would be two weeks before the series was back in action, traveling to Charlotte, North Carolina, for the sport's all-star event.

Meanwhile, Adam would travel to Loudon, New Hampshire, where the Busch Series was scheduled to compete on May 13.

"I spent so much time with Adam at the racetrack—going to the racetrack, being around the racetrack and being around race cars—that I felt like I needed to spend more time with Montgomery Lee and Austin," Kyle said.

Still, there was contact with his oldest son during the trip abroad. Petty said he and his daughter phoned Adam at the track "at least three or four times" during the flight overseas.

"Montgomery Lee thought it was cool that you could call from an airplane," he said. "So we called him in New Hampshire . . . and just told him we loved him."

Not long after his arrival in London, however, Kyle received a call from NASCAR president Mike Helton. There had been an accident.

On Friday, May 12, during a routine practice session at Loudon, Adam Petty's car had made contact with the outside retaining wall in the third turn. After spinning, it struck the unforgiving concrete barrier with full force. Traveling at approximately 130 mph, both the car and driver had come to a sudden, dreadful stop.

Nineteen-year-old Adam Petty, the hope and future of Petty Enterprises, was dead.

*   *   *

"The biggest thing," said Kyle, "has not been [the reactions] from the people you know. It's not been the outpouring or the calls from people you know or things like that. It was the people that you'll never meet and you'll never know."

These days are difficult ones for the Petty family. Nearly everywhere Kyle turns, it seems, he's faced with a reminder of his son. But nothing stirs the memories as much as the one thing that he simply can't escape, the one thing that has bound his family together for generations: the sport of auto racing.

He's a changed man. The heavy shroud of responsibility wears on a person, and few have as many concerns as Kyle Petty. What enjoyment the business side of the sport had sucked out of his career had been replenished by his son's burgeoning career. Now that was gone, too.

"After 20 years of racing a car, you just get jaded . . . jaded to people wanting autographs or doing this or doing that," he said. "For Adam, that was all so new that it added an element of excitement. To see him get excited that somebody from a TV station had done an interview or somebody had wanted an autograph. To see the excitement that he had for that, then it gave you a new excitement for the sport.

"It made you look at the sport differently."

Many thought the loss of his son would drive Kyle away for good. But while he did temporarily step aside, eventually the hold the sport had on him proved too great. There were things that needed to be done, employees whose livelihood rested on the continuation of Petty Enterprises.

Quitting, he said, was never an option.

"This is what we have always done as a family. My grandfather did it, my father did it, I've done it, Adam did it," Kyle said. "This is what we do. . . . Just because something goes bad or something goes wrong, you don't quit and go home. You keep plugging along at it.

"Like I said before, and sometimes it sounds a little crazy or a little stupid to say, but as much as Adam loved racing, he wouldn't stop, so there is no reason for us to."

As the dawn of the 2002 racing season approached, Kyle was as busy as ever: preparing for yet another year of competition, and making sure his teammates have the necessary tools and financial backing to be competitive in the growing sport. It had been nearly two years since his family lost both grandfather and son, losses that continued to wear on the family.

Still, they continue on.

Yes, they could have been farmers, as Richard said. Or grocers or lawyers or factory workers. But they weren't. Four generations of Pettys grew up to be race car drivers and changed the fabric of the sport forever.

And in the end, the sport changed them as well.

THE ULTIMATE TEST

For six decades Darlington Raceway has haunted
NASCAR's best, and the egg-shaped track is still the
hardest place on earth to win a 500-mile stock car race.

By Monte Dutton

N o architect planned Darlington Raceway. It was rather an ambi-
tious earth mover named Harold Brasington, who decided,
shortly after a visit to the Indianapolis 500, that he could build a
racetrack like no other in his South Carolina hometown.

Instead of an oval, Brasington built an egg, wider on one end than
the other. The owner of a heavy equipment company, Brasington made
a deal with another local businessman, Sherman Ramsey, to trade 70
acres of farmland for stock in the track.

They must have been crazy. Somehow, with an assist from a burgeoning racing tycoon from Daytona Beach, Florida, named William
H. G. France, it worked. It still works, despite the fact that the raceway
has been in operation since 1950.

The best racers always drive "by the seat of their pants." That's the
way Brasington built his racetrack. The reason Darlington is not a
standard oval is that Ramsey, his partner, had a little minnow pond

over behind what is now turn four. Ramsey was partial to his pond and the bait it provided for him and his friends. So Brasington narrowed the radius on one end and connected it to the other with a pair of straights.

It is popularly thought that such a thing could not happen today. It could not happen the same way, but it could happen. If a tiny pond existed on a plot of land designated for one of today's modern "super-speedways," nearby homeowners would probably use the pond as a means to deter the developers. They'd probably contact a sympathetic politician—and what politician isn't sympathetic, at least publicly?—and have the pond declared a government-protected "wetland."

Ah, but times have changed. In fact, times have changed a lot faster than Darlington Raceway has.

Until Labor Day 1950, when the first Southern 500 was held, no NASCAR race had ever been run on pavement. No NASCAR race had ever been run at a distance even close to 500 miles. Was Darlington revolutionary? Was it ahead of its time? Well, to give you an idea, the little track located very close to the middle of nowhere had an exclusive franchise on 500-mile stock car races until 1959, when France himself opened his two-and-a-half-mile speed palace in Daytona Beach.

Clarice Lane worked at the track when the first Southern 500 was held. Still works there, in fact. She recalled the confusion vividly, 52 years later. The organizers were expecting 9,000 fans; 20,000 showed up. Ticket locations had been unwittingly duplicated in some cases, and counterfeit tickets aggravated the situation even more.

"We had bought four tickets," Mrs. Lane said. "Harold [Brasington] had sold them to us. Well, we bought box seats down in front because everybody thought they wanted a front-row seat. Some people showed up from Virginia with tickets that said they had the same seats we did. We had bought four seats, and there must have been at least eight people crowded into those four seats that day.

"Everybody [presumably, the women] came in high-heeled shoes. We didn't know anything about racing, and there we were, down there in front, separated from the race cars by nothing but a barrier. Chunks of rubber hit us. We had oil on our faces. It was dreadful."

The race took more than five hours. One of the slower cars on the track won because it was allowed to run truck tires—some said illegally—and remained on the track while almost every other car was spending a good percentage of the day pitting for new tires. By race's end, crews had gone foraging through the infield, in some cases buying tires right off the passenger cars parked there.

Californian Johnny Mantz won the race in a black Plymouth with "98 Jr." on its sides. After the race, the chief technical inspector declared Mantz's car illegal. Bill France overturned the decision. The inspector quit in protest.

France was part owner of Mantz's car.

To the good citizens of the South Carolina Pee Dee—a region named for a river that drains it—it comes as a bit of a surprise that their racetrack, which was built at least a decade ahead of its time, is now seen as some kind of delightfully wicked anachronism by the drivers of the 21st century.

"I like it," Dale Earnhardt Jr. said recently. "I heard one day they might pave it."

That playful little slap was a reference to the track's surface, which is horribly abrasive thanks to the region's sandy soil. Darlington—not to mention another NASCAR track in nearby Rockingham, North Carolina—occupies an area known as the Sandhills, which is a band of, yes, sand that exists because in prehistoric times the Atlantic Ocean lapped up against the area. Now the Atlantic's tourist mecca of Myrtle Beach is about 75 miles away, but the thundering, 3,400-pound stock cars grind the sand into the asphalt as they rapidly drive around and around, and they have to replace their tires much more often than at other tracks simply because the deteriorating, pebbled asphalt takes a hefty toll on the rubber.

Another myth is the notion that Darlington Raceway was built for the speeds of 1950 and that it is somehow unfair for drivers still to have to race there at the speeds of the new millennium. This often-expressed view is a bit exaggerated. Actually, Darlington has been updated dramatically. When it opened, the track measured 1.25 miles around. Then it was lengthened to a mile and three eighths.

Up until 1968, the turns were much flatter. One end of the track was, for all practical purposes, good for only one lane of traffic at race speed. If the current drivers consider the layout hellish—and they do—they might at least consider the conditions that once gave rise to the popular term "Darlington Stripe."

Drivers still talk about the Darlington Stripe. Most have no idea what the term means. Their stripe is a vague reference to the fact that the racing groove is narrow—almost a sidewalk, really, when compared to other tracks—and slipping up, across the abrasive surface, to "tag" the wall is something they end up doing all too often.

The original, unabridged Darlington Stripe, though, was a good thing. Turns three and four were so narrow that it was impossible to go fast enough through the little alley without ramming the cars up against the guardrails intentionally. Drivers like Junior Johnson and Fireball Roberts "leaned" on the rails, they said, and when they did, sparks flew off their bumpers, and the friction left a "stripe" where the paint had been stripped away. It was a stirring sight, and while no one could really pass in that segment of the track, he could build up momentum to roar past his hapless opponents on the front straight and then through the wider turns one and two. Likewise, a skilled driver who knew how to use "the stripe" could keep faster cars driven by lesser men at bay for lap after lap.

Today's layout, which officially measures 1.366 miles and has relatively high-banked turns on both ends, was built for the speeds of 35 years ago.

It's a piece of cake, relatively speaking. On the other hand, Darlington is still unquestionably NASCAR's toughest track, and it is probably only rivaled, in terms of pure skill required, by the more spectacular but similarly diabolical concrete half mile situated in Bristol, Tennessee.

Harold Brasington liked races and loved building racetracks. He also built the Rockingham track, now known as North Carolina Speedway, in 1965. Brasington did not much care for administration, though.

Clarice Lane remembered Brasington's disinterested, and somewhat brief, days as the track president.

"Harold used to wander in and wander out," Mrs. Lane said. "He'd head out the door after dinner [in towns like Darlington, what other people call lunch is dinner, and what others refer to as dinner is called supper] and say, 'Clarice, I've got something to do. I've got to crawl around under the bed and round up enough pennies to buy my boy a bicycle,' and he'd wink.

"He must have bought a lot of bicycles," she concluded, "or else done a whole lot of crawling around."

Brasington was all too happy to get out of the way, though, when his apathy threatened the progress of his brainchild.

The man who really nurtured the legend was a high-spirited, glad-handing pepperpot named Robert E. Colvin. Bob Colvin was the sort of bald man whom people habitually called "Curly." He wasn't afraid, in the vernacular of the local farming community, to "get a little dirt on his hands." He was also a bold promoter who brought beauty pageants, parades, and appearances by Hollywood stars to Darlington for the Southern 500. Photographs from Colvin's tenure are full of the smiling faces of stars like James Arness and Ken Curtis, both from television's "Gunsmoke," and Clint Eastwood, then known principally for "Rawhide." Darlington Raceway had a mascot decades before anyone thought of the "San Diego Chicken." "Johnny Reb" greeted winning drivers in victory lane, waving a Confederate flag to the multitudes. Darlington—track and town alike—was not notably sensitive to the views of the black community in those days.

Colvin traveled the Carolinas, his garishly decorated "pace car" loaded down with cardboard signs he and others would nail to thousands of telephone poles. The Southern 500, proclaimed Colvin, was "the granddaddy of them all!" One of Colvin's first acts, upon becoming president of the raceway in 1952, was to build a radio network to carry the two annual races and spread the word throughout the South.

Darlington may be the only track in history that has had its attendance diminished by every construction project. In the mid-1960s, the Colvin public-relations machine proudly estimated its crowds at 80,000 or more. Today the track, having been enhanced by massive, high-rise grandstands on what used to be the back straight—the track's geography flip-flopped in 1998—draws crowds estimated at 60,000 fans, or 25 percent fewer, now that the grandstands are twice as large.

But Colvin made sure the stands were packed. Traditionally, the back straight was crowded with scout troops from across the state.

Colvin hired a Virginian named Ray Melton to man the public address microphone, and Melton's staccato delivery became another signature of the track. Melton spoke of Darlington Raceway as if it were the center of the universe. He coined terms like "high, wide, and handsome" to describe the cars as they zipped through the turns.

Unfortunately, on the morning of January 24, 1967, Bob Colvin died in his office of a massive heart attack. Despite the fact that he had been "Mr. Darlington" for nearly 15 years, Colvin was only 47 years old at the time of his death.

If anyone replaced Colvin as Darlington's leading ambassador, it was Harold King, who still works there and handles a variety of ceremonial duties within the community.

"I think, in retrospect, one of the worst things that ever happened to Darlington Raceway was Colvin's untimely death," said King. "For many years, we lost the spirit he brought to the track. Darlington sort of became lost—and trapped in one time and place—without Colvin's vision and energy.

"The times kind of passed us by for a long while. We lost a full decade of people who were coming along. If Colvin had lived, that never would have happened. He was the P. T. Barnum of our sport."

What never ended, however, was the pure spectacle of the Southern 500. Other tracks stole its limelight. In the '70s and '80s, the facilities at other tracks were being upgraded while Darlington Raceway was, for the most part, standing pat. Over time, while attendance at Darlington remained stable, the crowds at glittering edifices like Charlotte (now Lowe's) Motor Speedway, Daytona International Speedway, and Alabama International Motor Speedway (now Talladega Super-speedway) doubled and tripled, but at Darlington, everything remained basically the same.

A generation of new fans forgot about the track where it really all began.

"A lot of the new fans cannot capture the real significance of what they're looking at," observed King. "To them, nowadays it's like comparing the Taj Mahal to little Darlington."

Rather than a place of national renown, Darlington became more the pride and joy of its native state. The native South Carolinians David Pearson and Cale Yarborough exemplified the spirit of the Palmetto State. Pearson, from Spartanburg, became the track's all-time leader in victories, winning 10 races—three Southern 500s and seven Rebel 400/500s—between 1968 and 1980. Yarborough, born in nearby Timmonsville, became the all-time leader in Southern 500 victories, with five.

Pearson and Yarborough, like virtually everyone else who ever achieved a high degree of success at Darlington, were all-time greats.

"It meant a lot to me when I read where people said I was the best at Darlington," said Pearson. "As far as I was concerned, there never was another track like Darlington. It was the track that I called home, and, really, that's still the way it is today."

Even now, the number of drivers who have won at Darlington is astonishingly small, given the track's long history. Many prominent drivers—Lee Petty, for instance, and Curtis Turner, not to mention modern masters like Rusty Wallace—either never won there or haven't to date. Terry Labonte won the Southern 500 in 1980, when he was in his second full season, but has never repeated the feat. Richard Petty swept Darlington's two races in 1967 but never won there again in a

The field gets ready to begin the 1974 Rebel 450 at Darlington Raceway, a race shortened from 500 miles due to the energy crisis. Eventual winner David Pearson is on the outside of the front row in the famed Wood Brothers No. 21 Mercury.
DMP Archives Photos

career that lasted through 1992. Out of 200 victories, only three occurred at Darlington.

On the other hand, Darlington became the personal playground of greats like Pearson, Yarborough, Bobby Allison, Dale Earnhardt, and Jeff Gordon. Earnhardt won nine races, second only to Pearson, before his untimely death at Daytona in 2001.

"I think that's the legacy we have to preserve," said Darlington Raceway's current president, Andrew Gurtis. "When you look at our list of winners, it reads like the roster of a hall of fame. With very few exceptions—less by far than at any other track—only the greatest drivers of their time have won races at Darlington."

So while, in a figurative sense, its rocks may be jagged and its faces weathered, Darlington Raceway remains stock car racing's Mt. Olympus, even after lo these many years.

"There are probably really only 10 racers out there," said Dave McInnis, ex-South Carolina state legislator and circuit judge, now a member of the Darlington Raceway staff. "The rest of them are riders."

Watching a race at Darlington requires a great deal of sophistication and knowledge. The track's narrowness means that passing is difficult, and fast cars are often trapped deep in the pack. Implements that are helpful but not mandatory at other tracks—the stopwatch, the radio scanner (which allows fans to listen in on radio transmissions between drivers and their pit crews) and soundproof headset—are almost necessary to understand what is really going on.

It is not unusual for a stopwatch to reveal that the fastest car, at least early in a race, is running 22d or 23d. Identifying that car is often prophetic.

Bravado is a dangerous quality for drivers on Darlington race Sundays. Almost ad nauseum, drivers refer to the need to, in a phrase of seeming redundancy, "race the racetrack." What those drivers mean is that they must concentrate more on going fast around the track than on catching and passing other cars.

Pearson was famous for using traffic to his advantage. He had an extraordinary knack for timing his passes and forcing other drivers to make mistakes in traffic.

The great driver's son Larry won a Busch Grand National race at Darlington in 1996 after years of frustrations at the track.

"For years and years, all my daddy would harp on was that you had to pass people on the straightaways and time it so you didn't come up on them in the turns," the son said after his long-awaited victory. "For a long time, I didn't really understand what he was talking about. I finally figured it out after all these years. I still can't do it as well as he can, but at least I understand now what he means."

During Earnhardt's rookie year, 1979, he suffered a shoulder injury that forced him to miss several races. At his urging, Pearson, by then in the twilight of his career, substituted while Earnhardt was on the mend. Driving Earnhardt's car, Pearson won the Southern 500, which became a bit ironic when Earnhardt ended his career one victory shy of Pearson's career total at Darlington. It was not, however, the last of Pearson's 105 career victories. That came the following spring, in another car, but once again at Darlington.

"Nobody else ever looked like David Pearson driving around that racetrack," said Leonard Wood, who co-owned the No. 21 Mercury that Pearson drove during his heyday. "I couldn't explain the difference, but when David was driving a car on that track, I could tell it was him in it. He was so smooth and effortless. For everybody else, it looked like work. For David, it looked like the easiest thing in the world."

According to McInnis, Darlington is something of a Mecca. Fans from faraway locales make pilgrimages to the barren Pee Dee, hoping to find some illumination into what makes even the modern version of the sport tick.

On several occasions, longtime fans have designated the track as their eternal resting places. McInnis remembers one recent occasion when he oversaw the scattering of a Virginia fan's ashes at the track.

"The man had his tickets in his pocket on the day he died," McInnis said, "and he had himself cremated with them still there. The family came down and asked my advice as to what would be the best way to dispense with the man's remains.

"I told them, 'Well, the best seats in the house are off turn four. If I had a place to watch a race for eternity, it would be right here.' And that's where they did it. I said a few words, we all bowed our heads in prayer, and we scattered the ashes right there in turn four."

Darlington's modern champion, in another context, was James Henry Hunter, who served as president from 1993 until 2001. He then reluctantly moved back to Daytona Beach—he had been an official of NASCAR and International Speedway Corporation (which now owns Darlington Raceway)—to become a vice president of the sport's ruling body.

During Jim Hunter's tenure, however, Darlington was greatly renovated. Hunter oversaw the track's redesign, with huge grandstands erected in the names of onetime track president "Red" Tyler and Pearson, the most successful of all the drivers who had competed at the track. It was Hunter who made the controversial decision to move the start-finish line from one side of the track, where a highway behind the grandstands limited potential growth, to the other.

It should come as no surprise that Hunter is, yes, a native South Carolinian, which is to say he has a certain evangelical zeal about Darlington that is not always shared by non-natives.

Hunter had been a football player (at the University of South Carolina), a sportswriter, a public-relations man, and an administrator. Coupled with a love for Darlington that went back to his sportswriting days, he became the most colorful man to serve as track president since Colvin.

To Hunter, the preservation of Darlington Raceway was a sacred mission. Hunter knows, deep down, what many moneychangers do not: Every time a track like Darlington falls by the wayside—and every time another track is added that looks exactly like a half dozen others already in existence—the versatility required to be Winston Cup champion diminishes.

It is a track like none other. It is where Bill Elliott won the sport's first million-dollar bonus in 1985 and where a young driver named Cale Yarborough sailed completely out of the track in 1965. It is where Bobby Myers lost his life in 1957 and where Earl Balmer very nearly crashed through the press box in 1966. (From then on, that antiquated facility was referred to unofficially as "Balmer's Box.")

Few racetracks carry the ambience of a Wrigley Field or a Fenway Park. Few have ever called Darlington pretty, lavish, or, God forbid, user-friendly. It has been, at various times, nicknamed "The Lady in Black" and "The Track Too Tough to Tame." Its infield has long been renowned for the rowdiness of its inhabitants. It is still somewhat antiquated, and its renovation has been more gradual than similar projects at many other tracks. For more than a half-century, it has been visited by triumph and tragedy, great deeds and unspeakable horrors. With the possible exception of Indianapolis Motor Speedway, Darlington is the only track where the ghosts of long-dead heroes are *almost* visible, and the roar of old flathead Ford engines is *almost* audible.

There has never been anything like Darlington, and never will there be any motorsport facility that can match its quirkiness, originality, and checkered past.

"Darlington Raceway is a special place for me," Hunter said. "It always has been, and it always will be. I've never seen a bad race at this track."

THERE AIN'T MUCH HE AIN'T SEEN

From the dirt tracks to the superspeedways, Cotton
Owens knows as much about the rich lore of stock car
racing as anyone.

By Mike Hembree

The memories still bring a sparkle to Cotton Owens's eye—the good one—across more than a half-century of auto racing.

At 77, Owens, a pivotal figure in NASCAR's first 25 years, still keeps his hands in the good earth that was the foundation for what now is a multibillion-dollar industry.

Once one of the barnstorming modified circuit's greatest drivers, later a Winston Cup winner and leading team owner, he still has a sharp mind in matters mechanical. Owens now is linked to the sport that has defined his life through the adventures of his three grandsons.

At Cotton Owens Enterprises, a nondescript shop on the outskirts of Spartanburg, South Carolina, Owens's hometown and racing head-quarters throughout his career, the focus Monday through Friday is on auto salvage, which has been Owens's business since he left Winston Cup racing in the mid-1970s. Wrecked cars (mostly Chryslers—Owens is a Mopar man through and through) are delivered to Owens's

12-acre junkyard, and he milks them for parts before many are crushed and hauled away as scrap metal.

Weekends, though, often find Owens and his wife, Dot, and their family entourage racing again. Grandsons Brandon Davis, Kyle Davis, and Ryan Owens race four-cylinder cars built and maintained in Owens's shop on dirt short tracks in the Carolinas. It's a return to roots for Owens, known as one of NASCAR's greatest dirt-track drivers and a man once so dominant on the old ragtag modified tour that he earned the title "King of the Modifieds."

That was in the late 1940s and early 1950s, but the racing career of Everett Douglas "Cotton" Owens is so much more. He went on to drive and win in the formative years of the Winston Cup circuit, built cars for greats like David Pearson, Fireball Roberts, Junior Johnson, Bobby Allison, and Buddy Baker, and showed a knack for innovation that carries through to the not-so-stock race cars of the modern era.

All the more remarkable is the fact that Owens rebounded from a horrific wreck that should have ended his career (and could have taken his life) in the spring of 1951, years and years before he would make his mark at the top levels of auto racing.

Almost every great driver ultimately has The Big Wreck, one that serves as a pivot point, a crossroads. The psychological impact—not to mention the obvious threat to physical health (indeed, survival)—can be devastating. After a particularly brutal wreck, even one in which the driver suffers no significant injuries, the will to go a tick faster into the corner the next lap sometimes is diminished.

For Owens, the moment came in a modified race in Charlotte, North Carolina, in the otherwise promising spring of 1951. After success in modified racing, Owens had wandered into the growing but still infant Grand National (later Winston Cup) series in 1950 and saw

Cotton Owens in the early 1950s. Cotton Owens collection

his future there. The modifieds still paid good money, however, thus explaining Owens's arrival at the Charlotte fairgrounds track in a six-cylinder Dodge. It would be one of three or four stops he would make that week. The modifieds raced at every little bullring track on the map, drawing good crowds and generally putting on a wild, no-holds-barred show.

So it would be on this night.

Owens's car was strong in practice, and he knew immediately he'd be up front quickly. As he drove into first place on the back straight-away early in the race, his friend, Willie Thompson, crashed hard on the front side of the track, leaving his car on its roof.

"I had passed two cars going through three and four and was on the back bumper of Fireball (Roberts) about to lap him," Owens re-membered. "Fireball went around Willie. Then people came running out on the racetrack (toward Thompson's car). I could do anything with a race car and knew I had to do something quick. I flipped the car sideways and was going to go around the other side of Willie, but I had forgotten about passing those two cars in the corner. One of them hit me in the left door and turned me straight through Willie's car. I tore his car in half and went on through it and ran head-on into the bandstand (at trackside)."

It was not a pleasant sight. Owens's face had slammed into the steering wheel on impact. Owens and Thompson were rushed to a Charlotte hospital.

"I was having trouble seeing even while I was still at the track because the swelling of my face already had started," Owens said. "My face was knocked sideways, and half of my teeth were out. Willie was in there in the hospital screaming at the top of his voice to do some-thing for me. They took me over to another hospital, and I stayed there a couple of months.

"They wired up some bones in my cheek. They did the best they knew how back then."

A few months later, remarkably, Owens was racing again. He would drive for another decade, and then some. Most people never knew he raced many of those years on the ragged edge, wrestling with vision problems that plagued his left eye—and that bother him to this day.

He raced with double vision and a depth-perception deficiency, problems that eventually forced him to leave driving before he hurt himself—or someone else. He had four eye operations but still needs glasses to combat the double-vision problem.

"When I was driving, I just let my right eye override the left," Owens said. "I would just squint it to where I was actually just driving with one eye. I enjoyed racing so much it didn't bother me."

Owens would go on to win nine Winston Cup races against some of the top drivers of NASCAR's early years and to score dozens of victories at modified tracks large and small around the country. He raced with equal parts talent and determination, milking a paltry budget while raising a family and working late into the night on race cars in his backyard garage.

He would pop into places like Mobile, Alabama, where the locals tended to rule the roost and to deride outsiders and burn their rear ends.

"The old track there was built around a lake, and the back straight was the dam," Owens said. "Going through the first turn, there was a basin where the dam started. I found out I could run that car nearly wide open. It would jump, and I would sling it sideways and head it toward a telephone pole. When I hit the hump in the track, I'd miss the pole and straighten it out.

"I was rolling along and had moved from last to fourth when they stopped the race. Two guys were swimming out of the lake. I told the flagman, 'That's great, that guy jumping in there saving that driver.' He said, 'Save him, hell. He saved himself.' Two cars had gone in the lake.

"Anyway, I won the race."

People came to expect such things from Owens. As a teenager in Spartanburg, he had illustrated—boldly so, apparently—his proficiency with automobiles.

"Before World War Two, I had a '34 Ford," he said. "I absolutely was the terror of Spartanburg. Nobody ever knew what that car really looked like. They could only see a blur of it. When I left my house, I went down an alley and stopped. I took the spare tire off the back, took the mud flaps off, the muffler off, took the shades off the headlights. It was a different car altogether."

Then Owens—incognito—spent the evening roaring around town, spinning wheels, challenging other young hot-rodders, and generally confusing law enforcement. "By the time I got home, all that stuff was back on the car, and nobody ever knew it was me," Owens said. "One of my dad's friends would come over to the house—I'd be in the bed asleep by then—and tell dad, 'We think it's him, but we don't know for sure. But it's a '34 Ford.' Daddy would ask me about it, and I'd say, 'Aw, there's a bunch of them cars around town.' That's all I'd ever say. And there were."

Few were as slick—or as fast—as Owens's, though.

When people started racing in the Carolinas for real—on tracks, not on village streets—Owens knew he had found his calling. After serving in the Navy in World War Two, he returned to Spartanburg, started work at a wrecking yard and looked for a way onto the fast lane.

"I really had the fever," he said. "I had rawhided it around town enough to know what I was doing. A few of us built an old race car there in the junkyard and took it to the track in Hendersonville, North Carolina, one Saturday. The guys said they were going to see if they could get somebody to drive it. I said, 'Well, just give me my chance first.' I jumped in the thing, won the first heat race, started on the pole in the main and was leading when a switch fell off. I finished second."

Back home, Dot, Owens's wife, pregnant with their first child, didn't have a clue that her husband was launching an adventure. "I closed the wrecking yard at 12 o'clock and headed out to Henderson-ville and ran that afternoon," Owens said. "I came home about seven that night covered with red dirt, but I had money in my pocket. I've forgotten what story I told, but my mama said, 'He's driven that race car.'"

And so it began. Owens hit the modified circuit and soon became one of the hunted. Even when NASCAR's street-sedan Strictly Stock (later Grand National and, still later, Winston Cup) series began in 1949, Owens still leaned toward modifieds for years. The money was there.

"I could run a modified race and make $200 or $300 for 30 laps and be back home that night," he said. "And most of the time I'd get a $100 deal (from the track operator) just to come in and put on a show. I'd let them bang on me for most of the race and then just barely outrun them. I was running two or three or four races a week like that, and I could make more than I could running Grand National."

The modified jalopies eventually gave way to the shinier, more heavily promoted stock cars of Bill France's No. 1 series, however, and Owens moved into those ranks with the same level of ferocity. Opening his career in Pontiacs, he won for the first time on the old beach-road course at Daytona Beach, Florida, in 1957.

As the sport grew, so did Owens's reputation. When NASCAR left the beach at Daytona in 1959 for the giant new Daytona International Speedway, he breezed into town and set the fast speed—143.198 mph—for the inaugural Daytona 500 (he didn't win the pole because car preparations had delayed his arrival in Daytona).

The next season, Owens won the pole for the 500, reinforcing his stature at NASCAR's newest, fastest, scariest track.

He won a race in every season from 1957 through 1960, then scored four times in 1961. Even then, though, Owens was changing

Cotton Owens leans out of his car in 1957, the year he first won racing under Bill France's No. 1 series. Cotton Owens collection

the direction of his career. His eyesight, darkened in the Charlotte accident a decade earlier, remained a problem.

"I knew I had to get out of it because I was about to hurt somebody or myself," he said.

Owens turned to owning and managing his own team. He signed on with Chrysler, beginning a long and successful partnership, including a stellar run with driver and fellow Spartanburg resident David Pearson. Pearson won eight races in Cotton Owens Enterprises Dodges in 1964 and finished third in the point race. In a shortened 1965 season (Chrysler sat on the sidelines most of the year because NASCAR had banned its potent Hemi engine), Pearson won twice in 14 races.

In 1966 Pearson stormed to 15 wins and the series championship.

The Owens–Pearson partnership broke up 16 months later after a series of disagreements, but Pearson had built the foundation for what would be a 105-victory career, and Owens had proven his worth as a team owner and topflight mechanic.

Along the way, Owens also proved to Pearson that, despite his "official" retirement, he could still drive a race car. Owens ran two races in 1964—his final Winston Cup activity as a driver—to illustrate a point to Pearson, then an emerging talent Owens now calls the greatest driver ever.

"You had to let the pit crew help you, and David had just come off the dirt tracks and wouldn't listen," Owens said. "He would just ignore us on that part of it. So we went to Richmond (in 1964), and I decided to drive a second car and went out and beat him (winning the race, with Pearson second) on account of pit stops. It was right comical. He wouldn't even ride home with us. Then the following week, I went out and set a track record at Hillsboro (a notorious .9-mile dirt track in North Carolina). He absolutely tried to tear that dirt track up trying to catch me. That started the teamwork, and we started winning some races."

Owens, then 40 years old, finished second to Ned Jarrett in the race at Hillsboro, his final Winston Cup event as a driver. Later—much later—he would drive once more, in very different circumstances, for a very different reason.

Other leading drivers, such as Allison, Johnson, and Baker, would drive Owens's cars before his tenure as a Winston Cup team owner ended in 1973. Baker gave Owens one of his last hurrahs in 1970 by breaking the 200-mph barrier and establishing a closed-course speed record in an Owens Dodge in tire tests at the massive new Alabama

International Motor Speedway (now Talladega Superspeedway), NASCAR's biggest track.

Along the way, Owens worked overtime, developing safety innovations (he was the first to add significant protection to the driver's door by inserting extra bars) and modifying chassis components and setups.

"A lot of the stuff you see on cars today came out of our shop," Owens said. "Guys would drive for me and learn stuff and take it somewhere else. We always tried to stay a step ahead.

"If I was running today, I'd be up front somehow, or I'd quit. I wouldn't go to a track wondering if I was going to make the field. If somebody else could do it, I could. That's the way I always felt."

After leaving the racing circuit to operate his salvage business full time, Owens ran a few races as a favor to country western singer Marty Robbins, a close friend. Robbins, an occasional driver who enjoyed hanging around NASCAR garages, asked Owens to maintain his car for an abbreviated schedule. They raced a few events per season until Robbins died in 1982.

That should have written finish to Owens's racing career, but the grandsons changed his mind. "They wanted to run these little dirt tracks, and I tried my best to discourage it, but I saw I couldn't," Owens said. In 1988 the oldest, Ryan, announced at a family Christmas party that he wanted to stir up the Carolina dirt much as his grandfather had 40 years earlier, and Owens found room in his salvage shop to build a four-cylinder Plymouth for his grandson to race the following year.

Brandon and Kyle followed, and, at times, Owens has run a three-car team on an assortment of Carolina dirt tracks. Although the boys, now in their 20s, have moved on to "real" careers, they still race occasionally.

Each has won races, thanks in part to information "Pop" hasn't forgotten despite the fact he hadn't raced on dirt since 1964.

"It's the same old dirt and the same old techniques," he said. "There are better shocks, better tires and better springs now, but in a lot of ways, it's still the same. They still go around in circles.

"Dirt racing is a real good place to learn the tricks of the trade. Dirt is forgiving. The car can jump out from under you, but you can save it. And you learn the fundamentals of what a car can do. Once you learn those things on dirt, you can drive anywhere."

To assist his grandsons in that process, Owens jumped in one of the team cars at the age of 67 and ran a race at the now-defunct I-85 Raceway near Greenville, South Carolina. Ryan won. The grandfather was second.

"I wanted to know exactly what the chassis was doing," Owens said. "I came from back in the pack, and then I just followed him. He was running good that day. I don't know if I could have gotten by him."

Owens hopes to sell his business soon and "retire," although his definition of the word probably will differ from the standard version. He remains interested in Winston Cup racing but said the sport "has gotten completely out of hand. It's come to the point that you don't know what you're racing unless it's got [the manufacturer's name] written on it. You don't know if it's a Chevrolet, Pontiac, or Ford. I think they should go back to the standard-body cars. And engines costing 50, 60, 70 thousand dollars and more. That's ridiculous."

The changes through the years have been remarkable—some good, some unfortunate, Owens said. Money—and the quest for it—is the biggest difference. Now, top teams employ hundreds and spend millions. Owens ran the 1959 season with a team of two—himself and mechanic Arthur Coker.

"It really was more than you could do," he said. "The guys who did build their own cars back then should never have been able to drive them because they didn't have the rest it took to drive. I did the building, the hauling, the driving, the works. And we didn't have power steering [or] power brakes. We manhandled the cars. I've actually sat down to drive a race car to get relaxed."

What Owens had—and has still—is the vision.

STARS AND BARS

Benny Parsons made history, not merely by winning a championship, but by overcoming cruel fate and almost unimaginable adversity in order to do so.

By Thomas Pope

L uck, a wise guy once said, is the result of preparation meeting opportunity.

All the preparation in the world didn't prepare Benny Parsons for the misery that cloaked him and his team mere minutes after the field had taken the green flag for the American 500. The contingencies that crew chief Travis Carter had planned for didn't include some miscalculations and a worst-case scenario. As a result, Parsons could see the championship lead he held slipping through his fingers.

Shortly after high noon on October 21, 1973, in a flash, everything that Parsons and the L. G. DeWitt racing team had worked for since January seemed to have been in vain. On the 13th lap of the final race of the year, Parsons sped into a wreck that turned the passenger side of his car into a picture window.

Carter, Parsons's 23-year-old crew chief, went into the race confident that he had prepared for every possible scenario. He had filled a

111

truck with an array of spare parts, including an extra engine, ready to remedy almost any problem. What he hadn't conceived of was a race car missing a four-foot-wide section of steel tubing.

But as badly mangled as Parsons's Chevrolet was, the championship battle was far from over. Over the next few hours, his title hopes went from slim to fruition.

Did preparation make the difference? Partially. But in this case, the components of the equation were juggled. For Benny Parsons, opportunity was when luck met preparation. The luck? A car that didn't make the race was parked nearby, and one of the sport's greatest mechanics had the bold idea to ravage part of it and make a champion out of a former taxi driver.

The 1973 season hadn't been a dominant one for Parsons. Heading into the season finale at North Carolina Motor Speedway near Rockingham, North Carolina, David Pearson had won 10 times in 17 starts. Petty had won six events, Cale Yarborough four, and Bobby Allison and Buddy Baker a pair apiece.

Parsons's lone win had come on a hot day in early July at Bristol (Tennessee) International Raceway, whose towering 33-degree banks turned his chronic neck problems into withering agony. Parsons endured the pain as long as possible, then handed the wheel to a local sportsman standout, John Utsman, who drove long enough for Parsons to recuperate. Another driver switch was made when Parsons was ready to return to action, and even slowed by a pair of driver changes, he managed to win the race by a whopping seven laps.

That victory was coupled with amazing consistency. Parsons rolled into Rockingham having completed more laps than any other driver— over 9,000 of them in 27 races heading to NCMS—and every mile was worth points toward the title.

And for the DeWitt team, there was not a better setting than NCMS to cap off a championship season. L. G. DeWitt had come on board as a partner during the track's construction in the early 1960s, and his race team and trucking company headquarters were located just 12 miles from the speedway in the small town of Ellerbe.

Carter was homegrown, too, an Ellerbe kid whose prior mechanical experience had been with farm equipment, not race cars. Carter had joined the team part-time in 1971, then became a full-time employee in '72. A year later, as crew chief—"It wasn't hard to be a crew chief when there were only two or three people working on the car," he quipped—Carter had Parsons in position to win stock car racing's top prize.

The season had been scheduled to end at College Station, Texas, but when the track couldn't ante up the purse by a NASCAR deadline, the 1.017-mile Rockingham track wound up hosting the finale.

The weekend started well for Parsons, whose No. 72 Chevrolet was fifth fastest on the opening day of qualifying. Richard Petty, Parsons's closest pursuer for the crown, grabbed the pole position at 135-plus miles an hour, and David Pearson, who had led all but one of the 492 laps in winning at NCMS earlier in the year, joined him on the front row.

More drivers tried to make the race than there were positions for, and a consolation race decided the final spots in the field. Among the nonqualifiers was a Charlotte, North Carolina, driver named Bobby Mausgrover, and he would unknowingly prove to be the savior of Parsons's title bid.

With a lead of almost 200 points on Petty, Parsons's quest was to finish 15th or better to clinch the championship. Most insiders figured that he would breeze to the crown, so much so that prerace chatter centered not on the title chase, but on Allison's allegations that Petty and Yarborough had used illegal engines in the race at Charlotte two weeks earlier.

Thirteen laps into the American 500, the spotlight shifted back to Parsons with blinding intensity.

Johnny Barnes, a driver from Port Charlotte, Florida, had already been lapped twice when he hit the brakes to avoid running into the back of another competitor on the backstretch. Parsons, who had purposely slipped back to eighth, content to enjoy a calm Sunday drive, instead charged into a maelstrom.

"I thought I saw just a little bit of smoke, but when I came off of turn two, Johnny had spun and was sitting 90 degrees to the apron, right in the groove, and that was my first warning," Parsons said. "If we had been thinking, we'd have put a spotter on the roof of the press box with a radio to warn me of trouble, but we just didn't think of that."

Parsons jerked his car to the left to try to avoid a collision, but he didn't quite clear the obstacle, snagging Barnes's bumper with the passenger side of his car. Parsons's Chevrolet screeched to a stop, its engine silent and its driver stunned at the turn of events.

No one was injured in the crash, which ended the day for Barnes, Frank Warren, and Utsman. Dave Marcis, Darrell Waltrip, and Ed Negre drove away from the scene with minimal damage.

Parsons wasn't as lucky, though when his engine came back to life at the flip of the ignition, he thought he had escaped without serious damage. But as he put the car in gear and tried to drive back to the pits, it balked. The entire rear end assembly had been knocked out of whack, and its gears were unable to pull the car forward.

Disgusted, Parsons looked to his right.

"It was unbelievable," he said. "I had *no* right side.

"You can imagine how the adrenalin was flowing, getting ready for an event when you can win the championship, and then, just like that, it's over."

Minutes crept by before a tow truck arrived to haul Parsons's mangled car back to the pits. There were plenty of spare parts on hand to repair those that had been ruined and more than a dozen mechanics ready to lend a hand, and Carter was eager to get to work . . . until he saw the hole where the roll bars had been.

"My first thought," Carter said, "was, 'Richard Petty's going to win this championship again.' That's what I really thought."

As a crowd gathered around the wreckage, Barnes came over and placed a hand on Parsons's shoulder.

"Benny, I'm sorry, really sorry," he said.

"What happened?"

"I ran up behind someone going into the turn and had to get on the brakes," Barnes said. "I just lost control of the car. I saw you coming up fast and tried to keep the car off the rail."

Barnes walked away, and reporters eased in to try and elicit a comment from the dejected Parsons.

"I guess I should have spun the car out," Parsons told them. "But then I would have hit him sideways, and that would have bent the frame. Maybe I did the right thing. At least it seemed the right thing to do at the time."

As bad as the damage was, there was simply too much at stake to quit. Mechanics began swarming over the Chevy, dismantling the damaged pieces from nose to tail along the passenger side.

With the sounds of air guns, torches, and hammers filling the air, Parsons made his way to the garage area fence where his parents, sister, and numerous friends had gathered. "They were all crying," he said. "I guess I shed a few tears then myself."

He told them, "Well, it's over."

They had the parts to fix everything—everything except the shredded roll cage. "Who would have ever dreamed we would have needed roll bars?" Parsons pondered later. That blow, it seemed, would be fatal to their championship dreams.

Only it wasn't.

Ralph Moody and John Holman had built the powerhouse Ford operation of the '60s, doling out factory-backed machines of dominant lineage to drivers handpicked by the manufacturer. In time, the partners went their separate ways, and Moody had formed another company that built racing engines. One of his power plants was in Parsons's crumpled Chevy, and he was more than a curious bystander.

Moody pointed to Mausgrover's car, which hadn't made the race but was still at the track.

"Ralph said, 'Go get that car down there and cut the bars out of it,'" Parsons said. Shocked by Moody's bravado, he replied, "'That's not our car,' and Ralph said, 'Aw, that's OK. Go do it. I know those people.'"

One of the mechanics grabbed a torch and cut away the door panel of Mausgrover's car, then blazed through the roll bars. The bars were trimmed to match the remains of Parsons's roll cage and welded into place. Meanwhile, the rest of the crew was unloading the contents of the supply truck and got busy replacing the entire rear suspension and rear-gear assembly, the driveshaft, and brake drums. As unlucky as the 13th lap had been to Parsons's car, the team was fortunate that the front suspension had gone almost untouched in the crash.

As the repairs neared completion, Parsons and his crew found another reason to celebrate. Parsons frantically got the crewmen's attention by waving to them, and with one hand he held up four fingers, then the other, three. The crewmen looked up to see Petty's STP Dodge—No. 43—rolling into the garage, its engine silent, the camshaft snapped. The crewmen erupted into cheers.

Petty's brother and engine builder, Maurice, yanked out the pins holding the hood in position. He had his own idea about returning to battle—removing the broken engine and replacing it with a fresh one. And then, as Carter recalled, Maurice Petty saw the DeWitt crew cutting the roll cage out of Mausgrover's car for use in Parsons's.

"He just slammed the hood down and walked off," Carter said. "He knew if we could get the car back in the race, we would win the championship.

"When we saw Richard have trouble, we realized we had a chance. We had a fighting chance."

Seventy minutes and 133 laps after the massive rebuilding project had begun—"about a day's worth of work" had it been in the DeWitt shop, Carter said—Parsons and the No. 72 Chevy were back on the track. The fender that had read "Russell Bennett Motors, Rockingham, North Carolina." when the day began was reduced to "Russell" and "Rockingham." That sliver of sheet metal was all that remained of two fenders and a door, and the innards of Parsons's car were visible from its front bumper to behind the right rear tire. Viewed from the grandstands as it toured the track, the car looked like a skeleton on wheels.

"I was surprised when I came around and saw that Benny, with the chance to win the point championship, had his car torn up in that wreck," Pearson said. "But I was even more surprised to see him back on the track running."

But the championship battle wasn't over. There was still work to

Benny Parsons takes to the track with a severely damaged car in an effort to finish enough laps to win the 1973 Winston Cup championship. DMP Archives Photos

be done—miles to be logged, actually, since that was the foundation of the points system at that time—and Parsons ran at three-quarter throttle, trying to coax the car to the title.

That moment of relief came on lap 394, when Parsons glanced over to pit road to see his crew leaping up and down in celebration. Parsons wasn't yet ready to call it a day, though: "I wanted to stay out there a little longer just to be sure."

Parsons coasted along, minding his own business, racing with no one and giving the faster cars plenty of room to rocket on past him. That's easier said than done, Carter remarked, as the task of running at less than full speed to log miles is "the toughest job for a race car driver."

Eventually, a vibration developed in the car as the laps wound down, and it worsened by the minute. Parsons rode it out as long as he could stand it, then made the left turn onto pit road 23 laps from the finish.

A little more than 10 minutes later, Pearson took the checkered flag over Baker with a lap to spare. Yarborough's third-place finish allowed him to pass Petty for the runner-up spot in the standings. Parsons wound up 28th in the day's rundown, managing to coax out nearly 300 laps out of his rebuilt race car. His take at the pay window for the day: $625.

The championship celebration was somewhat muted. Parsons was more relieved than elated, and Carter took on the stoic visage of his boss, L. G. DeWitt.

"I just felt pleased," Carter said. "To me, it's what we were there for, and we accomplished that. And anything short of that . . . well, you just didn't do your job."

DeWitt invited the team members to his home for a victory lunch the following week, and also took them out to dinner at a club near the speedway. Parsons's big moment came the following February, when NASCAR honored the champions of its top three divisions—Grand National, Sportsman, and Modified—with a banquet at the Plaza Hotel in Daytona Beach, Florida, four days before the Daytona 500.

Parsons's Chevy had done yeoman work, not just on that day—October 21, 1973—but throughout the year.

"The car was unbelievably durable," Parsons said. "We only had the one car for most of the year. That car ran road courses, it ran big tracks, it ran short tracks, and it ran pretty decently on all of them.

"We were very fortunate, too. They had a couple of big crashes that year, one at Talladega, that took out a lot of the competition and allowed us to finish second or very high with a car that wasn't really capable of running in top 10. At Darlington, there was a big wreck that eliminated a bunch of cars, but my car would roll just fast enough that I could run on the apron, and I finished second, 13 laps down."

Parsons's driving career lasted through 1988, when he began a broadcasting career. His Hall of Fame career includes 21 Grand National victories, topped by the 1975 Daytona 500 and the 1980 Coca-Cola 600 at Charlotte. Surprisingly, it is those conquests, not the title and the mountain he had to climb to win it, that are his fondest memories.

"Winning the championship was great; don't get me wrong," he said almost three decades later, "but the negative thing to that, we won the championship, and a week or two weeks later, the Middle East oil embargo started, and we didn't know if we were going to race or not race in 1974. If we did race, would anybody show up, because gas was hard to come by for everybody? How would we get to race? Where would we buy fuel?

"All of a sudden, winning the championship wasn't the first thing on your mind."

That was only the beginning of the team's worries. Its attempt to defend its championship went sour at every turn.

"We tried to upgrade our equipment with the championship money we won," Parsons said, "and we felt like we had better stuff, but '74 was the most dismal year I ever had in my life. Nothing worked. NASCAR made everybody change over from big-block engines to small blocks, and it seemed like every part we bought broke. I broke connecting rods; I broke crankshafts. It was a disaster."

Parsons continues to enjoy being introduced as a former Winston Cup champion. Many of the crewmen who helped rebuild his race car that Sunday afternoon at Rockingham remained in racing decades

Benny Parsons waves from beneath the banner celebrating his points victory in 1973. DMP Archives Photos

later, and Carter is the co-owner of a Winston Cup team in Statesville, North Carolina.

The achievements of October 21, 1973, drove home a message that remains Carter's creed into the 21st century. "In racing, it's never over 'til it's over," he opined, "and that never changes."

COLUMBIA SPEEDWAY

Torn between the past and the future, a legendary track
bit the dust.

By Jim McLaurin

ou can no longer see the front gate that sat less than a hundred
yards off the main road. A mobile home dealership now obscures
the way. Even the old sign that read, "Columbia Speedway—
Racing Every Thursday Night" was chainsawed down years ago and
hauled off by Little Bud Moore as a souvenir.

The roofs on the concession stands and ticket booth have long
since succumbed to the elements, and now scrub oaks and pines poke
curious heads up through the cinderblock walls, as if to ask, "Where
did they all go?"

Even after two decades of idleness, however, the pavement is still
in pretty good shape. There are a few cracks where the weeds have
pushed their way through the old tarmac, but with a little work, the
track would be raceable in a couple of weeks. The irony is that the
pavement is the only thing that survived, because the pavement was
the thing that killed one of the South's legendary short tracks. All that's

left now of the place that was once a racing Mecca in South Carolina's capital city are the memories.

"Because of the tremendous amount of maintenance with dirt," said H. A. "Humpy" Wheeler, "and the fact that the superspeedway era was coming on and all, that it got to a point where everybody thought, 'Well, gee whiz. We'd be better off paving the thing. We'd be more modern and that kind of stuff.'

"So many of those tracks went out of business. Number one, it was much more expensive to compete on a paved track. Number two, some of those dirt tracks were two-groove tracks, and when they were paved, they became one groove, and there was no passing.

"It lost a lot of its drama, and drama is what sells tickets."

Wheeler should know what sells tickets. These days, he's running the show up at Lowe's Motor Speedway in Charlotte, and is considered a pioneer in the promotion of races and racetracks. Back in the mid-'50s, at the beginning of the golden era of Columbia Speedway, he was a fresh-faced young college student at the University of South Carolina, learning business during the day and, on Thursday nights, the business of racing. And what a classroom he had.

Most of the greats, near-greats, and not-so-greats of stock car racing history turned laps on the little half-mile oval. It was the site of the 38th race in NASCAR's Grand National (now Winston Cup) division on June 16, 1951, when Frank Mundy, a dapper young man out of Atlanta, took the pole position and then beat out Bill Blair for the checkered flag—in a Studebaker! Hall of Famers such as Curtis Turner, the Flock brothers (Tim and Fonty), David Pearson, and Speedy Thompson shared the track with guys with nicknames like Possum and Crawfish, Rock and Preacher.

Chevrolet got its first Grand National win there. Buck Baker got his first win in Columbia, and his son Buddy raced his first race there. The launch of the most storied career in stock car racing got no more than a one-sentence "mention" in the local paper on July 13, 1958: The final line of a story titled "Bob Welborn First in Race" reads, "Lee Petty's son, Richard, driving in his first competitive race, finished sixth."

You won't find it among Petty's 1,177 career Winston Cup starts, because it came in NASCAR's "Convertible division." But if you ask Petty where his first race was, he'll say Columbia.

Almost a year to the day later, Petty won the first race of his career at Columbia. Unfortunately, that one did not count among the 200 victories of NASCAR's winningest driver, because it, too, came in a ragtop. But if you ask Petty where he won his first race, see above.

What made it a special place? According to Jim Hunter, now NASCAR's vice president of communications but back then a reporter with Columbia's afternoon newspaper, just about everything.

The races were run on Thursday nights, which meant that it had no competition from other tracks, so it brought in the best from all over the Carolinas and Georgia.

"There was a regular trail that most of the drivers followed," Hunter said. "It was Columbia on Thursday nights, maybe Augusta or Savannah on Fridays, and Greenville-Pickens on Saturday nights. Columbia made it a long weekend and an extra race, so everybody who had a race car showed up.

"The boys from North Carolina that raced at Hickory or Asheville needed that extra paycheck, too, so the track always had great car counts, and with all that talent, great crowds."

It was also, Hunter said, maybe the first short track in history to have two press boxes. One, the official one, was on the outside, down the front straightaway. The second one was Mike Harkey's truck.

"Mike ran a landscaping business, which explains the flatbed truck, and he loved racing," Hunter said. "Joe Whitlock, who wrote for the morning paper, and I went to the promoter and told him we needed an infield press box so that if a driver fell out of a race or something, we could go talk to him.

"In the official press box, you couldn't drink beer or smoke or cuss or anything. It was a little different on Harkey's truck. It became the infield press box, but it was also the gathering place.

"Back then, hardly anybody covered the sport, so we knew all the drivers, and they knew us. When one fell out, he'd come down to the first turn where the truck was, crack open a beer, and talk. It was wonderful."

They say that there's a band of soil that reaches from the midsection of North Carolina through South Carolina and into Georgia where the clay is as close to perfect for dirt-track racing as anywhere on earth. Columbia was different.

"Greenville-Pickens was just like the Broad River, as red as red can be," said Haskell Willingham, a Columbia driver who raced the track when it was dirt and paved. "Closer to the coast, the tracks were more sandy. This place, the clay and the dirt were totally different. Everywhere else, you slid all the way around the track. But for some reason, when you'd run about 50 laps at Columbia, it was as hard as asphalt. It was just like running on a paved street."

The late Joe Whitlock, who himself became a legend among the men and women who wrote about racing for a living, knew why. In a story he wrote in 1988, Whitlock divulged the track's secret: Rock salt. Before the track was wet down for an evening's racing, he said, "Big

Ben" Metts would sprinkle 200 pounds of ice cream salt over the track with a hand-cranked spreader. Then Metts would climb into his big water truck and begin his counterclockwise laps, trickling just the right amount of water onto the dirt.

But the salt was only part of the secret. Knowing just how much water to put down was the other half, and Metts had his own method: "Rainy season or dry, cool weather or hot," Whitlock wrote, "he knew the precise moment when the race track was ready. It was the lap after he took the last nip of bourbon from the pint bottle nestled between his legs."

The track was fast and treacherous, and it made for some wild racing.

"The first time I ever saw Dale Earnhardt was when he was with his dad down to Columbia," said Phil Gunn, who was a volunteer helper on Lee Roy Yarbrough's team. "He was probably 12 years old. He was an aggressive young fellow back then. Joe Penland did something that night that irritated Ralph, and Dale snuck up behind him and hit him with a tire iron. He hit him in the calf and like to have broken his leg. Joe remembered meeting Dale."

Just as Yarbrough remembered "meeting" Tiny Lund. Lund, whose one claim to fame on NASCAR's Grand National circuit was winning the 1963 Daytona 500, was a gentle giant who ran a fish camp in Cross, South Carolina, during the week and raced all weekend. And he was gentle only when he wasn't on a racetrack.

"One night at Columbia, Tiny was not running his best, and he was notorious for hating Lee Roy, and Lee Roy did not like Tiny," Gunn said. "Lee Roy was leading the race and Tiny gets out there and was just messing around. The last lap, he got himself in position coming out of turn four, and just as Lee Roy was coming around him, he turned dead left.

"Ralph Earnhardt had dropped out of the race for some reason, and Lee Roy knocked Tiny up into the side of Ralph's trailer. He just about demolished our race car and Ralph's trailer."

Willingham, who watched them as a youngster and raced against them as a 16-year-old, didn't see that one, but he didn't doubt it at all.

"Tiny's heart was as big as he was," Willingham said, "but he'd flat run over your ass on a racetrack. He'd run over his own mother on a racetrack."

Rivalries stoked the fires, but nobody got burned. That was part of the attraction. Rivalries were common among the drivers and sometimes ended up in a tussle in the infield. Or among their fans in the grandstands. But not often. A good part of the track's success, Wheeler said, was that it was well run.

"The biggest thing I learned was that you can promote all you want to, but if you can't have a uniqueness to the track, which running on Thursday nights gave to Columbia, that's half the battle right there.

"The other thing I learned was that, when you run them at night, you've got to finish them early. That's one thing they always did at that track. By 10:15, it was all over. Everybody had to get up and go to work Fridays then; it wasn't like it is today. That's the only thing that kept it in business on Thursday nights, the fact that people came there knowing that they would get out at a reasonable hour.

"Also, I learned that a successful track needs to be a social gathering place, too. For fans as well as drivers and people associated with the business."

Like the Blackwell brothers up at Greenville-Pickens, the management in Columbia ran a taut ship.

"They were good racing crowds," said Willingham. "Very seldom a fight, almost none at all. I just think they wanted to see good racing, and the people who wanted to drink beer pretty much knew how to handle themselves. Another thing: I'll tell you, when Buddy Gooden had that track, he was really close to the Cayce police, and they had good security. And the crowd respected them.

"I'll bet, when I raced there, from '64 to '84, I can't remember seeing three fights. But it's like anywhere you go. If you start letting it get out of hand, it happens every week. I don't think he ever let it get started."

That, of course, is not to say that it never did. Back in the days before multimillion-dollar contracts and million-dollar motorhomes, most of the racers who did it full time depended on their meager share of the meager purses to make it to the next race, and they fought for it.

"They were very competitive," Willingham said. "Everybody was going for the 'change,' because they needed it to race the next night or next week. They didn't give anybody any slack.

"I was young. When I raced against Ralph, he was probably 35 and I was 16, and it didn't matter. He raced me as hard as he did someone he'd been racing with all those years. But you learned a lot, because they were very tough competitors and they'd been around."

"Little Bud"—not to be confused with "Big Bud" Moore, one of NASCAR's first big-time team owners—was a smallish guy from North Charleston who raced with both the big boys and the weekly racers. With his long hair and Coke-bottle glasses, he was also the one, depending on the length of your own hair, they loved or loved to hate.

"There were fierce rivalries," Wheeler said. "The rivalry that Ralph and Bud Moore had was the one you'd love as a promoter: The old wizened veteran versus the young upstart. Plus, Bud Moore sort of did things his way, and he was the James Dean of Columbia Speedway.

"He was wide open. The crowd loved him, because they knew if he didn't win the race, he'd wind up on his roof out in the parking lot.

"There was a considerable rivalry with "Tiger Tom" Pistone and Tiny Lund. They were wild on the racetrack together, and it was just nip-and-tuck and beat-and-bang. And they were really teammates. They went all over the place together.

"For some reason, Jim Paschal and Buddy Baker, when it came down to Columbia, something just happened to them when they got there. I remember they were beating and banging one night down there, and Buddy caught him coming off the second turn, and Paschal's car flipped almost the entire back straightaway. It was one of the worst wrecks I've ever seen on a dirt track."

Even the best couldn't save the Columbia Speedway.

Who was the best? Ask 10 old-timers, and you'd get 10 different answers. Penland and Willingham, the local boys, held their own against the upstate star, Spartanburg's David Pearson. Pearson beat Lund and Cale Yarborough and was beaten by them. In the track's latter years, Harry Gant and Jack Ingram, two interlopers from North Carolina who would become the backbone of NASCAR's Late Model (now Busch Series) division, had their supporters. Curtis Turner and Joe Weatherly, who came in with the big boys in the early years, were probably as good a two drivers as anyone who ever turned a wheel at Columbia.

But if you get down to it, even the fans of the others would give a nod in the direction of Earnhardt. He was a serious, professional racer

Bobby Isaac, knocked out of the 1968 Sandlapper 200, watches as race winner David Pearson (No. 17) and second place finisher, Charlie Glotzbach (No. 6) pass him. DMP Archives Photos

at a time when some of the others weren't. He was smart and dedicated to his craft. He was also ahead of his time.

"Ralph Earnhardt taught all of us back in '64, '65, how to keep records of previous racetracks," Phil Gunn said. "None of us was smart enough to figure that out. If you ever saw him race, he came to a racetrack prepared, on a flatbed trailer. He unloaded his car, ran about eight laps, and he was ready to race. That was it.

"Luckily, I was able to see his little book, and we learned from that and started keeping our own book."

And he was one hell of a race car driver.

"Ralph Earnhardt probably invented the 'oops' move," Hunter said. "You know, on the last lap, get your fender up under the guy's left rear and catch him coming off the fourth turn. Win the race and go over to the guy and say, 'Oops. My car's been pushing all night.'"

But neither Earnhardt nor Willingham nor any of the others could save the track from inevitable demise. The city grew up around it, and folks in the new housing tracts didn't like to have their Thursday nights interrupted by the deep-throated growl of race cars. It might have lasted longer had it remained a haven for the dirt-track stars, but the pavement was the final nail in the coffin.

Driving on dirt and asphalt required two different cars, and most of the meat-and-potatoes drivers who raced there on a weekly basis couldn't afford both. Since there was still good dirt-track racing in the Carolinas, some took their business elsewhere.

"It was too fast, and the local guys around here couldn't compete with the North Carolina guys who had been racing on pavement so long," Willingham said. "Not knocking the people who promoted it after Buddy Gooden had it, but they didn't know anything about racing. And when they paved it, the track was very fast.

"The local guys who put the meat on the table every Thursday before it was paved, they were having to bring cars in from out of town to race on the asphalt. Harry would come, Jack would come, and the Pressleys would come. The local guys who put people in the stands were pretty much out the door.

"The crowds fell off because there was no competition. Those guys would come down here and just blow you away."

FIREBALL AND MAX

The great Glenn "Fireball" Roberts died before his time,
but his memory lives in the heart of a writer who
befriended him.

By David Poole

Max Muhleman couldn't really see what had happened, but he
knew it was bad.

From a radio booth atop the front stretch grandstand at
Charlotte Motor Speedway, all he knew for sure was there had been a
wreck during the 1964 World 600. Junior Johnson and Ned Jarrett had
spun out coming off turn two, and another driver had wrecked as he
tried to miss them.

Muhleman knew there was a concrete wall running down the inside of the backstretch, a wall with gaps where cars could turn off the
track to cut into the infield if they needed to. Hitting one of those gaps
the wrong way could be very bad news.

A sick feeling in his stomach convinced Muhleman that something
was terribly, terribly wrong.

But there was only one thing he could really see.

The fireball.

* * *

Muhleman was writing about sports for a newspaper in Greenville, South Carolina, when his boss came to him with a new assignment. He wanted the young reporter to go just up the road to a half-mile dirt track at the Piedmont Interstate Fairgrounds in Spartanburg to cover a stock car race.

It was not, Muhleman felt, a dream assignment.

"I told him I'd rather cover a dog show," Muhleman said. "I didn't know a thing about it."

There was no dog show in the upstate region of South Carolina for Muhleman to cover, however. But there was racing—a sport still toddling out of its infancy—at least in any truly organized fashion.

Cars had been racing for years, of course, around dirt paths worn into a field or on horse-racing rings at county fairgrounds all over the Southeast.

The roots of the sport could be traced directly back to the hills of the Carolinas and Georgia, where illegal whiskey was delivered at night, daring men driving cars that had been souped up so they could outrun those being driven by the revenue agents trying to shut down this "moonshining" trade.

The law caught some, of course, but a lot of these good ol' boys managed to outrun or outfox the men carrying badges enough to stay in business. And whenever they'd have the time to talk amongst themselves, they would start bragging about how fast their cars would run and how well they could drive them.

Bragging led to arguments, arguments led to betting, and betting led to competition. Stock car racing was born.

By the middle of the 1950s, people around the South Carolina towns of Greenville and Spartanburg and thousands of other towns just like them across the South had only a few choices of how to spend their leisure time.

On summer evenings, the local mill might be playing baseball in a textile league, and there might even have been a Class C or D minor league baseball team around somewhere.

Or, they could go to the local dirt track, where once in a while, some of the guys they were starting to read about in the papers, the ones driving in something they called NASCAR, would come by and race against some of the local boys.

Max Muhleman didn't particularly like the idea of plucking particles of red-dirt grit out of his eyeballs for days to come, but his boss gave him little choice in the matter. So he went to the racetrack in Spartanburg and, much to his surprise, didn't mind it so much.

"The drivers didn't mind talking to me, even though I was a reporter and they didn't know who I was," Muhleman said. "Some of them even seemed to like it."

Some of the drivers, it turned out, also were pretty interesting fellows.

Guys like Edward Glenn Roberts, who was born January 20, 1929, and who, as a lad in central Florida, was a tremendous high school athlete. He was particularly gifted as a pitcher, with a blazing fastball.

Before he started driving race cars in the late 1940s, he'd already picked up a nickname: "Fireball."

Fireball Roberts won the 18th race ever run in what is now known as NASCAR's Winston Cup Series. Back then, on August 13, 1950, it was called the Grand National division, and at Occoneechee Speedway in Hillsborough, North Carolina, Roberts drove a 1949 Oldsmobile, No. 71, to a victory over Curtis Turner in a 100-lap race.

He raced only occasionally in NASCAR events over the next six years, but in 1956 he hooked up with car owner Pete DePaolo and won five races, driving the No. 22 that would come to be associated with his name. He won eight times the next year and six times in 1958 and became about as big of a deal as a man could become driving stock cars.

He was six feet two inches tall with broad shoulders and the kind of rough-hewn good looks that central casting might call for in a swashbuckling pirate—or a race car driving daredevil.

Roberts was a star, just the kind of guy a young sportswriter who'd developed an affinity for racing in spite of his initial misgivings might look for to interview at a race.

"I was at Darlington Raceway one day," Max Muhleman recalled. "There weren't a lot of reporters around NASCAR back then—you could have a press conference and put everybody in a large closet."

The reporters who were around didn't need an appointment to interview a driver. They didn't have to elbow their way through crowds of fans seeking autographs to get close enough to ask a question, either.

So on this day at Darlington Raceway, Muhleman kept hanging around until the handful of others had drifted away from a bull session with Roberts. Eventually, Muhleman began questioning Roberts on how a driver decided what line to run around a given track.

"Somehow in there I wound up telling him I thought I could run around the Darlington track in a certain amount of time," Muhleman said.

Roberts laughed him off. "I'll bet you a steak dinner you couldn't do it," he said.

Muhleman put down his notebook and started to take off.

Glenn "Fireball" Roberts showcases his "rough-hewn good looks" for the camera in 1957. DMP Archives Photos

"Hold it, hold it," Roberts said. "Anybody crazy enough to try that deserves a steak dinner."

Over that steak dinner, a friendship was born.

Muhleman wound up liking racing so much he went to work for the *Charlotte News*, an afternoon daily in Charlotte, North Carolina, which was rapidly becoming a hub for NASCAR racing and its racers.

The *News* and its rival morning paper, the *Charlotte Observer*, were among the first group of major Southern daily newspapers to cover NASCAR events on a regular basis. In the days before drivers and crew chiefs all had $750,000 motor homes that allowed them to reside inside a fenced-in lot at the track, everyone stayed at the same hotels wherever the circuit took them. Drivers, officials, media—nearly everybody—shared the same bars and restaurants, too.

Roberts and Muhleman enjoyed that part of the racing kinship, but their friendship was something more. When Roberts came to Charlotte to race, he often stayed at Muhleman's apartment. They sometimes sat for hours talking about anything but racing. Muhleman was as fascinated by his friend's interests off the track as he was impressed by his skills on it.

"I had this reel-to-reel tape recorder, and I asked Fireball if I could tape some of those conversations," Muhleman said. "We decided that we would do his autobiography."

By 1959 Roberts had hooked up with Florida neighbor Smokey Yunick, proprietor of the self-proclaimed "Best Damn Garage in Town" in Daytona Beach, Florida. Yunick built fast race cars, and Roberts seemed hell-bent on finding out just how fast a human being could make them go.

"If Fireball would have had a tire that could have stood up under the punishment he put on them, his record would be something that would have never been equaled," Yunick wrote in his autobiography, which was released after his death.

"In those days you could hear the tires blow. The deal was, the guy leading was running the tire test. How in the hell he could have set there for nearly four hours waiting for that 'boom,' knowing it was gonna hurt, is hard to understand."

In those days, when a driver went into a bar or nightclub—and drivers of that era did that a lot—the first moment anyone in the house band noticed him, the band struck up a song they felt appropriate for that driver. Whenever Roberts came in, the band would usually play a country western tune that became Roberts's unofficial theme song. The song was "Hello Walls."

Roberts won the 1962 Daytona 500 in one of the Pontiacs built by Yunick, but Smokey says he decided right after that it was time for Roberts to find a new line of work. Roberts thought Yunick was crazy, which was certainly not the only time the colorful legend met with that evaluation, and kept on racing.

By early 1964, however, Roberts was beginning to think about his future. Joe Weatherly, one of the sport's top stars, had been killed in a crash at Riverside, California, that January. Roberts was working on a divorce from his wife, Doris, and had plans to marry a woman named Judy Judge, who was the sister of Yunick's wife. He had a deal in the works to quit racing and make a living doing public-relations work for the brewery that produced Falstaff beer.

Muhleman knew about his friend's plans, so he knew that the World 600 on May 24, 1964, might be the last time he'd get to see Fireball race at the 1.5-mile track in the town where he worked for the local newspaper.

Normally, Muhleman would have been in the infield to cover the race. There weren't elaborate media facilities in 1964, not even at the bigger tracks like Charlotte. There wasn't much in the infield, either, so if Muhleman had been inside the track, he would have been able to run over to the backstretch to see whose car had been in the wreck.

But a Charlotte radio station had decided to broadcast the World 600 and had recruited Muhleman to join former driver Fonty Flock as "expert" commentators on the broadcast to assist anchor Sammy Bland.

From their radio booth near the start-finish line, they couldn't see much of the backstretch—at least not where the wreck happened.

"You could see them, but you couldn't see them real clearly," Muhleman said. "Then there was this huge plume of smoke, a tremendous gasoline fire. I got this sick feeling."

Muhleman tried to spot Roberts's car—by this time he was driving a purple Ford still carrying the No. 22—among those circling back around the track under the yellow flag. He couldn't find it.

"Fonty whispered in my ear," Muhleman said. "'It's Fireball.' Our view was so obscured, I just think Fonty had an intuition."

Flock was right.

Today's race cars have a fuel cell consisting of a 22-gallon container inside a metal box, with a valve that allows the fuel to be put in but protects it from running out. In 1964 Ralph Moody had begun working with the first generation of fuel cells by building a strong box around the tanks. But NASCAR officials had ordered them removed from cars Moody helped prepare, because the boxes had not been approved.

Today's drivers also wear several layers of protective clothing, including a flame-resistant driver's suit. In 1964 drivers were first beginning to wear clothing that had been treated in flame-resistant chemicals. Roberts had an allergic reaction to the chemicals, however, so his clothes were not treated with the flame retardant.

Roberts had seen Johnson and Jarrett spinning and tried to dodge the wreck, but he spun, too, and slid backward into one of those openings in the inside wall along the backstretch.

The car flipped on its roof, and the gas tank ruptured. Fuel began to run down into the cockpit of Roberts's car, soaking the underside of the roof that was now on the ground right under the head of the trapped driver. Roberts yanked at his harness, trying to get free, as the huge plume of orange flame and black smoke Muhleman could see erupted. Jarrett climbed from his car and scrambled over toward Roberts's Ford. Inside, Roberts was upside down and unable to get loose from his belts.

"Help me, Ned, I'm on fire," Roberts screamed.

Jarrett finally managed to pull Roberts loose and drag him away from the inferno. Roberts was still alive, but only barely. He was burned horribly. Those who saw him afterward would say his legs looked like charred logs.

He was taken to a Charlotte hospital. Muhleman was there, but he wasn't allowed in to see his friend. Immediate family only. Muhleman thought about getting a nurse to help sneak him in, but decided against it. The reports were actually somewhat optimistic at times.

The burns were terrible, but it was infection the doctors feared the most. On June 30, more than a month after the accident, Roberts's condition took a dramatic turn for the worse. He had pneumonia, and the infection was in his bloodstream.

On the morning of July 2, Muhleman was at his desk at the *Charlotte News* when the word came. Fireball Roberts was dead.

Just like he did back on that day when his boss first sent him to the racetrack in Spartanburg, Muhleman did his job. He spun a piece of paper into his typewriter and wrote a column about a fallen hero—and a fallen friend.

"Fireball Roberts, perhaps the most nearly perfect of all stock car drivers, is dead, and it's like awaking to find a mountain suddenly gone," he wrote.

Muhleman compared his friend to Mickey Mantle, to John Unitas, to Bob Cousy—the greatest sports heroes of the time.

"He was a master craftsman in one of the world's most dangerous professions, but he brought such talent and class to it he seemed beyond the risks that others ran," Muhleman wrote. ". . . He had a keen appreciation of life, which included good books, good music, and art in any form. He was a remarkably able speaker, articulate and entertaining and always at ease.

". . . It can safely be said that no man gave his profession more of himself than Fireball Roberts. He ran only to win, and he ran in a manner that inspired respect as well as excitement. There will never be another like him."

"I really liked writing," Muhleman said.

After Roberts's death, though, he decided that he might like to try something else. He had a job offer from the Ford Motor Company to join its public relations staff, working on the Cobra sports car program. When his wife said she wouldn't mind relocating to California, Muhleman put racing and writing into his rearview mirror.

From PR, he moved into sports marketing. His first big sports client was an ice hockey league, but eventually the circle would be drawn to its close.

Muhleman returned to Charlotte and spent nearly three years helping the city land its first major league professional franchise, the NBA's Charlotte Hornets. Following that, he spent six more years working to bring the NFL to Charlotte, playing a major role in developing the concept of permanent seat licenses in the process.

It's hard to be in sports marketing in Charlotte without having your hand in NASCAR, and eventually Muhleman Marketing took on some racing clients.

What goes around comes around, especially in a sport where you always wind up right back where you started.

But some wounds simply never heal.

For two years before his friend died, Muhleman would sit and talk for hours with Roberts. They talked about racing, about religion, about baseball, about books, about politics, about everything.

Muhleman had most of it on tape, planning to use it all in that book he somehow never got around to doing.

He kept the tapes. He just never could bring himself to listen to them.

"I always said I was going to do it," Muhleman said of the book he never wrote. "For a while, I waited because there were some things on there, some personal things . . ."

He leaves the sentence, like the book and the friendship, unfinished.

THIS CIRCLE IS UNBROKEN

Greenville-Pickens Speedway, once a key part of Winston
Cup's short-track landscape, roars again as a test site
for top teams.

By Mike Hembree

The NASCAR Winston Cup series underwent the equivalent of
major surgery in the 1972 season, as officials trimmed its schedule
from 48 races to 31.

Lost in the transition, as NASCAR attempted to put more empha-
sis on major events for its new sponsor, the Winston cigarette brand of
the R. J. Reynolds Tobacco Co., were several short tracks that had
served as key building blocks in racing's early years.

Gone, with one clean fall of the ax as NASCAR began what be-
came known as its "modern era," were Hickory (North Carolina)
Speedway, Columbia (South Carolina) Speedway, Smoky Mountain
Raceway in Maryville, Tennessee, South Boston (Virginia) Speedway,
Bowman-Gray Stadium in Winston-Salem, North Carolina, and
Greenville-Pickens Speedway in northwestern South Carolina.

They were relics of another age, a time when stock car racing was
about beating and banging and fussing and cussing, a distant cousin of

the largely politically correct sport now thriving in the 21st-century world of blanket television coverage and multimillion-dollar sponsorships.

Fans and operators of the small bullrings had reason to question the future. Without NASCAR's top stars, the future—if, indeed, there was one—looked grim.

Some did not survive. Others milked weekly shows for enough dollars to get by.

A few—perhaps best exemplified by Greenville-Pickens Speedway—made the transition with hardly a whimper.

Today, GPS is working on its second half-century of auto racing with all engines cranked and any potential problems in the rearview mirror. And its success is due in no small part to the fact that Winston Cup, which left in a rush 30 years ago, is a frequent visitor to the flat half-mile track again.

This time, NASCAR's No. 1 series comes through the speedway gates not in its race-day finery but in its work clothes. GPS has evolved into one of the most important off-site testing facilities in the NASCAR universe. Several days a week, from March through late autumn, the track's asphalt is being traversed by Winston Cup, Busch Grand National, and Craftsman Truck vehicles, as teams run tests for upcoming races.

Winston Cup teams are limited to seven tests per season at tracks that host series races, but tests at other tracks are unlimited. GPS, located within a couple hours' drive time from team shops in the Charlotte, North Carolina, area, is an ideal choice. The track's size and surface work well for the missions of most teams, and it doesn't hurt that the transporters rolling onto the track property are greeted—as in days of old—by "family."

Track operator Tom Blackwell has been a fixture at GPS since 1956. He and his brother, Pete, who died in May 2000, were the speedway's "Mr. Inside" and "Mr. Outside" for decades, Pete running the front office just outside turn three and Tom patrolling the pits and working the technical side.

Although slowed by open-heart surgery, Tom, 73, continues to work at the track ("Retire? Why do that? What else would I do?" he asked) and greets Winston Cup visitors with the same good-natured kidding he tossed toward Richard Petty, Bobby Isaac, and David Pearson in the 1960s, when all of them were young and the racing world was seen through a different prism.

"Todd Bodine was here not too long ago," Blackwell said, smiling at the memory. "Most of the guys know I'm going to give them hell. One of the team guys told me when he was signing in to give the driver hell when he showed up. I saw Todd getting out of his van. When he was signing in, I said, 'I'll tell you one thing. You need a driver for this damn car. You ain't got no driver at all.' He didn't know how to take it."

You take it, throw back your own insult of the day, and move on. That's how it's always been at Greenville-Pickens and how it always will be under the Blackwell banner. Little changes from season to season at the little oval tucked away in the Carolina Piedmont.

The track runs a weekly show of Late Model Stock, Street Stock, and Charger division racing and also hosts NASCAR's Goody's Dash and All Pro touring series. Winston Cup, Busch, and Truck teams running tests fill up much of the rest of the calendar.

Attendance for the speedway's weekly shows is remarkably good and predictably steady. Many of the same fans sit in the same seats, week after week, or park their pickup trucks on the terraced bank on the backstretch. Threatening weather is the only thing that hampers GPS crowd numbers, and special events overflow the grandstands. Blackwell said the biggest crowd in the 56-year history of the speedway—10,000-plus—turned out for the 2001 season opener when officials dedicated the track backstretch in memory of Dale Earnhardt, who had died at Daytona International Speedway a few weeks earlier.

The Earnhardt name runs through the history of GPS like water through a delta. Ralph, Dale's father, raced at the speedway for several years and won the track championship in 1965 and 1966. Dale, a precocious youngster, traveled with his father and played in the infield while his dad circled the dirt track. A creek ran through the center of the infield in those days, and, more often than not, Dale met his dad after the race with muddy clothes and a wary smile.

"His daddy used to whip his butt here all the time," Blackwell said. "He was always in trouble."

Dale would go on to drive his way to seven Winston Cup championships and into the hearts of millions, but he never forgot his ties to GPS, one of the tracks he considered home. For more than a decade, Earnhardt returned to the track every September to sign autographs. Although he normally detested long autograph sessions, Earnhardt always insisted that Labor Day Monday be kept open on his schedule for Greenville-Pickens, and he left town with a payday considerably less lucrative than for most of his personal appearances.

"He told us that the only reason he came here was that he felt like we were family," said Blackwell.

And it was no doubt special to Earnhardt that his father's name is forever a part of the speedway's unique salute to its champions. The name of every GPS track champion—beginning in 1957 with Grady

Track champions David Pearson (left) and Butch Lindley, two of the best short-track drivers in stock car racing history. Greenville-Pickens Speedway collection

Hawkins—is painted on the speedway's backstretch wall, a sort of Everyman's Hall of Fame that includes David Pearson, Jeff Hawkins, Butch Lindley, Robert Pressley, and such local hotshots as Donnie Bishop, Buddy Howard, and Marty Ward.

The day after Dale Earnhardt was killed, hundreds of fans came to the track to remember and mourn. They left flowers, Earnhardt caps, and T-shirts at a makeshift memorial in front of Ralph Earnhardt's name on the backstretch wall.

The circle was not broken.

*   *   *

Greenville-Pickens began with horses, not horsepower. The track, which opened in 1946, was built for horse racing, although that sport didn't prosper, and the 64 stables built outside the racing oval never hosted a horse, according to Blackwell. Concrete blocks used in the stables eventually became part of the frontstretch grandstands.

The speedway hosted its first automobile race July 4, 1946. In town to run the show was traveling promoter Bill France Sr., who was working on a plan to start a national sanctioning organization for stock car racing, a vision that would be realized with his formation of NASCAR the following year.

Admission to the first race was $2.50. Newspaper advertisements referred to the track as the "$100,000 Greenville-Pickens Speedway" and also announced that the new facility would have a "section reserved for Colored."

Ed Samples, an Atlanta barnstormer, won the first race, leading the last of 40 laps and winning $500. He would be the first big name in a long list of great racers to run the half-mile—both those who put their names on the outside wall as champions and those who raced in the Winston Cup (then Grand National) series, men like Petty, Pearson, Bobby Allison, Curtis Turner, Fred Lorenzen, Fireball Roberts, Cotton Owens, Lee Petty, the three Flock brothers, Junior Johnson, Herb Thomas, and Ned Jarrett.

The track had a dirt surface until 1970, its next-to-last year as a Winston Cup speedway. For years, it was part of a regional loop that allowed drivers to run at Columbia, Greenville-Pickens, and tracks in neighboring North Carolina and Georgia on successive nights, creating wild weekends of mayhem as drivers settled scores from the previous evening.

GPS, though, cut its own brand and separated itself from many of the other half-mile dirt tracks in the South. In its dirt days, the surface was prepared and maintained well, drivers remember, and the fans were . . . well . . . very enthusiastic.

"Little Bud" Moore, a Charleston resident who traveled north to compete against the GPS locals (never a good idea), remembers rough-and-ready fans at the track "who would cut you—even the men." He was escorted from the track by local law-enforcement officers on more than one occasion. Robert Pressley, another invader, drove down the mountain from Asheville, North Carolina, to win the track champion-

Maurice George (No. 29) and Ralph Earnhardt (No. 8) race through Greenville–Pickens Speedway's second turn in its dirt-track days. Greenville-Pickens Speedway collection

ship in 1988 and remembers some overly aggressive fans shadowing him on the way home one Saturday night.

Ned Jarrett, who suffered a serious back injury in a 1965 crash at GPS, remembers the track as one of the smoothest when Winston Cup ran there on dirt.

"It fit a smooth driver, someone who had a soft touch with the accelerator," Jarrett said. "Petty was good there, and Pearson. The track didn't favor those dramatic-type drivers who threw the cars into the corners, like a Junior Johnson or a Curtis Turner.

"The long straights and the relatively short turns made it a little unique. The banking—when it was dirt—was totally different from most places. It was pretty flat coming off two, but three and four had some banking, so you could drive in there pretty hard, and you could get off four pretty hard. In turn one, you went in right up next to the guardrail and came down low and had basically a flat surface to exit on. If you didn't make it, you hit a big dirt bank."

Moore called GPS "a good ol' race track" in its dirt days, "one you could run a 100-miler on and it stay in shape. It might get rough in a couple of places, but everybody who ran there was used to that. I've been to a lot rougher places."

The track trick, Tom Blackwell said, was a lot of water. He knows because he dumped most of it on the clay surface from the bowels of some of auto racing's ugliest water trucks, mutant vehicles that still roam the land at dirt facilities.

"We had a bunch of water trucks over the years," said Blackwell, who figures that, counting water laps, pace laps, and laps driving the track's cleanup truck, he's the speedway's all-time lap leader with no debate. "I turned them over and did about everything you could do to one," he said. "But we got the track in good shape by soaking it from about four o'clock to midnight every Friday. Then all we had to do was smooth it out a little on Saturday, and it was ready to go."

The brothers Blackwell arrived on the scene at GPS late in 1956, buying the track after attending a few races at a nearby speedway in Anderson, South Carolina.

"We started hanging around the race track over there, and that's something we probably never should have done," Blackwell said. "Then we started talking about building one. We couldn't find the land. Then a guy told us to talk about buying this one, and we worked it out."

The original 37-acre track property has grown to 150, and Blackwell also runs a wildly successful carnival-type fair every September on the grounds.

Through the years, he and his brother maintained close ties with the France family. GPS joined NASCAR in 1951 and continues to run under NASCAR sanction, making it No. 2 only to Bowman-Gray Stadium in North Carolina for consecutive years as a weekly track under NASCAR's banner.

"I'll never forget Bill France telling us one day that racing was going to be one of the biggest things we had ever seen," Blackwell said. "'It's coming,' he said. 'Get ready for it.'"

The Blackwells got a glimpse of that future in April 1971 when, after discussions with NASCAR and ABC, the track hosted the first NASCAR race broadcast from start to finish by a television network. ABC was interested in fitting a full race into a 90-minute segment of its popular Saturday afternoon "Wide World of Sports" program, and GPS fit the template.

"They were looking for a race they could get in in an hour and a half," remembered Pete Blackwell in a 1999 interview. "They had gone through the result sheets from the year before and saw that we had finished a race in about an hour and 25 minutes. They asked me if I thought we could do that again. I said, 'Sure,' although there was no way I could be sure."

NASCAR cut the starting field from 30 cars to 24, thus trimming the likelihood of caution flags and speeding the progress of the race, which finished in 1:16 with Bobby Isaac taking the checkered flag. The network had plenty of leftover time to do postrace interviews.

Announcers Jim McKay and Chris Economaki were ABC's lead announcers for the historic day. They were assisted by an array of technicians, including a man who was stationed inside the men's rest room. He stayed on the phone line to network headquarters in New York to keep tabs on the signal transmission.

The day was an overwhelming success for the Blackwells. They were afraid attendance would be paltry because the race was scheduled to be televised, but an overflow crowd turned out, no doubt boosted by curiosity. "Everybody wanted to be here to see it," Pete Blackwell said. Tickets were $5.

Winston Cup drivers returned to the track—for the last time, as it turned out—in June that year, and, perhaps fittingly, NASCAR all-time victory leader Richard Petty won the last major league race at GPS. Tiny Lund finished second, a lap down. Also in the race, the 29th Winston Cup event at the track, was little-known Richard Childress, who finished 23d. He won a few dollars for the bank account that one day would make him one of Winston Cup racing's most successful team owners.

Twenty years earlier, on August 25, 1951, the track had hosted its first Winston Cup race. Bob Flock won that one, outrunning such future Hall of Famers as Buck Baker, Herb Thomas, Lee Petty, and Curtis Turner. The total purse was $3,600.

In more than a half-century of racing, GPS has held events for almost every kind of four-wheeled vehicle, and dirt motorcycles were popular at the track in the 1960s. Longtime track steward Bill Blackwell, a cousin of the owners, remembers a cycle racer hitting a guardrail in the third turn, vaulting out of the track and landing in a nearby pine tree. He stayed with the cycle as it bounced down the limbs of the tree, Blackwell said, before landing on the ground—and in the hospital. He was back at the track before the day's racing was over.

Through the years, the Blackwells remained friendly with most Winston Cup drivers, visiting Daytona every February to tour the garage, visit teams, and make plans for future events. Tom Blackwell saw two races on the old beach-road course at Daytona and had been to every Daytona 500 through the 2001 season. Recovering from December surgery, he missed the 2002 race.

GPS was rediscovered by the Winston Cup community several years ago. "The Stavola brothers started bringing their cars down to test, and then everybody found out about it," Blackwell said. "Now they all come. We have had as many as 13 Winston Cup drivers at one time."

When the brightly colored transporters pull into the old track, telephone lines in the neighborhood, located about four miles west of Greenville, begin crackling. "Hey, Jeff Gordon's at the racetrack," Fan A will tell Fan B, and soon hundreds of people are driving out to the track to watch the big boys test.

"Dale Earnhardt came here to practice a couple of days in December before he won the Daytona 500 (in February 1998)," Blackwell said. "A guy at the track said he could rub the No. 3 (Earnhardt's car) for good luck and he'd win Daytona. So Earnhardt goes down there and wins, and everybody figures the guy has the magic touch. A couple of weeks later, Bill Elliott came in to test, and the first thing he asked was, 'Where's that guy?'"

Blackwell also can run through a string of Winston Cup drivers who have tested at GPS one week and won the next. There's no magic in the old asphalt, though; it's simply a convenient, well-run track that gives teams a reasonable facsimile of Martinsville Speedway and other Winston Cup tracks that fit into the "flat" mold.

"It's a good place if you have a new brake package you want to sort out," said Lee McCall, crew chief for Winston Cup driver Sterling Marlin. "It's a nice, smooth track and a good track to test on. We want to try to go to places that are somewhat similar to places we race on, and it fits."

Winston Cup crew chief Donnie Wingo said the turns at GPS don't provide a lot of grip, making it a perfect spot to check the strength of brake systems. "You have to use a lot of brakes there, and if you can make a car turn there, you can make it turn at Martinsville," he said. "When we want to try new things, we'll go to a place like that and kind of nail down what we want to do before we go use one of our seven official tests."

So, on a historic half-mile track where Turner, Petty, Baker, and Isaac once roamed, this new generation of Winston Cup drivers burns laps over and over, plowing the same landscape, seeking the same hot groove.

It is the circle that remains unbroken.

SOUL SEARCHING

Once one of NASCAR's most engaging personalities, Kyle
Petty now searches for a new direction as he tries to
cope with the tragic death of his son.

By Jeff Owens

I t was qualifying day at Charlotte Motor Speedway, and reporters
had packed the infield media center for an appearance by Kyle Petty
and his dad, "The King."

Kyle and Richard always draw a crowd. Though Richard has been
retired for seven years and Kyle hasn't won a race in four, they are still
two of NASCAR's most popular celebrities. Fans and the media
flocked to them like disciples, clamoring for their attention as if they
were royalty, which in a sense they are, presiding at the helm of
NASCAR's first family.

Though Richard is still one of the most famous sports figures in
America, it was Kyle, the prince of this royal family, who attracts the
most attention. Why? Just look at him.

Richard is the creation of an era when NASCAR was John Wayne
cool. He sports a flashy, designer cowboy hat, shiny boots, his trademark shades, and one of the widest country grins outside of Nashville.

Kyle, meanwhile, is the anti-king, pulling into the parking lot atop a Harley, his ponytail snaking down his back, earrings glistening in the sun. He is hip, cool, and a biker dude all rolled into one. While his dad is a throwback to the old days—when cars and drivers were Strictly Stock—Kyle is stuck in a time warp between '60s hippie and Generation X.

Though father and son, they are as different as night and day. Yet, in a way, they are the same, because each has his own unique personality, his own compelling identity. In Kyle's words, they are who they are, not what someone else wants them to be, which is rare in today's image-is-everything world.

As Kyle stepped to the podium, he held in his hand a die-cast version of his father's famous No. 43. It was Petty blue and designed to commemorate the royal family's 50th year in racing. Though it was a souvenir a collectible company would make a mint off of, the media covered the event as if it were breaking news. This was, after all, the Pettys. Only an appearance by Dale Earnhardt or Bill France himself could garner such attention in the NASCAR world.

Moments later, Kyle did not miss the irony when he caught himself criticizing NASCAR's big-money marketing machine. Oh, the hypocrisy, he said, as he remembered that, just minutes earlier, he had been hawking his own die-cast cars. "You guys should be writing about what goes on on the race track, not what somebody who sells toy cars tells you," he said, laughing.

That's Kyle Petty, able to take on Big Business and Big Brother while poking fun at his own family, which has made its own fortune off NASCAR. You want irony, perspective, and some of the best analogies in sports? Talk to Kyle Petty.

After photos were taken and autographs signed—no one in sports signs more autographs than the Pettys—Kyle was surrounded by reporters, each wisely seeking the opinion of NASCAR's most outspoken personality. As intelligent and well read as any professional athlete, Kyle was the best interview on the Winston Cup circuit for one reason: He always spoke his mind. He told it like it was, no matter whom he offended or what controversy he incited.

When he said NASCAR was boring, he meant it. When he said that the drivers of today were "fake" and that sponsors were ruining the sport by forcing drivers to change, he was speaking the truth. He said what others believed but were afraid to say in public.

He went by the motto of another sports star who marched to the beat of a different drum. Of the dress-wearing Dennis Rodman, Petty said, "When he looks in the mirror at night, he can't say he sold himself out or he changed the way he was just to get an NBA job."

The same could be said for Petty. He is who he is, and if you don't like it, too bad. He's not about to change for anyone, no matter how much money is on the table.

"I kind of look at it like Richard Petty," he said of his famous dad. "He wears cowboy boots and a cowboy hat, and that's just who he is. This is just who I am. I've had sponsors before who said, 'Cut your hair.' I'm like, 'Keep your money.' You can't, because that's not who I am, and the guy sitting in the grandstands is going to know that's not who I am."

Sadly, a year later Kyle Petty was not the man he used to be. Death will do that to a man. Where money and success couldn't break him, death did.

A year after Kyle held court in Charlotte that bright, sunny day, death snuck into his life and stole his pride and joy, taking his 19-year-old son, Adam, in a race car crash at New Hampshire International Speedway.

Kyle Petty has not been the same since. Oh, he still has the long hair and earrings, and he still rides a Harley, leading a group of NASCAR stars across the country every year to raise money for charity. But part of him is missing, part of the soul that made him who he was.

"That kid was his best friend," said Felix Sabates, Kyle's onetime car owner. "Kyle and Adam were inseparable. If you lose your best friend, it's pretty tragic. To lose your best friend and your son at the same time, I don't know how you cope with that."

In a sense, the whole NASCAR world lost a friend. From the time he was a toddler, Adam Petty was around stock car racing, playing in the infields with boys like Jason Jarrett and Justin Labonte, while their daddies raced.

When it was his turn to join the race, Adam spread excitement and joy throughout NASCAR like few rising stars ever have. He was a cross between Davey Allison and Dale Earnhardt Jr., all charismatic legacies destined for the big time.

"We were putting a lot of our future and a lot of things in the basket with Adam to sort of carry the torch for us," Richard Petty said.

"Kyle's dreams and Richard's and Petty Enterprises' were basically being tailor-made for Adam," former championship driver Darrell Waltrip said. "He was their future. The future of Petty Enterprises was basically riding on his shoulders."

From the time Adam was 14, nearly every move Kyle made was for his oldest son. In 1997 he left Team Sabco, where he had won six races, to start his own Petty satellite operation, one designed to build a foundation for Adam. When he moved back to Level Cross, North Carolina, to help run the family business a year later, it was to get

Petty Enterprises ready for Adam. When the team decided to switch to Dodge in 2000, it was for Adam. And when it made plans to expand to three teams the following year, the driver of the new team was supposed to be Adam.

"He spent a lot of time and a lot of effort on Adam's racing program, because that's what made him happy," Sabates recalled.

Never had Kyle been prouder than on September 30, 1998, the night Adam held off Winston Cup veteran Mike Wallace to win at Charlotte in his first career ARCA (Automobile Racing Club of America) start. Afterward, Adam stood in victory lane, holding a Charlotte Motor Speedway trophy and grinning from ear to ear. They say his smile was infectious, and that night it surely spread, because his father and grandfather stood next to him, flashing the same toothy grins.

Eight months later, as Kyle stood near the same spot, his reflection bouncing off a Petty blue Pontiac, he talked of his lifelong dream. Dale Earnhardt Jr., the son of the seven-time champion, was about to make his Winston Cup debut at Charlotte. Kyle dreamed of Adam doing the same, following his father toward a checkered flag.

"I'm looking forward to racing against Adam," he said. "I always looked forward to racing against my father. Of all the things I've done, that's one of the things that is most special to me, being able to say that, for a period of time, I did race against him. . . . That's what is so cool about this sport, that you can go out there and have those kinds of personal relationships on the racetrack. It carries over for a lifetime."

Except when one of those lives is cut short. Earnhardt Jr. got to race against his dad, spending a full season with him before his father died on the last lap of the 2001 Daytona 500. Kyle and Adam never made it that far.

Adam made his first Winston Cup race on April 2, 2000, at Texas Motor Speedway. Ironically, Kyle failed to make that race, pouring all his efforts into Adam's big-league debut. Though disappointed at missing the field, he was proud of his son, who was speeding toward a dream of his own.

"All I ever wanted to do was be like my dad and do what he did," Adam said before the Texas race. "Me and my dad are really close, and that's one thing that's really neat. He is a big kid, and I'm a big kid trying to grow up and do what he's done. We're like best friends."

But all those plans came to a screeching halt a month later.

"All of my hopes and dreams and what I tried to work for was for Adam, to be able to build something for him," Kyle said in one of his first interviews following his son's death. "Now that I feel like we finally built it to a point where we could capitalize on it, he's not here to take advantage of it."

Rarely has a sport been as shaken as the NASCAR world was by Adam Petty's death.

The first fourth-generation athlete in major-league sports, he had the driving talent of his grandfather and the charisma of his dad. When he walked through the garage, flashing his familiar smile, his happy-go-lucky demeanor seemed to light up the whole sport, pumping it full of hope and promise. For all that had gone wrong in recent years—rising costs, disgruntled fans, uncontrollable greed—Adam Petty represented all that was good about NASCAR. He was the faithful son following in the footsteps of his father, carrying on the richest family tradition in racing.

All that changed in a flash when his Chevrolet slammed into the third-turn wall at New Hampshire, killing him instantly. When news of his shocking death spread through the NASCAR community, it plunged the sport into a deep sorrow it had never felt before. Drivers, crewmen, family, and friends all felt they had lost a child of their own.

"He had such a great future ahead of him," said Chris Hussey, Adam's crew chief. "[Death] was the last thing on our minds. When you're young, you're Superman; you think you're invincible. That's the way I thought of him. I thought he was Superman. I thought he was invincible."

"He was such a wonderful kid," said Barry Dodson, Petty's former crew chief and a longtime family friend. "I watched him grow up. He stayed with my children when he was little. We changed his diapers.

"I've been to too many funerals," Dodson added, tears streaming down his face, ". . . but this one really hurts."

Not only had NASCAR lost a talented young driver and a rising star, but also a family member had lost a son. And sons are not supposed to die, not the sons of fearless racers.

"There is nothing that I can think of that could be any worse than to lose a child," driver Ward Burton said after Adam's death. "It's a horrible, horrible thing."

No one knows that better than Dodson. He lost his teenage son and daughter in a traffic accident in 1994. Though he resumed his racing career, he has never gotten over their deaths.

"You expect your mom and dad to go, you don't want your brothers and sisters to go, but you never want to have to bury a child," he said. "Nothing compares. When you bury a child, a part of you dies, too."

When Kyle and Patti Petty learned about the September 1994 deaths of Trey and Tia Dodson, they sped down Highway 151 from Charlotte to Darlington, South Carolina, racing to comfort a friend. Six years later, Dodson returned the favor. He was waiting for Kyle when he returned from Europe a day after Adam's death. He spent the next few days consoling, coaching, and preparing Kyle for the long days ahead.

Though Patti and Kyle comforted Dodson following his loss, they could never quite fathom what he was truly going through . . . not until Adam died.

"I was such a fool to think I knew how y'all felt," Patti told Dodson. "I thought I did. But I had no idea."

"You just don't know until you walk the walk," Dodson said.

Dodson walked that walk, and it nearly crippled him. He joined Kyle's team following his children's death but plunged into such a deep despair he could barely work. He ended up leaving the team before season's end.

"Barry just completely fell apart," Sabates said. "He couldn't cope with it. I had an uncle who once said, 'It's very hard to feel the weight of the box unless you carry it on your shoulders.' I knew what Barry was going through . . . but I could not imagine it."

As he struggled to cope, Dodson led Petty to victory lane one last time. On June 4, 1995, on Dodson's 42d birthday, he and Kyle won the Winston Cup race at Dover Downs International Speedway, taking advantage of an early 20-car pileup that opened the door to victory lane.

To this day, Dodson believes he was somehow destined to win that race, giving him the opportunity to honor his children the only way he knew how, the way racers do.

"I said a little prayer that day, and Trey and Tia helped us win that race," Dodson said. "I know in my mind and in my heart that is what happened. They were watching over us that day."

As they celebrated the win in victory lane, Kyle leaned over and whispered in his friend's ear, "This is for Trey and Tia."

"Kyle said it was his biggest win, and he dedicated it to Trey and Tia," Dodson said. "Now I wish he had saved it. I just wished he had saved it for Adam."

For months following Adam's death, Dodson and others tried to comfort Kyle. But nothing they could do or say could comfort a man and a family whose life had been changed forever.

"Back then, Kyle summed up my life as being in sort of a free fall," Dodson said. "Now, here he is in the same free fall."

A week after Adam's death, as the NASCAR community mourned, Kyle's friends pondered the future of the Petty family, openly wondering what life held for someone who had suffered such a terrible loss. Would Kyle return to racing? Could he? Or would he hang it up, ending his career and taking his public persona into seclusion?

"If it was one of my little girls, and something happened to her at a racetrack, I don't know if I could ever stand to go back again," Waltrip said. "I don't know if I could stand to look at a race car again."

Said Geoffrey Bodine, the survivor of a horrifying wreck just three months before Adam's fatal crash: "If I had lost a child in auto racing, something I had done all my life and something that was my life, I don't think I could make it. I don't think I could deal with it."

If anybody could deal with such a loss, though, it was supposed to be Kyle Petty, a spiritual leader and, emotionally, one of the strongest men in racing. He had seen enough tragedy in his life to build a strong fortress.

As a child, he watched his father accidentally run over an eight-year-old boy, killing him during a drag race in Georgia, a burden his father would have to carry the rest of his career. At age 15, he stood and watched as a water tank blew up in his father's pit at Talladega, killing Richard's 20-year-old brother-in-law and Kyle's uncle. Then, in his first season of professional racing, Adam accidentally ran over his own crew chief, killing him, during an ASA event in Minnesota, and saddling himself with a tragedy no teenager should have to bear.

But the Pettys are a strong lot, able to handle enormous trials that would break a normal family. They somehow lean on each other, trusting their strong family bond and a deep faith in God. Following the 1998 accident, it was Kyle and Richard who comforted Adam, teaching him to deal with death and loss.

"I turn to the Lord now for a lot more guidance. He helps me a whole lot," Adam said a few months after the fatal accident. "I went away a boy, and I . . . I won't say I came back a man, but I had to grow up a lot."

But there are some tragedies, some burdens that are too heavy for even the strongest to bear. Following Adam's death, friends and family worried about what might happen to Kyle. Dodson worried that he might try to maintain his public image, continuing his role as one of NASCAR's great ambassadors while hiding his inner pain. Dodson knew from experience that it wouldn't work.

"He's always been the type to bottle everything up," Dodson said. "No matter what the problem was, no matter whether he was being successful or not, he was always the same Kyle. But you can't bottle this up. You can't bottle death."

Kyle and his team skipped the two races following Adam's death. But on June 2, Kyle returned to racing, joining his Winston Cup team at Dover and, incredibly, driving Adam's Busch Series car at the same track.

And true to form, he stepped right back into the limelight, sharing his sorrow and pain during a tearful press conference.

"I don't think I've ever had anything affect me anywhere close to this," he said, wiping tears from his face. "I've just been devastated by this. But this is the only thing I know to do, to go and get back (to racing)."

Quitting, he said, was not an option, not for a family raised on stock cars. Racing was in his blood, just as it had been in Adam's, and he couldn't dam up those veins. Adam and his memory would not allow it.

"Quitting never crossed my mind," said Kyle, who, a year later would watch his youngest son Austin follow Adam into racing. "This is what we have always done as a family. My grandfather did it, my father did it, I've done it, Adam did it. This is what we do. We look at ourselves in a lot of ways like a bunch of farmers. Just because

Kyle Petty gives his two sons, Austin (left) and Adam, their first view of the family profession at Charlotte Speedway in 1986. DMP Archives Photos

something goes bad or something goes wrong, you don't quit and go home. You keep plugging along at it. Sometimes it sounds a little crazy to say or a little stupid to say, but as much as Adam loved racing, he wouldn't stop, so there is no reason for us to stop."

So Kyle soldiered on. And he knew no better way to honor his son than to drive his race car.

"It was incredibly hard for Patti and me to go back to Adam's race shop," Kyle said. "You'll never know how hard it was to walk through those doors and see those cars sitting there with his name on it, and see his seats in the car and his uniforms and stuff like that. But at the same time, there is nothing Adam loved more than race cars, being around his crew and racing people."

It was just as difficult for Kyle to return to the racetrack, a place where he and his son had spent most of their life, playing together and racing together.

"Coming in here and just rolling through the front gate of the racetrack, knowing Adam wasn't here, was pretty hard," he said. "I didn't take it too good, because being at the racetrack on Thursday nights were our time. It was mine and Adam's time."

Time they would never share again. Without Adam, Kyle is not the man he used to be. He is not the same outgoing personality fans and the media used to flock to. Instead, he buries himself in his work, focusing on his race cars—Adam's race cars—and trying to rebuild Petty Enterprises, once one of NASCAR's proudest organizations. Each week on NASCAR's grueling Winston Cup circuit, he straps on his helmet, one bearing Adam's name, and climbs into his race car, which also carries his son's name, and continues his quest for one more trip to victory lane.

He now shies away from the spotlight where his star once shone so bright. And out of respect for the grief they know is still there, fans and the media no longer flock to him as if he were a spiritual guru. Yet his pain and suffering are still way too public. Just as Earnhardt Jr. had to cope with the public spectacle following his father's death, so has Kyle had to bear his cross in the open.

As he walked down the streets of Chicago a year after Adam's death, a man walked up to him, reached for his hand, and told him he was sorry about his son's death.

"It's been a year and a couple of months, but it's still so incredibly public," Kyle said two days later. "Most people who lose a son or a father, their immediate family knows it, but when they go on vacation, nobody knows it. They can probably escape it at some point in time. But for myself or for Dale Jr., no matter where you're at, it's always there."

Always reminding him of the incredible void in his life, the emptiness that has changed his perspective and reshaped his attitude about a lot of things, including racing. "I think it changed the way I look at the sport in general," he said.

"I've always said this, but I believe it now more than ever . . . this is just a sport. It's not the end of the world. You go to Indy, and if you don't make the race, you go home. Big deal. I don't see that as a major problem anymore. . . . You look at a lot of things differently."

Death will do that to a man, even a man as strong as Kyle Petty.

WHERE LEGENDS RACED

For a span of six decades, historic old Nashville Speedway hosted the Who's Who of racing, provided a playground for country music celebrities, and served as a career springboard for some of NASCAR's greatest drivers.

By Larry Woody

Marty Robbins, the late, legendary country western singer, loved fast cars almost as much as he loved strumming guitars. He took on NASCAR's biggest, baddest tracks, such as Daytona and Talladega, but his favorite playground was his hometown track, Nashville Speedway, a tough little five-eighths-mile asphalt bullring nestled just south of downtown Music City at the State Fairgrounds.

During one sultry Saturday night fender bender, Robbins had survived an inordinate (even by the track's crunching standards) number of crashes and was leading the race when he suddenly veered onto the apron, screeched into the pits, and hastily began to unbuckle his helmet.

His crew chief rushed over and shouted frantically over the roar of the combatants still slugging it out on the track: "What'n hell's wrong, Marty? Tires? Brakes? Gas? What? What!"

"Ain't nothin' wrong," drawled Robbins. "We're runnin' late with all those cautions and I've gotta get over to the Opry. Sorry boys, but I gotta go."

Beverly Hamilton, aunt of Winston Cup star Bobby Hamilton, chuckled as she recounted the late 1950s story.

"My daddy, Preacher Hamilton, was Marty's crew chief that night, and he wasn't too happy about his driver pulling in while he was leading. But that's what Marty did just about every Saturday night when he wasn't on the road: He'd go out to the Fairgrounds and race as long as he could race and still get to the old Ryman Auditorium in time to do the final set on the Opry. Marty preferred the last set because that gave him more time to race. He'd change from his racing uniform into his Opry outfit on the way from the track, and he'd often walk out on stage still sweating from the race."

Such tales are woven into the rich fabric of the historic old track: fast cars and Opry stars, colorful drivers with names like Paddlefoot and Chubby, Smut and Bullet Bob, Coo Coo, and Flookie.

The track was the training ground for a fleet of young hotfoots who would go on to gain fame in NASCAR's big leagues: Coo Coo Marlin, Darrell Waltrip, Sterling Marlin, Jeff Green, Bobby Hamilton, Jeremy Mayfield, Casey Atwood.

"There's not a weekly short track anywhere that has produced as many great drivers as that old place," said Gary Baker, one of a number of operators of the city-owned speedway. "It could have its own Who's Who of stock car racing. Man, if that track could talk, the stories it could tell."

Well, since it can't, I'll tell a few for it.

Like the time an out-of-town driver came in for a race and local fans didn't know he was equipped with a prosthesis: an artificial leg. Midway through the race, he was involved in a terrible crash. Silence descended over the packed grandstands as rescue workers rushed to the scene, where the car sat crumpled against a guardrail. Slowly, through the smoke and dust, there came a wiggle of movement inside the car. The window net was raised, and a relieved cheer began to rise from the crowd . . . only to turn to a gasp of horror when a leg, with driving shoe attached, was tossed out the window!

The Speedway was managed during its formative years by Bill Donoho, a tough, crusty former Nashville assistant police chief who packed a pistol and took no lip. Many an irate driver went storming furiously into Donoho's office to vent a grievance, only to meekly emerge a few minutes later, hat in hand, and quietly tiptoe away. Donoho never lost a debate.

Well, almost never. He finally met his match in Cale Yarborough, who proved to be just as hard-damn-headed as Donoho during a $50 feud. Cale claimed that Donoho came up $50 short on some promised "appearance money" after a race. Donoho—worth millions—refused to shell out the measly 50 bucks, "on principle, because I paid Yarborough exactly what I said I was going to pay him, and he won't get a cent more!"

After one Grand National (now Winston Cup) victory at the Speedway, Yarborough refused to come to the press box for the customary postrace winner's interview, out of spite for, "that no-good, lyin' Bill Donoho!"

The feud festered for years before Donoho finally relented and grudgingly forked over the disputed $50 to Yarborough. As the two mule-stubborn old combatants grudgingly shook hands, a witness jokingly remarked that Donoho appeared to have his other hand on his pistol, while Yarborough had *his* other hand on his wallet. At any rate, that $50 should go into the Motorsports Hall of Fame. It represents the only argument ever lost by one of NASCAR's toughest promoters.

As ornery and cantankerous as Donoho could be, he also had a seldom-seen soft side. Before hosting a Grand National race in the early 1970s, he heard about a young driver who was down on his luck. He had lost his ride and was driving a taxi up in Detroit.

Donoho called the kid and asked if he'd like to come to Nashville to race. The kid said he had no car. Donoho said he'd find him a ride. The kid said he had no money to travel to Nashville. Donoho said he'd send him some. The kid had no place to stay. Donoho put him up at his house.

The kid's name was Benny Parsons, who, after getting his career on track, would go on to win a Daytona 500 and a Winston Cup title and would become one of the sport's favorite drivers and a popular TV commentator.

"To this day I don't know why Mr. Donoho took such an interest in me," said Parsons. "At the time I certainly wasn't a big-name driver who could help sell tickets. Maybe he just felt sorry for me. All I know is that he did me a huge favor during a tough time and never once asked for anything in return."

When Donoho died several years ago, Parsons was the only prominent out-of-town driver who came to his funeral.

Nashville Speedway has been running since 1958, but long before then—back at the turn of the century—races between newfangled motor cars were held at the Fairgrounds site, known then as Cumberland Park. In 1904 racing icon Barney Oldfield came to town to show off his famed Peerless "Green Dragon." Later, driving on the dirt oval scratched out of the rocky bottoms, Herbert H. Lyles would set a world record by going eight miles in a dizzying 8 minutes and 29 seconds.

Oldfield returned in 1907 to better that record by covering two miles in two minutes and one-fifth second.

When the Speedway went NASCAR, the pioneers of the sport rolled into town: Lee Petty, Buck Baker, Fred Lorenzen, Fireball Roberts, the Flock brothers, Joe Weatherly, Glen Wood, Cotton Owens, Rex White . . . eventually to be joined by latter-day stock car stars like Richard Petty, David Pearson, Buddy Baker, Cale Yarborough, Bobby Allison, Neil Bonnett, Dale Earnhardt . . . the best of the best.

Then there was the homegrown talent, steel-willed weekend warriors who migrated to the Fairgrounds—like singers drawn to Nashville with a guitar and a dream—and went on to find NASCAR stardom. At the top of the Speedway's honor roll is Darrell Waltrip, who arrived in Nashville from Owensboro, Kentucky, in the late 1960s in search of challenge and opportunity.

Richard Petty (No. 43) passes high above a collision to stay on course at the Nashville Speedway. Fairgrounds Speedway

Waltrip found both. He used the Speedway as a springboard into NASCAR's big leagues. (He won his first of 84 Winston Cup races on his home track in 1975.) Today the three-time champion looks back on those early days with fondness . . . and a bit of amusement.

"It was pretty wild back then," Waltrip said. "Those old local boys didn't take kindly to some loudmouth kid from Kentucky rolling in and winning all their races. I used to joke that every Saturday night I had to run two races: one on the track, and another for the exit, after the race. When there was a dispute—which was about every Saturday night—they tended to settle it with a lug wrench instead of a rule book."

Waltrip had some memorable battles with Coo Coo Marlin, who won a record four track championships and whose son, Sterling, won three local titles and went on to capture back-to-back Daytona 500s. After one grueling battle, Waltrip's winning car was protested by Coo Coo and the flock of family members who served in and around his pits. As he sat on the pit wall, watching his car be dismantled by inspectors, Waltrip was asked how he thought the episode would turn out.

"Don't know," shrugged Waltrip. "I can't see my race car. It's covered up with Marlins!"

"Darrell was a good driver," Coo Coo would grudgingly concede years later, "but he had good equipment. And he liked to run his mouth too much." Old rivalries die hard.

When Sterling came along, he was virtually unstoppable. With a pretty blonde at his side—Paula, who would eventually become Mrs. Marlin—Sterling rode roughshod over the competition. Some of his fume-choked challengers accused Marlin of cheating. Marlin grinned and dismissed any advantage he might have had as "superior reading of the rule book."

In the old days, the fans often came for the promotion and stayed for the race. The Prince of Promoters was Jimbo Donoho, flamboyant son of the Speedway operator. Along with stock car racing promotions, Jimbo also dabbled in various country music enterprises. Once, amid a widely publicized dispute with legendary singer Webb Pierce, Jimbo dumped a load of catfish into a swimming pool he and Pierce co-owned. At the Speedway, Jimbo brought in everybody from Jerry Lee Lewis to Dynamite Bob to help draw a crowd.

Dynamite Bob's prerace show consisted of blowing himself up in a coffin (packed with flour, to enhance the dramatic effect). The exact connection between the stunt and a stock car race was always a bit fuzzy, as was Dynamite Bob after a few performances.

Another Bob, "Bullet Bob" Reuther, won the first track championship and earned a reputation as a driver not to be trifled with. Once, after being spun out, Bullet Bob cut across the track infield, lay in wait on the backstretch, and T-boned the offender when he came past. Reuther, godfather to Winston Cup star Bobby Hamilton, was wild and reckless, but also a talented racer. He once held a speed record on the old Daytona Beach course and raced successfully on short tracks throughout the South and Southeast, but his heart never left his hometown Fairgrounds battlefield.

There was plenty of humor at the old track. At the start of one race, a den of newborn puppies was disturbed as they slept in a culvert on the backstretch. They waddled out onto the track, and the field of cars went swerving and spinning to miss the little dogs. The flagman began frantically waving the yellow flag.

"Ladies and gentlemen," deadpanned track announcer Joe Williams, "the race is under caution due to a litter on the track."

It wasn't all fun and frolic, heroes and hijinks. The Speedway, like other tough little tracks, had its moments of trouble and tragedy. Two drivers died on the track, and several more were seriously injured over the years by crashes and flames. Many of the badly injured racers were competing for a $50 purse and $5 trophy. No driver ever got rich racing at the Fairgrounds.

The 15,000-seat Speedway lost its two annual Winston Cup races in 1984 when the track became bogged down in management problems. But Gary Baker, who continued to run the weekly series for a few more years, said the end was in sight long before then.

"The track had become too old and outdated to keep up with NASCAR's growth," Baker explained. "It is in a cramped, landlocked location, with no room to expand. Our only hope to keep Winston Cup was to build a big, new track at a new location, and I was never able to get it done."

Veteran promoter Bob Harmon took over the track for several years. During that period, Dale Earnhardt Jr. came in occasionally to gain experience against the tough local talent. One night he was joined by his racing brother and sister, Kerry and Kelley. All three Earnhardt kids were caught up on a crash on the first lap.

"We argued over who had to call our dad and give him the news that we'd wiped out three cars in one wreck," Kerry recalled a few years later. "I think we finally made Kelley do it. We figured he'd be easier on her."

Today the Speedway continues to host Saturday night specials, with area drivers swapping sparks and sheet metal for purses that hardly cover their gas and tire bills . . . just as they have done for decades.

Some dream of making it big, like some of their predecessors. Most, however, race for what Coo Coo Marlin called "the pure hell of it": for the action, the excitement, the unmatchable rush provided by roaring engines and high-octane adrenaline.

How long it can continue is debatable. Weekly racing is an archaic sport trying to survive in a new, challenging world. The NFL and NHL have come to Nashville. The Opry has moved from the old Ryman. No sweaty stars rush onstage there anymore, fresh from the racetrack. Local stock car racing has become an afterthought.

The bigger races—NASCAR Busch and truck and Indy Racing League events—are now run on a new $125 million track called Nashville Superspeedway, even though it is located 40 miles from Nashville, in another county. The old Fairgrounds track has been left behind.

The track was scheduled to close at the end of the 2002 season, but a group of area businessmen took over the lease and hope to keep it running. Still, despite their best efforts, the track faces an uncertain future. Not even Dynamite Bob can compete with the NFL, NHL, and 100 TV channels.

Someday the motors are sure to fall silent for the final time at the tired old Fairgrounds. All that will remain will be the ruins of scarred concrete walls looming through the weeds and the whispers of old ghosts carried on warm summer breezes.

And the stories . . . all the sorrowful, funny, rich, sad, inspiring, wonderful stories. They will live on.

The old track, you see, does know how to talk.

THE MAN WHO MADE IT LOOK EASY

David Pearson was never charismatic and seldom
profound. In the opinion of many, he was merely the
greatest stock car racer who ever lived.

By Monte Dutton

David Gene Pearson was my boyhood hero. He was, to me, what
Clayton Delaney was to Tom T. Hall, what John F. Kennedy
was to Bill Clinton, and what Alfred Hitchcock was to Martin
Scorcese.

Of course, I didn't wind up being a race car driver, a guitar picker,
a politician, or a motion-picture director. As Pearson himself might
have said, "Them's the breaks, I reckon."

I'll never know what it was like to be David Pearson. Pearson has
never been inclined to wax poetic on his greatness. I'm not sure he's
ever understood it. He managed to do things with a stock car that I
never saw anyone else do, and the only person unimpressed was Pearson himself.

Reviewing Pearson's career can be a daunting task, especially in his
presence. The celebrated winner of 105 NASCAR races is maddeningly matter-of-fact in discussing a career that was positively spectacu-

lar. A bit of trial and error yields a successful formula: Go elsewhere for the anecdote or the legend, then confront the great man with it. Grudgingly, Pearson will concede that, yes, it happened. Set him off a bit, or get him to laugh, and he will provide a few details.

Everything is still a competition, a race of sorts, for this gracefully aging product of a textile mill village. During his driving career (1960–86), Pearson would evade questions by repeating them back to the interviewer.

"David, how does this victory stack up against the other great victories of your career?"

Pearson would scratch his head. "I don't know. How would you rank it?"

Ah, the Silver Fox. He remains reticent, but not modest. He knows full well how great he was, but he chooses not to draw attention to his accomplishments with idle boasts. That Pearson retired at just about the time stock car racing began its extraordinary growth spiral is fitting in a way. Tennis star Andre Agassi set the standard for the 1990s when he proclaimed, in so garish a vehicle as a television commercial, that "Image is everything." To Pearson, image is nothing. Performance is everything. As such, he would not be comfortable with anything in the racing mainstream of today except the money.

"When I had good equipment, I always figured I had as good a chance as anybody," he says. It is as close as he will come to a boast.

A case can be made that Pearson was the greatest of them all. He won 105 races, second only to Richard Petty's 200, but he made only 574 starts to Petty's 1,184, meaning that his winning percentage (.183) was higher than Petty's (.169). During what is known as NASCAR's modern era (1972–present), Pearson won 45 races in 206 starts, for a winning percentage of .218. Only Jeff Gordon comes close, and Pearson was winless during his final six seasons. From 1972 through 1980, Pearson's winning percentage was .283, and during the time he drove for Stuart, Virginia's Wood Brothers, it was .301.

In an era in which injuries were frighteningly common, Pearson was never seriously injured in a race car. Practically no one, save the still-youthful Gordon, shares that distinction.

In fact, no less an authority than Bobby Allison noted the uncanny similarity between the driving styles of Pearson and Gordon.

"Jeff Gordon is the only driver I have ever seen who reminds me of David Pearson," said Allison, himself a winner of 84 Winston Cup races. "Gordon knows when to go and when not to; he instinctively knows how to pick and choose. You'd swear he was beat, and then all of a sudden he roars to the front when it counts. Pearson's the only other driver I've ever seen who could do that."

The subject touches a chord with Pearson.

"The more I watch Gordon, the more impressed I am," says Pearson. "Gordon's like me in that people don't give him credit for driving hard. When I was with the Woods, they made out like I was sandbagging, like I could drive it to the front any time I wanted to, and just stayed back there playing possum. That's because they couldn't see nobody working on the car."

Therein lies one of the great secrets of the 1970s. The Wood Brothers knew more about tire stagger than anyone else, so much so that they did most of their adjustments on Pearson's No. 21 Mercury Cyclone by changing the inflation pressure in the tires. Leonard and Glen Wood had learned the art while pitting Jimmy Clark's Lotus in the Indianapolis 500 during the 1960s. When Pearson pitted, all the Wood Brothers crew seemed to do was change the tires and add fuel. The prescribed adjustments had already taken place when the tires were inflated. Meanwhile, other teams adjusted the spoilers and moved weight around, and when no one saw the Woods doing it, they all just figured the driver was biding his time. It was a magnificent secret that the family team from Virginia was unwilling to advertise.

"I was driving hard, but there were times when the car wasn't right," he recalls. "But we never gave up, not me and not the team. That's the way Gordon and his team are today. They ain't beat 'til the checkered flag waves, and we weren't, neither."

That having been noted, Pearson did have a wonderful flair for the dramatic. One year at Charlotte Motor Speedway during the World 600, bonuses were posted for the leader of laps 100, 200, and 300 of the 400-lap race. Pearson started out front but spent most of the day in the nether reaches of the top five. Each time the money was on the line, however, he drove to the front. By day's end, he had captured the pole, race, and each of the 100-lap awards.

Pearson once won 11 poles in a row at the 1.5-mile track. H. A. "Humpy" Wheeler, the track president, became obsessed with figuring out the source of Pearson's superiority. When he thought he had it figured out, Wheeler had one end of the track repaved and modified.

"The next time we raced, Pearson won the pole again," Wheeler recalls. "When we handed him the check, in victory lane, with the flashbulbs popping and everything all a-glitter, David whispered in my ear, 'You know what? You fixed the wrong side.' All the while, he kept on smiling for the cameras."

By far the most famous of Pearson's victories was the 1976 Daytona 500, in which he and Petty crashed on the final lap. With Petty's Dodge stricken 15 yards shy of the finish line, Pearson, who had had the presence of mind to keep the engine in his rumpled Mercury running, crossed the finish line first at no more than 40 miles per hour, smoke swirling from the tires.

Eddie Wood, then a crewman but now the team's co-owner, remembers what Pearson said on the radio that day.

"What happened?" Wood asked.

"The bitch hit me," Pearson replied.

"Where's Richard?"

"Stopped up here shy of the finish line."

"Well, I'm coming," Pearson said, finally reengaging the clutch.

Another race at Daytona, a year and a half earlier, epitomized the Pearson knack for the dramatic even more. It has been lost in all the lore surrounding the 500 of '76, but as an example of Pearson's virtuosity, unflappable demeanor, and plain old guts, it was his masterpiece.

The 1974 Firecracker 400 was a race Petty was determined to win. In both 1972 and 1973 Pearson had finished first, Petty second. Before the start of the race, Petty sent word to Pearson that it was not going to happen again.

"One of the boys in Petty's crew came up to me and said, 'Richard says to tell you that he ain't gonna be embarrassed again,'" Pearson remembers.

In those days, when a race at Daytona or Talladega drew to its conclusion, it was generally considered advantageous to be running second when the white flag waved. The famed slingshot maneuver—the second car would interrupt the flow of air by pulling out of the "draft" to shoot by the first—was almost impossible to defend.

Pearson led with Petty second and the rest of the field trailing by nearly a quarter of a lap. Pearson gradually slowed, trying to force Petty to pass him, but lap after lap, Petty just slowed with him. When the white flag waved, Pearson took a rather extreme, and spectacular, measure.

At the line, Pearson feigned mechanical failure, lifting his foot off the accelerator and "mashing" the clutch. As his Mercury suddenly slowed, Petty had to swerve to the right to avoid him. Then Pearson sped off after him, trailing by almost 200 yards as the new leader entered turn one. Down the backstretch, the Mercury tracked down Petty's Dodge like a heat-seeking missile. Pearson passed Petty in turn four and won for the third year in a row.

Petty was angry afterward, saying that Pearson had meant to embarrass him. It was the only rift between the two great drivers.

A few days later, though, the city of Spartanburg, South Carolina, held a day in honor of favorite son Pearson, and Petty showed up to pay his respects.

Recalling this most spectacular of victories, Pearson is predictably modest.

"The way I figured it, there wasn't any gamble to it," he says. "I was going to finish second either way. Might as well give it a try."

Pearson and Petty finished 63 races with one first and the other second. Pearson won 33 of them.

Cotton Owens, for whom Pearson won the first of his three championships in 1966, speaks of his former driver as if he wore a cape.

"David Pearson was the best race-car driver who ever lived," says Owens, himself a retired racer. "There is no doubt in my mind about that. We had some good times together. I loved him like a son, and I think that's probably why we split up.

"We had just gotten to the point where we were too close. It's just like when you're raising a boy, and it gets to the point where you and him are both hardheaded. David and I just got to where neither one of us was listening to what the other one said."

A favorite Owens story concerns the time, during the mid-1960s, when Chrysler Corporation decided it wanted to put Pearson in the Indianapolis 500. A tryout was arranged at the 1.522-mile track in Hampton, Georgia (then Atlanta International Raceway, now reconfigured and known as Atlanta Motor Speedway), in an Indy roadster normally driven by the late Don Branson. Owens and Pearson drove to the track.

Pearson was leery from the start.

"The steering on those cars was awfully quick," he says. "Just the slightest flick of the wheel would put you out of control. The only time I had ever driven a car that was even close to being like that had been on a dirt track, and I was afraid I was going to put that thing in the wall just because I wasn't used to anything like it. I tried to get them to change the steering ratio, but they said that's not the way we do these things and that I'd get used to it."

Reluctantly, Pearson returned to the track and brought the roadster up to speed. Within three laps, he was circling the high-banked oval at a considerably faster pace than Branson.

The Chrysler delegation exulted. When Pearson returned to pit road, Chrysler executive Frank Wiley ran out to greet him. As Pearson crawled out of the cockpit and pulled off his helmet, Wiley yelled, "Well, David, what do you think?"

According to Owens, Pearson looked the Chrysler executive square in the eye and replied, "I can't stand these things. Too much air in your face."

That was the end of Pearson's Indy car career. He and Owens drove back to Spartanburg.

Pearson won the first Sports Car Club of America Trans-Am race he ever started. He became the second driver ever to win three championships—Lee Petty was the first—and he only ran the entire NASCAR schedule five times in his entire career. To Pearson's way of thinking, he won the championship the only times he really put much effort into it. During his prime, he and the Woods competed only in the major events, where both money and competition were at a premium.

Pearson's 1973 season, in which he won 11 races in only 18 tries, is considered one of stock car racing's supreme accomplishments, comparable on a lesser scale to Petty's phenomenal 1967 championship in which he won 27 times in 48 events, including 10 in a row.

Petty himself has often been quoted as saying Pearson was the finest driver against whom he ever raced.

David Pearson poses behind the wheel in 1973, the year he won an astounding 11 races in only 18 tries. DMP Archives Photos

"Whenever there was a big pileup in front of me, if I could, I always tried to find David and follow him," Petty says. "If anybody could get through it, it was Pearson."

Petty's longtime crew chief and first cousin, Dale Inman, adds, "I always thought Cale Yarborough was the toughest. To me, there were times when Pearson kind of lost interest. It seemed to me like he was only in it to win, and if he didn't have the car to do it, he didn't give it as much effort. But Richard's the one who was in there racing against all those guys, and if he says Pearson was the best, then I guess I'd have to agree with him."

Today Pearson dabbles in racing, keeping himself available but not obligated. He shows up at a few races each year, particularly at Darlington, the only major league track in his home state and the one where he is still considered the acknowledged master.

Widowed, Pearson works out at the YMCA to keep his ailing back at bay, eats breakfast at the same diner most mornings and trades old stories with lifelong friends, and tools around the city on his Harley. Bypass surgery has slowed him down a bit and made him watch his diet, but he looks healthy and energetic. He still looks like he could win the Daytona 500, thanks to his broad shoulders and barrel chest. Occasionally, some young hotshot's daddy puts Pearson on retainer to take the boy around a particularly vexing track and give the kid a few pointers. Pearson still knows how to go fast.

"One thing I've always been blessed with is the knack to figure out how to go fast, even if it's a track I've never seen," he says. "Usually I can look at it and figure out the way around."

Pearson's legend has perhaps been diminished by his reluctance to talk about it. He laughs easily, remains intensely competitive and proud, but seems singularly unimpressed by his own career. He is cooperative, but just doesn't have much to say.

His name will always be paired with Petty's, and as a folk hero, it will always pale. Petty was racing royalty. He instinctively knew how to act and talk. He was perfectly matched to his era. Pearson didn't care about that, and he always had the figurative dirt under his fingernails. Petty was a heroic figure, a veritable white knight; Pearson was a stouthearted commoner from the wrong side of the tracks. Pearson left the mill village semiliterate, and while the school of hard knocks taught him well, he never became completely comfortable in the world outside.

In the cockpit of those glorious race cars—Cotton Owens's No. 6, the No. 17 of Holman and Moody, and most famously, the Wood Brothers' No. 21—Pearson was more comfortable than anyone, though. In the 1970s, when inquisitive medical researchers first attached sensors to racers, seeking to study their reactions in competition, they were astonished to find that Pearson, at 200 mph on the high banks of Daytona or Talladega, was as relaxed as if he had been lounging in a backyard hammock. The heart rate of Pearson racing was the same as that of Pearson resting.

Dale Earnhardt, similar in many ways to Pearson, revered him. The next-to-last of Pearson's 105 victories was as a substitute for Earnhardt, who suffered a shoulder injury during his rookie season and chose Pearson to drive in his stead in 1979. It is a bit ironic that the track where Pearson won in a car built for Earnhardt was Darlington, where Pearson wound up winning 10 races and Earnhardt nine.

David Pearson had so much natural ability that he took it for granted. Perhaps that was—and is—his great secret. He made legendary achievements seem routine.

It's because, to him, they were.

•

COLOR MY WORLD

Humpy Wheeler has never forgotten the excitement he felt as a 12-year-old boy waiting for something big to happen. That's the feeling he tries to create every time he opens the gates at Lowe's Motor Speedway in Charlotte.

By David Poole

Never, Humpy Wheeler says, underestimate the importance of anticipation.

"Most people live black-and-white lives," says Wheeler, president of Lowe's Motor Speedway in Charlotte, North Carolina, and the greatest showman of his auto racing generation. "They want a little Technicolor in them, and they need to have something in their lives to look forward to.

"That's how great annual events happen. People get such a charge out of getting ready to go and anticipating it, that when they get there, the event becomes what they hoped for. Great events people create the illusion that something is going to happen at their event that's so great and unique that you have got to be there. Then, they make that illusion become reality and work every angle possible to make sure that's how it is."

From that basic philosophy, Wheeler has built his image as

NASCAR's version of P. T. Barnum, a man willing to try just about anything to make a race at his track unique and memorable.

He has staged circuses along pit road, arranged for military "invasions" of his frontstretch, had daredevils make jumps in everything from motorcycles to school buses, and tackled projects that nobody, including himself, was sure could even be done.

It's a way of thinking, Wheeler says, born during his boyhood in a small North Carolina textile mill town called Belmont, about 25 miles away from the racetrack Wheeler has helped guide for more than 25 years.

Perhaps the first signs of where Wheeler would wind up in life came as early as his very first words. The Wheeler family lived then in Bessemer City, North Carolina, next door to a man named Ned, who spent a lot of his time working on his hot rod in the yard.

So when it came time for young Howard's first words, he didn't say "da-da" or "ma-ma." He said, "Ned's car."

When Howard Wheeler Sr. played football at the University of Illinois, he got caught smoking Camel cigarettes. As he ran laps for punishment, his teammates began taunting him by calling him "Humpy." The nickname stuck and, against his son's resistance as a teenager, eventually passed down a generation to Howard Jr.

The Wheelers wound up in Belmont because Howard Sr. was athletic director at Belmont Abbey College, a Catholic school run by Benedictine monks. While the younger Wheeler grew up in a Catholic home and attended parochial high school in Charlotte, he was also a product of the rough-edged environment found in the working-class town his family called home.

"Every day I was in culture shock," Wheeler says. "I would be up at the abbey with my father and the monks; then I would be thrown right into the mill town and the mill boys. My grandfather worked as a carpenter, building mill houses, and my mother ran a mercantile store next to the mill. It was like going from one world to another."

Wheeler inherited some of his father's athletic talent. He played football well enough to play in college at the University of South Carolina. Out of necessity, he also learned to box.

"I can't believe how, over the years, people have glamorized all the mill village stuff," Wheeler says. "Look, people were mean. Poverty breeds meanness, and there was a lot of poverty. To survive as a kid, you had to toughen yourself to deal with all of that. . . . In the 1950s, the biggest sport in the wintertime in the Carolinas, as far as numbers, was boxing. All of these little mill towns had boxing teams."

Wheeler showed an entrepreneurial spirit at a young age as well. When he was 13, he started a bicycle shop in his backyard.

Why a bicycle shop? "There wasn't a bike shop in Belmont," he says.

Belmont did, to the young Wheeler's endless fascination, have a store downtown that sold just nails, nuts, and bolts.

"The old man who was in there had bolts up to the ceiling and a ladder to reach them," Wheeler says. "I'd go in there, and he would show me a standard thread, or a forced thread, and why they made them that way. . . . He wasn't all that busy."

He also hung around the local Chevrolet dealership, standing around and watching the mechanics work, handing them tools and asking them questions as they repaired the cars. He dragged enough used parts home from the dealership's trash bin to annoy his mother, who wasn't particularly fond of having a junk heap in her backyard.

When he could escape Sunday afternoon visits with his folks— "You didn't want to sit around in somebody's parlor and watch dust motes and eat crackers," he says—Wheeler would walk out near the highway and watch new cars, the flashy models going to and from Charlotte, go by.

Ever since Ned's car, automobiles had fascinated Wheeler.

"The Charlotte Speedway was only about six miles away, and I would hitchhike over there," he says. "In those days, you didn't worry about a nine-year-old kid hitchhiking; it was no big thing. You just found somebody to walk in with you, because, if you were under 12, it was free with an adult."

Around age 15, Wheeler started helping out a guy who lived near his house with the race car he worked on in his backyard.

"I went to Kings Mountain with him, and his driver didn't show up, and he didn't want to drive," Wheeler says. "Two guys named Frosty Spearman and Horace Porter ran the track. It had real long straightaways, and you about had to stop at the end of them and turn left. . . . I finally convinced him to let me take the car out and practice it."

Wheeler talked his way into driving in the race and drew the pole position for the first heat.

"When I got in the car, Frosty came over and asked me if I'd ever driven before," Wheeler recalls. "I said, 'You've never heard of Howard Wheeler? I can't even believe you'd ask me that question.' I never did lie to him. I got passed by every car in the field on the first lap."

Wheeler learned quickly, however. Later on, while in college at South Carolina, Wheeler was racing at a track in Newberry, South Carolina, and convinced the track owner to cut down on the size of his track to make it tougher to drive. Wheeler then went out and found the widest car he could find, an old Packard. He painted it orange and got some of his football buddies to help him work on the car. The car was so wide that, if Wheeler ever got out front, it was nearly impossible to pass him. He won a few races that way.

But Wheeler knew his future was not behind the wheel. He spent more time working around tracks than he did driving and tried to learn something at every track he saw. He finally got a chance to apply some of that when he wound up running Robinwood Speedway, a dirt track in Gastonia, North Carolina, next door to his hometown.

Wheeler did just about everything there is to do in running a race-track, from selling the tickets to working with the local media and from enforcing the rules—the boxing background sometimes paid off there—to cleaning the bathrooms and preparing the surface for a Saturday night of racing.

One Saturday the water truck he used to wet down the surface, to keep the dust from flying so bad his ticket buyers wouldn't be washing red grit out of their hair for a week, broke down.

"I called the volunteer fire department to see if I could borrow one of their water trucks," Wheeler recalls. "It was a dry time of the year, and they were really afraid to let me use it. I had reached the end. So I called up a buddy who had a septic tank business. I said, 'Look, I'm in a bind out here.' He brought the truck out there, and we worked on the track.

"I went home to clean up, and I got back to the track around four o'clock. I am telling you the smell was unbelievable. I just hoped the wind would blow the right way. I couldn't cancel the race; we'd already sold the tickets. We had the race, and people were complaining. I finally got on the loudspeaker and said, 'The paper mill is at it again.' I apologized for the smell. That got me off the hook a little bit."

It's a long way from Robinwood Speedway in Gastonia to Charlotte Motor Speedway. Wheeler had a lot of stops along the way, most notably a stint in the mid-1960s when he worked for Firestone's racing tire operation. "That was my real degree in motorsports," Wheeler says. "I got to travel to all the big tracks and watch the people who ran the tracks and how they ran them."

In 1975 Bruton Smith hired Wheeler to help him run the 1.5-mile Charlotte track, beginning a partnership that would change the face of racing.

Wheeler's first big challenge came in May 1976, a time during which the only motorsports story getting much attention anywhere was Janet Guthrie's bid to make the Indianapolis 500 field.

"We were getting killed," Wheeler says. The Charlotte track's 600-mile race is held on the same day each year as the Indy 500. "Even the *Charlotte Observer* was covering Indy more than us."

Wheeler had to do something. He called Guthrie in Indianapolis and told her that, if she didn't make the race there, she should come to Charlotte and try to run against the good old boys. "Every time I talked to her, I represented failure," Wheeler says. "She didn't even want to talk to me."

But Guthrie failed to make the Indy field. Wheeler arranged a Winston Cup car for her to drive at Charlotte and even got Kelly Girl to sponsor it. Guthrie made the World 600 field, and the tickets flew out of the windows.

"We sold every ticket we had here, even the singles," Wheeler says. "Usually you always have them left over. We had women coming to the track by themselves in taxis."

In the 25 years since, it has been Wheeler's job to keep selling those tickets, and there are thousands more to sell these days. The Charlotte track now has around 167,000 seats, including several thousand in more than 100 luxury suites stretching from the exit of turn four to the exit of turn two.

It was the first track to have a "Speedway Club," an upscale restaurant and club facility open year-round.

The track hosts two Winston Cup events, plus The Winston all-star race, each year. In trying to sell all those tickets, Wheeler says he tries hard to recreate that feeling he had as a 12-year-old boy anticipating an upcoming event, and to remember how bored he felt when he just sat there waiting for something he'd been excited about to get started. One race day at Charlotte, Wheeler was standing at the back of the press box during one of his prerace extravaganzas. He overheard a couple of reporters griping about the show.

"What's next?" they asked. "Dancing bears?"

"I thought it was funny," Wheeler says. "I decided we'd get a damn elephant in there." The next year, the prerace show was a full-blown circus. NASCAR officials were petrified that an elephant might step on one of the cars and worried about how the track would clean up the stuff the animals "left behind." But the show went on.

Since the Coca-Cola 600 takes place on Memorial Day weekend, its prerace show has in recent years taken on a military theme, with mock invasions and various other maneuvers often being used to "rescue" the track's costumed mascot, "Lug Nut."

In 1985 Wheeler got a chance to marry his short-track background with his big-track promotional skills when The Winston all-star race began. The Charlotte track hosted the first running of the event and, after a disastrous trip to Atlanta the next year, returned for the next four years. After 1991 Wheeler's track was again in danger of losing the event.

At a meeting in Winston-Salem, North Carolina, headquarters of

"NASCAR's version of P.T. Barnum," Humpy Wheeler poses in circus regalia in front of an elephant statue . . . Harold Hinson

series sponsor R. J. Reynolds Tobacco, Wheeler was trying to come up with something to excite Sports Marketing Enterprises president T. Wayne Robertson. And he was failing.

"I kept throwing ideas at him, and nothing was getting to him," Wheeler remembers.

Until, that is, Wheeler said he planned to light the track and hold the Winston on Saturday night, short-track style. That got Robertson's attention.

The rest of the Charlotte track's staff who'd accompanied Wheeler

. . . and sits atop the real thing in a prerace circus.
Harold Hinson

to the meeting looked at each other. They'd never heard the idea of lights.

That's because it was the first time Wheeler had thought of it. "I told them I didn't have the slightest idea how we were going to do it, but we were going to do it," Wheeler says.

Wheeler tried one of his own ideas, a wide band of light placed atop the wheel fence. He set up a test in turn one of the Charlotte track.

"I brought a bunch of people in. We were going to test in the pace car, and everybody was looking at me like, 'Who's going to do this?' I had to do it, and I almost killed myself. I went down into the first turn, and I'm telling you, I couldn't see anything."

Wheeler eventually got Musco, a company from Iowa, in on the project. The company built a 25 percent model of the track's turn four in an airport hangar near its headquarters. The project, featuring lights bounced off mirrors, included 16 patent-worthy concepts.

"As soon as I saw it, I said, 'How simple!'" Wheeler says. "I knew it would work."

Of course, he didn't tell anyone he knew that it would work until April, a month before the scheduled running of the Winston. Promotion is about creating drama, Wheeler says, and he believes it is, at least in part, a talent that can't be taught.

"I think if you have the gene, you can learn the rest of it," Wheeler, now 63, says. "If you don't have that gene in you, you can acquire the skill, but you will never be a great promoter. You may be a good one. So many people bash themselves because they're not 'creative.' I say to them that it's not a question of being creative; it's recognizing creativity and being strong enough to apply somebody else's idea to what you're doing. If you don't have creative ideas, you have to at least be able to recognize them."

The people who work alongside Wheeler sometimes also have to recognize that there are limits to even what a showman like Wheeler can pull off.

There was another fellow from Belmont, named Reginald "Moon" Huffstetler, who had a gift for being able to tread water for long periods of time. He was so good, in fact, that he wanted to take a shot at the world record. So Wheeler set up a pool at the Charlotte track during race week one May, and Huffstetler set the record. The next year, he broke his own record. The next year, he did it again.

Before long, Wheeler was looking for something to spice up the act. At a meeting of his staff one day, somebody jokingly suggested that a shark be placed in the pool with Huffstetler. The movie "Jaws" was popular at the time. "Moon vs. the Shark: one must die." Everybody had a big laugh.

Except Wheeler. His staffers could see his mind working.

"I'd seen those shark documentaries with the guys wearing those chain-mail suits taking pictures," Wheeler says. "I thought we could put Moon in one of those."

One of the staffers pointed out that Huffstetler would have trouble treading water hour after hour wearing chain mail. Plus, another feared, animal-rights protesters would be all over the speedway for trying such a stunt.

"If they don't show up," Wheeler said, "you dang well better hire some."

One day a member of the office staff brought in a copy of a supermarket tabloid. In the middle photo spread was a monstrous car-chewing, smoke-belching contraption called Robosaurus. "We've got to have that," Wheeler said. It was the prerace show's feature attraction at the next race.

A stunt man who called himself Jimmy the Flying Greek contacted Wheeler. His gimmick was driving a school bus up a ramp and jumping cars.

"I thought it was so stupid it might work," Wheeler says. "I thought it was a good idea, but I wanted to see it. I called up Lanny Hester (another promoter) and told him it was a good idea, and he ought to do it at Bristol. I went up there for it, and it was a disaster.

The bus went up in the air, landed, and knocked the whole front axle off. The axle went down the track, ran into the first turn and knocked a big hole in the track surface."

Wheeler believes it's his responsibility to face the music when things go wrong. Not this time.

"I got the hell out of there," he says.

Jimmy the Flying Greek figured out what went wrong and brought his act to Charlotte. He was a hit.

"There is a real social difference between watching an event on TV and actually being there," Wheeler says. "Very few people brag about seeing something on television. They may give you the information about what was on, but they don't brag about it. But if they went to the Super Bowl or the Coca-Cola 600 or whatever, and it was a great experience, or something unusual happened, they're going to boast, 'I was there.' That means, 'and you weren't.' They don't say that, but it makes them unique."

There's a landfill behind turn three at the Charlotte track. Years ago, that area was a deep ravine that dropped off quickly beyond the track's walls. Wheeler figured he could have a stunt pilot in one of his prerace shows fly a steep dive into the ravine. An explosive charge would then be set off, implying that the plane had crashed. Minutes later, the plane would emerge from the smoke and fly back across the crowd, wagging its wings in salute.

His assistants were appalled at the idea. The stunt would mortify the fans. Wheeler gave up on the idea.

Well, at least for a time.

"It can still be done," he says, his eyes dancing with anticipation. "I know it can."

NASHVILLE'S FASTEST FAMILY: THE HAMILTONS

Racing's past, present, and future can be found dangling
from the branches of the Hamilton family tree. Four
generations deep, they were racing stock cars well
before NASCAR came along.

By Larry Woody

There are varying accounts on how Charles Robert Hamilton acquired his nickname, "Preacher."

"I've heard that it was because he was kind of bossy and always preaching to people he worked with," said his daughter, Beverly. She paused and added: "And I've always heard that it was because of his, uh, colorful language. He cussed so much that some of his buddies started calling him Preacher, I guess from the old saying, 'He was so aggravating that he could make a preacher cuss.'"

She paused again and chuckled. "I sort of suspect that the second one might be the correct version. But I really don't know for sure. All I know is that from the time I was a little girl, everybody called my daddy 'Preacher.'"

If Preacher Hamilton could cuss up a blue streak, he could drive one, too. Around Nashville, where he grew up, Hamilton developed a reputation in the early 1940s for flat burning the tires off his homemade race cars. He raced whenever and wherever he could find a track—on an old downtown dirt oval called the Cumberland Bowl, on the little bullrings gouged out of cow pastures around Middle Tennessee, on forays down into Georgia and Alabama, and over the mountains into the Carolinas. He even made a few trips to Daytona to check out a beach course somebody had laid out.

Preacher Hamilton was a racing original, a stock car pioneer and the patriarch of a family that would turn out some of the sport's leading leadfoots. Son Bud raced on the local level and became famous as a car builder for country western singer/racer Marty Robbins. Grandson Bobby—who was raised by Preacher and came to idolize him—would go on to fame in NASCAR's Winston Cup big leagues. Great-grandson Bobby Jr., began racing as a teenager at Highland Rim Speedway, a little track 20 miles north of Nashville, worked his way into the NASCAR Busch Series, and plans to make an eventual move into Winston Cup. Bobby Jr.—Little Bobby—is believed to have started racing shortly before his boyhood friend, Adam Petty, did. (The records are hazy on what, exactly, constitutes an official race in some of the lower, semipro divisions.) But if Little Bobby did, indeed, race before Adam, that would make the Hamiltons the first fourth-generation racing family in history, ahead of the exalted Petty clan.

It all began with Preacher.

"My daddy was a great driver back then, but the sport wasn't organized—NASCAR wouldn't come along for several years—and it didn't get much recognition," Beverly recalled. "He raced all over, and he won just about everywhere he raced, but none of the drivers made much money back then. They raced mostly for the fun of it."

The racing bug bit Preacher's son Bud, but the liquor bug bit harder.

"My father was an alcoholic," said Bobby, somberly. "There's no use trying to sugarcoat it. Alcohol ruined his life and destroyed our family. I hate alcohol for what it did to us. To this day I don't like to be around it."

Bud and Martha Hamilton split up when Bobby was 18 months old, and Bobby was sent to live with his grandparents.

"Bobby and I grew up together, more like sister and brother than aunt and uncle," said Beverly. "Every once in a while, Bud would move in with us for a few weeks or months, when he had no other place to go. But he didn't have much to do with Bobby. Bobby spent most his time with his granddaddy."

"I didn't dislike my dad; I just never really knew him," Bobby said. "My mother worked all the time to help support me. I remember one time when I was racing at the Fairgrounds, I was too broke to buy a set of tires, and I asked my mother if she could help me out. Somehow she came up with the money—I guess she went to the bank and borrowed it—and gave it to me."

Despite his battles with the bottle, Bud loved to dabble in racing, especially in the mechanics of the sport. His driving career was limited to mostly the local level, and after a serious crash at Highland Rim Speedway, he gave it up. But he was an ace mechanic, and he and Preacher began to build and work on race cars for other drivers. They built and maintained many of the cars driven by Marty Robbins, who, in addition to being a national singing celebrity, was also a serious racer.

"Bobby and I spent a lot of time together when we were kids," said Ronny Robbins, Marty's son. "While our fathers were working on their race cars, Bobby, Beverly, and I would play around the garage, riding

Father and son "Preacher" (left) and Bud (right) Hamilton flank racer and country music star Marty Robbins, for whom they built and maintained cars. Beverly Hamilton

our tricycles. I noticed that Bobby always seemed to drive his faster than the rest of us."

Growing up on the tough streets of East Nashville—the proverbial Wrong Side of the Tracks in Music City—Bobby wasn't certain what his future held. He tried a variety of jobs, working as a mechanic and driving a tow truck for Martin's Wrecker Service. But there was always a craving, a yearning, perhaps a calling.

"I'd always been interested in cars and racing, I guess because I'd grown up around it," Bobby said, "but I never really thought much about driving professionally. Racing was considered something you did for the hell of it, not something to make a living at. I started racing at Highland Rim when I was 15, 16, and was doing work for other teams in exchange for their spare parts. I never had a nickel back then."

Bobby married young. Little Bobby was born; the marriage dissolved. Bobby remarried, and his wife Debbie took Little Bobby as her own.

Meanwhile, in the early 1980s, Bobby began racing at Nashville Speedway, where the crowds were bigger, the competition tougher, and the opportunities greater. His natural talent quickly became evident. He won the track championship in 1987 and 1988, and in the process he caught the eye of another former Nashville champion, Darrell Waltrip.

"They were running a Busch race at Nashville one weekend and Darrell came over and asked me if I would qualify his car for him," Hamilton said. "He had to be in Charlotte for the Winston or something and wasn't sure he could make it back in time. I told him sure—Darrell Waltrip has been my hero for years—and after I got the car set up and qualified, Darrell told me it was one of the best-handling cars he'd ever driven. That made me feel good, getting praise like that from a driver like Darrell."

Afterward Hamilton got a call from prominent team owner Rick Hendrick, for whom Waltrip drove. Hendrick was assisting some Hollywood producers with a racing movie, *Days of Thunder,* and they needed a driver to run some laps in an upcoming race at Phoenix to provide some movie footage. Hendrick offered the job to Hamilton.

Hamilton did such a good job driving the "movie car" in the 1989 Tom Cruise film that he caught the attention of several Winston Cup team owners. He ended up landing a job with Tri-Star Motorports, not one of the mega-teams, but at least it was a start.

It was 1990 and suddenly the one-time Nashville wrecker driver found himself in the big leagues. The next season he won Winston Cup Rookie of the Year, and his career set sail. Hamilton would get a series of rides, including a stint in Richard Petty's famous No. 43 Pontiac shortly after Petty's retirement.

"I like everything about Bobby Hamilton," Petty said at the time. "First of all, he's a heckuva race driver who knows cars and how to work on them. I think that's important; a lot of drivers can't do that nowadays. Also, I like him as a person. He's a good, honest family man. And he gets along good with the fans. I've always thought that was critical in this sport. The fans are the people who pay our salaries and make it possible for us to race. Some drivers don't seem to appreciate that. Bobby does."

Hamilton's rags-to-racing-riches career rise seemed, appropriately, like a Hollywood script.

"The movie deal got me a lot of attention," Hamilton said. "I guess I was just at the right place at the right time, but I'd put in a lot of work to get myself in that right place. Running all those races at Highland Rim . . . racing at Nashville. All that helped get me connected to Darrell Waltrip, and Darrell helped get me connected to Winston Cup."

Hamilton, who at one point in his career was too broke to afford a set of tires, currently has winnings in excess of $13 million. He also has built a successful, 32-employee team that fields entries in the NASCAR Craftsman Truck Series.

Perhaps remembering the kindness of Waltrip several years ago, Hamilton took an interest in a teenage driver named Casey Atwood, a Nashvillian who launched his career at Highland Rim Speedway. In 2000 Atwood made his Winston Cup debut and the next year competed full-time as a driver for the high-profile Ray Evernham Motorsports. Atwood is considered one of the sport's brightest, most promising young talents, and he credits Hamilton for steering his career.

"There's no way I could have got where I did as fast as I did without Bobby's help," Atwood said. "Nobody in my family raced. I had no NASCAR connections. Bobby was the one who introduced me around, told me what I needed to know, and opened doors for me."

Hamilton, at times, seemed to assist Atwood more than he did his own son, Little Bobby, who was struggling to get his racing career jump-started. At one point Little Bobby moved to North Carolina, where he thought the opportunities might be better.

"At times I didn't understand why my dad wasn't doing more to help me," confessed Little Bobby. "Yeah, it hurt my feelings a litttle. But now, looking back, I can see what he was doing. He wanted me to get out and learn on my own. I know now that he was always there if I'd needed him to fall back on."

"I love Little Bobby, and I was willing to help him," Hamilton said, "but I felt that it was important for him to do as much as he could on his own. I knew that would be the best thing for him in the long run."

"Bobby doesn't show a lot of emotion," said Beverly, who oversees Hamilton's growing racing business at his Lebanon, Tennessee, headquarters. "The men in our family were all like that. But we know how much he cares about Little Bobby."

Indeed, Hamilton was so shaken over the 2000 death of Adam Petty in a crash at New Hampshire International Speedway that he tried to talk his son out of racing.

"We had been really close to the Pettys, going back to when my dad drove for Richard," Little Bobby explained. "Adam and I used to play together, hang out together, talk about our plans to race someday. When Adam got killed, my dad really took it hard. I've never seen him so upset.

"A few days after Adam's funeral, my dad sat me down and asked me if I really wanted to keep racing. He didn't come right out and ask me not to, but I could tell that was what he wanted. I told him that I was determined to race, and that was it. There wasn't anything he could do to talk me out of it."

"I just told Little Bobby that I loved him and would support him in whatever he decided to do," Hamilton said. "I wanted to make sure he didn't feel any pressure to drive a race car just because his daddy drove one. There aren't any shoes he needs to fill. If he wants to do something else for a living, that's fine with me. That's what I told him."

Two other drivers would die in 2000, then the 2001 season opened with the fatal crash of Dale Earnhardt in the Daytona 500. Hamilton was so distraught over Earnhardt's death that he asked reporters not to discuss it with him.

Meanwhile, his own son was moving up, becoming a force in the Busch Series and itching to join his father full-time in Winston Cup.

"Do I worry about him? Hell, yeah, I do," said Hamilton. "Every second he's on that track, I worry myself sick. But I know that I can't stop him, no more than anybody could stop me when I was Little Bobby's age. I was determined to go racing, and, by God, nobody was gonna keep me from it.

"Richard and Kyle (Adam's father) will tell you that Adam felt the same way. It's in their blood, and they're gonna do it. We can't stop them. All we can do is to make sure they have the best, safest equipment possible and try to teach them to keep their heads out there and not do anything stupid. Other than that, it's out of our hands. All we can do is worry. And pray a lot."

While Bobby is noted for his reserved, taciturn manner, Little Bobby is more open and outspoken.

Following the grim rash of on-track tragedies, Little Bobby was critical of NASCAR for not moving faster on a number of safety measures.

"I love this sport," he said, "but I don't want to die for it."

As for his once-strained relationship with his father, "We're closer than we've ever been," said Little Bobby. "My dad is not big on hugging and kissing and showing a lot of public emotion, but I know how much he loves me. I can tell, and that's all that matters."

Toward the end of his father's life, Bobby and Bud would reconcile.

"My dad was always a big Richard Petty fan, and it really pleased him when I started driving for Richard," Bobby said. "He'd come to some of my races, and we'd spend time together. He was at Phoenix when I won my first race, and that meant a lot to me. I think it meant a lot to him, too."

Bud Hamilton died just as his son was blossoming into a major racing celebrity. Friends say that Bobby grieved terribly—but quietly, privately, as is the Hamilton way.

What does the future hold for the Hamiltons? Bobby admits he's not sure how much longer he wants to keep chasing checkered flags. He has hinted that retirement may not be too far down the road. Little Bobby, meanwhile, is squirming to move up and start mixing it up with the big boys. It's just a matter of time.

Safe to say, the Hamilton name will continue to remain prominent in racing lineups for many years to come.

Somewhere up there, the colorful, crusty old codger who started it all is watching. Preacher Hamilton, who launched a racing dynasty that has spanned seven decades, is smiling down as his grandson and great-grandson continue to carry the family banner into the asphalt wars.

Any angels in Preacher's vicinity might be advised to wear earplugs.

DRAFTING, DANCING, AND DEATH ON THE EDGE OF THE CONTINENT

Daytona has produced moments of auto racing glory but also has seen the dark side.

By Mike Hembree

T he hard winter wind blows seemingly forever down the back-stretch at Daytona International Speedway.

It rolls in with a level of predictable ferocity from the north, making landfall where the Atlantic Ocean breaks across the hard-packed sand of central Florida. It crosses the very passing lanes of the old Daytona beach-road course, where men (and the occasional woman) raced cars with wild abandon and considerable skill in the relative quiet of the 1950s.

The wind often arrives in huge, in-the-face gusts, whipping flags across the vast expanse of the speedway property into a frenzy. Caps fly. Hot-dog wrappers swirl like pregnant confetti.

On the track, the wind is nobody's friend. Almost always acting as a headwind on the long backstretch, it whips waves on Lake Lloyd in the speedway infield and carries seagulls in from the east. It once carried Cale Yarborough, running directly into it at 200 miles per hour, hell-bent for stock car racing history in Daytona 500 qualifying, into a hellish flip in the third turn, his car suddenly thinking it could fly and lifting off the track, into the sky and onto its roof. Yarborough had recorded an astonishing speed of 200.503 miles per hour—drivers had flirted with the 200 barrier at Daytona for several years—on the first of two qualifying laps. On the second, the car took flight.

That was February 1983. Yarborough lived to run another day. Into the Daytona wind again.

This is what you remember about Daytona. The wind blows. The clouds scatter. Seagulls land, feed and fly, land again. The thunder roars up from 43 cars whipping through the fourth turn. Forty-three accelerators hit the floorboard as they pass under the grandstand, the cars' collective rush of wind fighting the green flag in the starter's hand.

It is the perfect storm.

Here, on two and one-half miles of the most famous asphalt in the world, you deal with what nature and Bill France Sr. throw at you. A mechanic and sometime driver who forged his sport into shape and gussied it up for the Madison Avenue suits who eventually would come knocking on his door, France dreamed of this track in 1953. Wrestling one financial struggle after another, he saw it open on former swampland near the Daytona Beach airport in 1959.

In building the speedway, France had corralled the Atlantic wind, caught its fury. It moved around his speedway's high banks, built to astonishing heights so that the cars could go fast and the fans could see them. It pushed them down the sweeping trioval, then battered them in the face on the long backstretch.

Some—ultimately many—figured it out. They came to the sparkling new track—a monster like none of them had ever seen—in the winter of 1959, pulled their swift cars into the infield, and gaped at the wonder of it all.

It stretched beyond their wildest dreams. They were innocents in a land of plenty.

Mechanic Bud Moore hauled a 1959 Chevrolet to the first 500 and rode along the high banking himself to understand the true nature of the landscape. It was not, after all, a façade.

"I couldn't believe my eyes," he said. "It was so big, so enormous. After we got inside and got in a (passenger) car and drove around it, I couldn't believe the banking. We stopped in a turn and tried to walk up it."

Soon, they were playing with its air, testing its wind, trying to figure what would work where, what was safe and what wasn't, where the ragged edge could be found.

Junior Johnson, more stubborn than most, wily, smart, a man who became one with the cars he drove, might have invented the draft at the track. Pushing forward, always pushing, he discovered the second year at Daytona—1960—that by placing his front bumper within inches of the car in front of him, a seemingly daring move at the astonishing speeds they were running on this virgin ground, he actually could go faster. The craziness of the wind in this new environment made two cars linked together faster than one, made slow cars slick, made the weak strong.

"We were running a Pontiac in that race (with Jack Smith driving)," Moore said. "We were leading the race when Jack called (on the two-way radio) and said that something was wrong. We had broken three lug bolts off the right front wheel. We had to change the hub. We got it back out, laps behind.

"Junior was running a Chevrolet for Ray Fox. Smokey Yunick had

Fireball (Roberts) in a Pontiac and Bobby Johns in a Pontiac. With about 10 laps to go, Smokey came over to me and said, 'How about telling Jack to get up there and draft with Bobby and get him away from Junior? Junior's catching him.'

"Jack did. Jack got to pulling him 12 miles per hour faster than he was running. Coming off two, the back glass flew out of the back of Johns's Pontiac, he spun out, and Junior won the race. Smokey came over to me and said, 'Damn, I didn't tell you to pull him that damn fast.' It had sucked the back glass out of the car." Johns later said the wind rushing through his Pontiac caused a lifting effect.

That air again.

Even in 1959, at the first race, drivers had noticed an odd phenomenon. Swept along in the rush of a line of cars, they felt a vacuum effect that served as a "slingshot" that could propel them past the car ahead. For many years to come, before the modern arrival of the dreaded carburetor restrictor plate, the slingshot pass was a Daytona staple.

On pit road in those early years, mechanics marveled at the speeds.

"Everybody thought it was just too dangerous at first, but they got used to it," said longtime mechanic Ray Fox Sr. "The cars handled better after a while. In 1960, when Junior won the race, he said it was amazing that he could catch a car's draft and pass them back with only a little 348-cubic-inch engine in a Chevrolet. He won the race with good common sense and good drafting."

Racers accustomed to half-mile dirt tracks, power slides through short, tight turns and beating and banging against friend and foe in tight-quarters racing found themselves riding the tail of a dragon. It was as if the carnival had come to town. It was a monster midway.

"We didn't know what kind of speeds we were going to run or how to set the cars up," said Cotton Owens, a driver and mechanic. "I went down there for the first race with a stock 1958 Pontiac. The rear end was one and a half inches lower than the front end. I'd go into the corner, and I could turn the steering wheel from one side to the other and the car wouldn't even turn. The wheels were off the ground.

"Everybody was amazed at the place. We drove in there and looked at the thing, and you couldn't see from one end to the other. It was the biggest thing we'd ever seen. It was scary. You didn't feel the sensation of the speed, but the car would raise up, and you'd have no feel of the race track. When you'd back off the accelerator, the front end would drop back down, but then you'd put your foot back in it and go into the next corner and it'd raise up again.

"Nobody liked that feeling, because you'd have no feel of the steering wheel."

It was big, bad, and frighteningly unpredictable.

For those reasons, and others, soon it would become sacred ground, following Darlington in South Carolina onto the grand tapestry of Southern speed. It was a place that would become a Mecca for all who drove fast cars in circles, a destination for all who would run harder, ever harder, into the first turn.

Daytona.

Bill France Sr. worked his way through an amalgam of financial wrangling to construct the giant speedway. From conception to reality, the track evolved through the 1950s, as France dealt with government officials, money moguls, and the scruffy nature of the land where the speedway was rising.

The massive (480 acres) speed plant had been on France's drawing board for years. Before the opening of the track, racing at Daytona had meant competition on one of the strangest courses in motorsports history: the Daytona beach-road course. Using 1.5-mile sections of the hard-packed sand on the beach and the parallel Highway A1A, a narrow two-lane asphalt road, officials designed a temporary track. Drivers raced north on the beach portion of the course, slid and bumped through the north turn, ran onto the asphalt section that normally carried beach traffic, raced toward the south turn, and returned to the sand.

Beach racing, which began in 1936, developed into a remarkably successful enterprise after France, who had moved to Daytona Beach from Washington, D.C., took over promotional chores in 1938. Thousands stood on the sand dunes and along the A1A section (the only public road ever to be used as part of a Winston Cup race course) to watch some of stock car racing's early daredevils face the unique challenges of the course. The races were scheduled with great respect for the tides. At low tide, there was plenty of racing room on the sand. But, if the tide rolled in sooner than expected (its progress sometimes accelerated by strong offshore winds), the races sometimes had to be shortened. Cars occasionally wound up racing—even rolling—in the surf.

The beach races were a natural follow-up to single-car timed speed runs on the sand at Daytona Beach and Ormond Beach, its sister to the north. The speed runs, which started in 1903, drew the famous and infamous to the Florida eastern shore in all manner of exotic and powerful machinery. They tested the Atlantic sand until 1935, when land-speed runs moved to the wide-open spaces of the Bonneville Salt Flats.

Despite financial losses in the early years, the beach-road course races became a successful substitute and filled the Daytona area's need for speed. As housing and businesses began crowding the beachfront in the 1950s, however, France realized that the days of racing cars on the sand were limited. He looked west five miles to find land to build the Indianapolis Motor Speedway of stock cars.

The track, built at 2.5 miles to match Indy's size but severely banked to create faster speeds, opened for the 1959 Daytona 500, and the race was all France could have hoped for. The finish was one of the closest in racing history, with Lee Petty edging Johnny Beauchamp in a battle so tight that France needed three days of studying photographs and films to certify the winner.

Johnson won the following year as cars raced perilously close in the magic of the still-developing Daytona draft, and the track's reputation grew.

Soon, Daytona became every short tracker's dream, a place to run wild and free and as fast as God and Bill France would allow.

It also would be a killing field.

Even before the beginning of the beginning.

Marshall Teague was part of a Daytona Beach–based run-and-gun gang of racers—a collection that also included Fireball Roberts and Ray Fox Sr.—who ran the ragtag circuit of short tracks in Florida and Georgia after World War II. Handsome in a burly sort of way, with a prominent nose and dark hair swept back from his forehead, Teague turned away from few challenges. A 1939 graduate of Seabreeze High School in Daytona Beach, he, Roberts, and Fox went looking for adventure in the largely unorganized but energy-filled stock car racing environment of the 1950s, and they found a lot of it.

Teague, an expert mechanic who ran a service station and garage in Daytona Beach, won the AAA national stock car championship in 1952 and 1954 and raced in the punishing 2,000-mile Mexican road race in 1952. He gained a significant spot in stock car racing history by driving Hudson Hornets to considerable success and thus attracting the first sponsorship support package from a car manufacturer.

Bob Jacobsen, a race fan from Baltimore, in a letter to Mitzi Teague, Marshall's widow, expressed his admiration for the driver:

"I was at Jacksonville Naval Station in 1952 and got to see Marshall race Fonty Flock in an Olds all afternoon on that little dirt bullring. They can talk all they want about Bill Elliott, Harry Gant, and all the smooth drivers today, but Marshall could teach them all a lesson in smooth driving. Being a Hudson owner and fan at that time, Marshall was my hero. I went down to the gate and slipped my program through to the flagman, and Marshall signed it sitting in his car while waiting for the green flag."

Teague, who also raced in the Indianapolis 500, was one of the first men to drive a race car on the fresh Daytona International Speedway asphalt. He was testing an Indy car at Daytona February 11, 1959, barely 11 days before the track was scheduled to open with the first Daytona 500. Twenty-four hours earlier, Teague had turned a lap at more than 170 miles per hour in the car. On the morning of the 11th, he expected more speed, saying he had been "just playing around" the previous day.

Instead, Teague crashed the car in a particularly violent wreck in the second turn. The car rolled and tumbled and stopped about 500 yards from the turn. The driver's seat was ripped from its anchors, and it landed 150 feet from the rest of the car, with Teague's body still held in the seat harness. He was killed instantly.

Out on this new frontier of speed, in the chill of adventure, the first pioneer had fallen.

* * *

Over the decades to come, 33 other people followed Teague onto the Daytona death list, a long and grim roster that grew to include raw rookies, racing unknowns, longtime veterans, and the man who drove race cars better than anyone else in the history of the speedway.

Don MacTavish lit up the racing world in New England in the 1960s like few other young drivers. Outgoing and bright, accomplished at every track he visited, he was considered a future star. He had raced since his teenage years.

Twenty-six and looking to broaden his horizons, MacTavish came to Daytona in February 1969 to run in the Permatex 300 Late Model Sportsman race that served as a preliminary to the Daytona 500. It would be his next step toward the top level of stock car racing.

It also would be his last. That day became one of the most shocking in the history of the track. Of any track.

MacTavish drove car No. 5, a 1966 Comet. Racing out of the fourth turn on the ninth lap, his car lost its grip and hit the outside wall. The right front of the Comet hit a gate that covered an opening in the track wall, and the impact ripped the front end from the car, which lurched violently into the air. The engine, transmission, and other parts flew a dozen ways, scattering across the track.

With virtually its entire front end torn away, the remains of the car spun on the track and stopped. MacTavish's body was slumped over the steering wheel, facing oncoming traffic with no protection. Cars slid and swerved, attempting to avoid the No. 5 and the parts and pieces littering the track.

Sam Sommers, a Georgian in a Ford, was in the mix of drivers trying to negotiate the hellish scene. He didn't make it through. What was left of MacTavish's car sat facing Sommers on the track.

Sommers slammed into the car, throwing it into the air yet again, battering MacTavish's body.

Safety workers ran to the scene and were stunned by what they found. Sommers was shaken. The front end of his car was crushed by the impact of the wreck, but he was not seriously hurt. His larger concern was his role in the death of MacTavish. Gruesome photographs of the first part of the accident made it clear, however, that MacTavish was almost certainly dead before Sommers's car made its exit from the fourth turn.

Many photographs of the accident remain. Some do not. Some were so vividly repugnant that the prints and negatives were destroyed.

MacTavish, of Stillwater, New York, was the seventh fatality at Daytona International Speedway.

There would be other hard rains.

Ricky Knotts, a 28-year-old resident of Mattawan, Michigan, rolled into Daytona Beach in February 1980 towing the same dream as hundreds of young drivers before him. He had raced on Sportsman tracks in Michigan, Indiana, Wisconsin, and Missouri and, with the help of his father, Richard, put together a shoestring effort to attempt to run the 500 that season.

He had seen the lights of the big carnival.

It would be his first time on a superspeedway.

On the Thursday before the 500, in a qualifying race, Knotts was involved in a trioval crash with Blackie Wangerin. On the race's 15th lap, they were attempting to pass a car driven by Slick Johnson. Knotts and Wangerin hit and started spinning, and Knotts's car slid wildly out of control across the track's grassy apron. The grass did little to slow

Knotts's speed, and the passenger side of his car met the inside retaining wall with violent force.

He was killed instantly. Television replays showed his body slumped in the seat just after the impact. The hospital report said he had massive head injuries.

The garage area was unusually quiet after the race. Richard Knotts struggled to come to grips with the sudden loss of his son. They had made the trip to Daytona essentially on their own, with no crew or support personnel and little money, hoping against hope to work their way into stock car racing's big show.

"I know Ricky left us doing what he loved," the father said.

A. J. Foyt, the great Texan who would finish 31st in that Sunday's 500, who had seen friends and fierce competitors die in race cars, who himself would suffer injuries of nearly every sort in a brilliant racing career, paid for Ricky Knotts's body to be transported home to Michigan.

Others, so many others.

Bruce Jacobi, critically hurt in a Daytona 500 qualifying race in February 1983. He died almost four years later, never regaining consciousness.

Don Williams, in a coma for a decade after head injuries suffered in a February 1979 Sportsman race, died May 21, 1989.

Neil Bonnett and Rodney Orr, dead within three days of each other in crashes during 1994 Daytona 500 practice on opposite ends of the long track, one funeral following another.

Motorcycle racers. A powerboat racer on Lake Lloyd. Winston Cup driver Billy Wade, testing tires. Goody's Dash drivers. Go-kart racers.

*   *   *

Then, The Man.

Dale Earnhardt owned Daytona as surely as Castro owns Cuba. Although Richard Petty won seven Daytona 500s, Buddy Baker ran its high banks with shocking speed and a wild eye, Jeff Gordon figured out its quirks very quickly, and Bill Elliott whipped around its banks at 210 miles per hour in qualifying, absolutely no one ran Daytona like Earnhardt.

They said he saw the air that whipped across its banks, over its race cars, into the windshield of his black No. 3. He worked it like a master craftsman, humbling lesser men, making the road his own.

Including qualifying races, Busch Grand National races, International Race of Champions events, and Winston Cup races, Earnhardt won 34 times at Daytona. In 1998 he finally answered the only lingering question, winning the Daytona 500 after two decades of bad luck of the most miserable sort in his sport's biggest race. It was the capstone of his career. No other driver in any form of racing has won half as many Daytona events as Earnhardt.

On February 18, 2001, Earnhardt figured to have a good shot at his second Daytona 500 victory. He started seventh, a spot behind his son, Dale Jr., who raced out of the Dale Earnhardt Inc. (DEI) shop. Also strong throughout Daytona SpeedWeeks was Michael Waltrip, a teammate of Junior's and Senior's close friend.

As the 500 roared into its final lap, Waltrip, winless in a long Winston Cup career, had the lead in one DEI car; Earnhardt Jr. was second in another. Third, and trailing by enough space to rule out a second 500 victory for himself, was Earnhardt Sr.

As Waltrip and Junior approached the checkered flag, Earnhardt

The Dale Earnhardt statue outside Daytona, where "The Intimidator" won 34 times and died in a crash in 2001. Mike Hembree

was busy in a pack of cars entering the fourth turn. As they wrestled for third place in the wild sort of dash that has become typical of last laps at Daytona and Talladega, its sister track, Earnhardt was pushed down to the track apron. His car wiggled and then turned hard right, sending him into the wall. A millisecond before Earnhardt's car slammed into the concrete surface, Ken Schrader hit it in the passenger side.

The Earnhardt and Schrader cars dropped down the banking and rolled into the grass even as fans in the frontstretch grandstands were celebrating Waltrip's landmark victory. Schrader jumped from his car, ran to check on his friend and quickly summoned rescue workers.

It was too late. Earnhardt was dead.

A firestorm of controversy followed as NASCAR responded to the loss of its greatest star. A six-month investigation resulted in the conclusion that a number of factors came together at one horrible moment to produce the environment that killed Earnhardt. A hard hit to the lower left portion of his head caused a fatal skull fracture.

It was the hardest of ironies that Daytona, home to so many tragedies, had never—until Dale Earnhardt's last lap—taken a life in the Daytona 500.

In the infield, as night fell on that black Sunday, the U.S. flag, at half-staff, flapped in the wind.

THE FORGOTTEN LANDMARK

When North Wilkesboro Speedway president Enoch
Staley died in 1995, it set off a chain of events that
sealed the fate of the legendary North Carolina facility.
Two other track owners, Bruton Smith and Bob Bahre,
each purchased half of the track, and at the end of 1996,
one race went to Smith's new site in Texas and the other
to Bahre's in New Hampshire. The final race at North
Wilkesboro, won by Jeff Gordon in the fall of 1996, left
barren one of NASCAR's truly historic venues.

By Kenny Bruce

The question comes up, from time to time, concerning the future
of North Wilkesboro Speedway.

"If NASCAR would give us a (Winston) Cup date, yeah,
we'd put one up there," said Bruton Smith.

The familiar grin spread across his face, and his eyes twinkled as
he scanned his audience knowingly.

A comment like that ought to get 'em to talking up in Wilkes
County.

Only the folks up in Wilkes County no longer care. As a matter of
fact, they quit caring a long time ago. Smith knows it, and so does
anyone else associated with stock car racing.

Smith is an incredibly wealthy man, thanks to his nearly 200 automobile dealerships, racing-related endeavors such as 600 Racing, and a
corporation known as Speedway Motorsports Inc.

SMI, a publicly traded company on the New York Stock Exchange

(NYSE: TRK) has among its holdings some of the grandest stock car facilities in existence; namely Atlanta, Bristol, Texas, Lowe's, and Las Vegas Motor Speedways, as well as Infineon Raceway. The company is also one-half owner of another facility, the one known as North Wilkesboro Speedway.

In Smith's financially charged world, North Wilkesboro's finest hour came in 1995, when SMI took possession of 50 percent of the facility, purchasing interest from track co-owner Jack Combs. With that transaction, Smith had secured what he believed would be a second Winston Cup date for his brand-new Texas Motor Speedway, a sprawling 1.5-mile facility then under construction north of Fort Worth.

Six months later, another track owner, Bob Bahre, purchased the remaining 50 percent interest in North Wilkesboro from the family of track founder Enoch Staley. Before he passed away in 1995, the one thing Staley stressed to family members was that his half of the track was never to fall into Smith's hands. It didn't, but the measure also ensured that the facility would likely never again host a Winston Cup event, either.

"You can't make money there," said Smith, cutting right to the meat of the problem. "What are you going to do? We're only a 50 percent owner.

"I'm not going to take our two pieces of capital, money and our human capital . . . I'm not going to waste any of that up there. As I said, we're only a 50 percent owner."

Smith got his date for Texas, but it wasn't the much sought-after second date. When the 1997 NASCAR Winston Cup schedule was announced, Texas Motor Speedway had one Cup event on its schedule.

Bahre, meanwhile, had a second date for his New Hampshire International Speedway.

And North Wilkesboro Speedway, one of only two facilities that had hosted NASCAR events since that inaugural season in 1949, had none.

Terry Labonte reached a glove-covered hand over and flipped the ignition switch, bringing the engine tucked underneath the hood of his No. 5 Chevrolet to life. Nothing about the process felt any different from any of the hundreds of other times he had done the same thing. But this time, it *was* different. This time, the whole stock car racing world was watching, or at least that seemed to be the case.

On April 14, 1996, Labonte traded in one nickname for another. The Iceman became the Ironman. A former Winston Cup champion, Labonte was starting his 513th consecutive race, a mark reached only once before in series history, a mark previously achieved by only one man: Richard Petty.

It seemed only fitting that, just a few hours later, Labonte wound up in the winner's circle. And just as fitting, perhaps, was the site of his conquest: North Wilkesboro Speedway.

Five months later, when the series returned for a second time to the tiny .625-mile track, history may not have been made, but it was certainly still being written. Jeff Gordon, the defending series champion, the kid who would be king, dominated the event en route to his fourth victory in his last five starts. It was his 10th and, as it turned out, final victory of the season.

Gordon, only 25 and already a Winston Cup champion, didn't win the title that year. Labonte, his teammate, did, overcoming his young adversary in the waning weeks of the season to collect his second career championship.

Still, it was a proper finish for North Wilkesboro that year, a speedway so rich in stock car racing lore. The final two races for North Wilkesboro Speedway left their marks on the sport like brands on cattle, scorching the track's final resting place in the NASCAR record book.

NASCAR, the sport born and bred on the backs of a generation of hardworking, blue-collar men, was going places. Cleaning itself up as it prepared to head to the wide-open spaces of Texas and the shadows of L.A. To the bright neon lights of Las Vegas. To Kansas City and Chicago and Lord only knows where else.

Only North Wilkesboro wasn't going along for the ride. After 48 years and 98 events, the end had finally arrived.

Drivers pose for a group picture prior to the last Winston Cup race at North Wilkesboro Speedway on Sept. 28, 1996. DMP Archives Photos

The rich rumble of the engines died that day; the smell of hot rubber wafted over the grandstands a final time. As the last hauler pulled out of the infield, track workers swung the crossover gate shut, the clang of metal meeting metal ringing hollow. North Wilkesboro was finished. And some say an era of stock car racing was, too.

"That was like our Daytona," said Labonte. "We put more effort into Wilkesboro than we did Daytona."

And for good reason. North Wilkesboro was the home track of Junior Johnson, one of the sport's legendary figures. A winner of 50 races, Johnson was a former moonshiner from nearby Rhonda, North Carolina, who parlayed common sense and an unorthodox understanding of the rules into a multimillion-dollar racing empire. As an owner, his teams won 6 championships, 140 races, and 128 poles. And when the series hit his neck of the woods, Johnson's teams were, more often than not, favored to come away with the victory.

Labonte, who has been around the series since 1978, has seen the sport change over the years. And he, like many others, knew North Wilkesboro wasn't keeping up with the torrid growth.

"You know, it was just, for me, it was a good racetrack, and we have won some races there. But our sport has definitely passed it by. The facility was not like a lot of the ones we go to now. Then it went on the auction block, and the two (race) dates went other places.

"I like the short tracks, and that was a fun track for me to race at. And it was close to home, too. I kind of miss it, but I understand why we don't go there."

From the very first day it opened in 1947, two years before the formation of NASCAR, North Wilkesboro exuded something of a country charm. Not the sanitized, "Cracker Barrel" feel so many folks today mistake for country, though. It was more like the feel one got by racing hell-bent down a dirt road, kicking up a rooster tail of dust as the tires fought for something solid to bite into. And the tightening of one's skin as that dust settled and dried on bare, sweat-covered arms. From day one, North Wilkesboro was country.

Even today, the town of North Wilkesboro itself, a tiny 5.5-square-mile rest stop located in the foothills of the Blue Ridge Mountains, boasts a population of barely 4,000. And that makes it the largest town in Wilkes County.

North Wilkesboro, like many other tracks around the country, could best be described as functional at a time when functional was all that was required. It was the perfect setting for a sport as rough and rowdy, as colorful and carefree, as the Old West.

Stock car racing put North Wilkesboro on the map. It brought thousands of folks to this quaint little town twice a year. Many more fans turned on the television and were whisked away to one of the sport's legendary landmarks.

For a while that was enough. Before long, though, the popularity of the sport began to explode. New tracks were being built. Money was being poured into those already in existence. As the sport evolved, so did the tracks. Amenities such as paved parking lots, shuttle buses, and more and better rest room and concession facilities went from being mere afterthoughts to legitimate concerns. Sponsor suites suddenly became a way to court those who had the deep pockets necessary to make many of those improvements.

Gone forever were the days when one could carve a track out of a dirt field, throw up some wooden bleachers, and nail a few posters to a handful of telephone poles.

For a time, track officials did their best to keep up with the fast-paced growth. As late as the early 1990s, seats were being added and upgrades were being completed. Still, it wasn't enough. Even with upgrades, North Wilkesboro always seemed to be a decade behind.

In the end, even NASCAR wasn't opposed to vacating the North Wilkesboro premises. In Smith, the sanctioning body had an owner who understood the need to provide a first-class facility. And by sending one of Wilkesboro's dates to Texas, it took the sport into yet another major market. In Bahre, it had a second, some would say unnecessary, presence in the Northeast.

Kenny Wallace, making his Winston Cup debut, spun his entry on lap 320 of the First Union 400 at North Wilkesboro. The year was 1990, a year that had already seen series favorite Dale Earnhardt lose the Daytona 500 on the last lap, then bounce back to win back-to-back races at Atlanta and Darlington.

It was no surprise that Earnhardt was battling with another former champ, Darrell Waltrip, for the lead at North Wilkesboro when the yellow flag was displayed for Wallace's incident.

Most of the lead-lap cars had already made pit stops under green flag conditions. But Brett Bodine, making just his seventh start for car owner Kenny Bernstein, hadn't and, as a result, was running in the top spot. Officials, unsure of the running order, radioed down to the pace car, instructing its driver to pick up Earnhardt as the leader. Bodine, just ahead on the track, was allowed to circle the track and take up residence at the rear of the lead-lap cars. With nothing to lose, he also took the opportunity to make a quick stop in the pits for fresh tires.

After a number of laps were run under the yellow flag, as NASCAR checked its scoring, Bodine was credited with the lead. Those drivers on the lead lap were eventually brought around to fall in line behind the Quaker State–sponsored Buick. With fresher tires and prime track position, Bodine was able to hold off Waltrip and Earnhardt to score his first career victory. It came in his 80th start and vaulted him to fifth in the season's points standings.

Weird? Perhaps. Strange? No doubt.

Both Waltrip and Earnhardt complained that the scoring snafu had cost them a chance at victory. But while officials eventually admitted they had made a mistake, their final statement called it "irreversible" and said no change in the official finishing order would be made.

Bodine's victory might have raised a few eyebrows, but in reality, it was just one of numerous historical footnotes that can be linked to North Wilkesboro Speedway. The site has been the scene of many memorable moments, both good and bad, in the sport's history.

Some of the more noteworthy:

- In 1962 teams got their gas from fuel trucks in the infield instead of the more familiar fuel pumps used today. But because of the high number of cars still competing in the latter stages of the race, the gas supply eventually ran dry. A truck sent to obtain more fuel earlier had failed to return. As a result, crewmen were sent scurrying through the infield with hoses and buckets in an attempt to siphon gasoline from passenger cars.
- On Friday, April 15, 1966, as teams began arriving for the Gwyn Staley Memorial, Ford Motor Company announced an end to its racing efforts because of rules concerning its new overhead-cam engine. Officials said the new piece was "too heavy" and "couldn't be competitive" under the NASCAR regulations handed down with its initial approval. The race-day crowd that weekend was

only 6,000, approximately one-half what was expected, because of Ford's decision.

- Problems with its tires forced Goodyear to pull its new radial tire from competition at Daytona in 1989. The radials were reintroduced later, in April at North Wilkesboro, and were underneath Dale Earnhardt's race-winning entry.
- Through the years, a number of drivers made their Winston Cup debuts at North Wilkesboro. In addition to the aforementioned Wallace, Willy T. Ribbs (1986), Hut Stricklin (1987), and John Andretti (1993) made first starts on the short, tight oval.

Ribbs became the first black driver to start a Winston Cup race since Wendell Scott in 1973.

Tim Richmond didn't win his first Winston Cup race at North Wilkesboro, but the flamboyant Indy 500 Rookie of the Year did earn his first short-track series victory there in 1984.

Although races at North Wilkesboro certainly had their share of accidents, few ever left any driver with serious injury. That wasn't the case, however, for Lou Figaro of Inglewood, California. Figaro died in a local hospital from injuries he sustained the day before when his entry flipped three times during a race in 1959.

Two other notable deaths occurred on the day of North Wilkesboro races but didn't take place at the track. In 1990 rookie Robbie Moroso was killed in an automobile accident after returning home from the Wilkesboro event. He had finished 21st in the Tyson/Holly Farms 400 earlier that afternoon.

Some two decades before Moroso's death, the sport lost one of its more colorful figures the Sunday of the fall Wilkesboro race. Curtis

Turner, who had quit driving just two years earlier, died when his plane crashed near DuBois, Pennsylvania.

A few other historical oddities from the old five-eighths-mile oval whose front straight ran downhill and backstretch ran, predictably, uphill:

- Race winner Tim Flock immediately announced his resignation as driver for car owner Karl Kiekhaefer following a win at North Wilkesboro in 1956. Kiekhaefer was the series' first successful multicar owner, and his entries had posted 21 wins in the previous 14 months when Flock resigned.
- In 1957 Johnson, the local hero, finished 20th in his first race back at North Wilkesboro after serving an 11-month, 3-day sentence in an Ohio federal penitentiary for moonshining.
- In the 1961 fall race, Rex White made only one pit stop during the 320-lap event on his way to the victory.
- Herb Thomas, a two-time series champion, came out of a five-year retirement in 1962. His first start of the season came at North Wilkesboro, where he finished 14th.
- Marvin Panch, a 17-time race winner, showed up at North Wilkesboro late in the 1963 season after spending seven months recuperating from injuries sustained in a sports car accident. He promptly won the 250-lap event.
- Johnson swept both North Wilkesboro events during the 1965 season. The first, the Gwyn Staley 400, was Johnson's first at his home track since 1958. Before the race, he had changed his car number from 27 to 26 for "good luck."
- That fall, in the Wilkes 400, Johnson nabbed his 13th victory of

the year. As it turned out, his 50th victory was to be his last as a driver in NASCAR competition as well.

- No driver has ever dominated the series in a single season like Richard Petty did in 1967. In addition to winning a record 27 events, Petty also strung together 10 consecutive victories during the second half of the season. That, too, was a record. And win number 10 in the streak came at North Wilkesboro.

In the fall of 1958, Johnson had his hands full while racing for the win at his home track. At some point in the latter stages of the race, a fan—some have said it was an uncle of Johnson's—tossed a fruit jar at one of Junior's closest competitors. The fan was escorted off the track property.

And Johnson eventually won the race.

That wasn't the only time an overzealous "attendee" had chosen to throw caution, as well as a cold beverage, to the wind. In 1964 Petty appeared en route to the victory when someone tossed a bottle onto the track. Following the caution period for clearing the debris, David Pearson managed to close on Petty and eventually passed him for the lead with only four laps remaining.

Another bottle-tossing incident took place during the fall race of 1980. In that instance, the broken glass was no more dangerous than the large pieces of asphalt that continued to break apart under the pounding of the heavy stock cars. Even the pace car spun out while trying to exit pit road. In all, 113 laps of the event were run under caution.

Following the race, the track surface was finally repaved.

Petty saw another bottle-tossing incident erase his chances to win in 1981; his car ran over the glass, and the cut tire that resulted took his entry out of contention.

Fans even managed to disrupt the festivities in the winner's circle at North Wilkesboro. In 1972 Petty emerged with a victory after a fierce, fender-banging duel with Bobby Allison. Afterward, an intoxicated fan crashed the victory-lane celebration, apparently to lodge an informal protest.

His case didn't get far. Petty's brother, Maurice, hit the party crasher over the head with his brother's helmet.

Each October, the Brushy Mountain Apple Festival is held in downtown North Wilkesboro. According to officials, it's the largest event in Wilkes County. Now that NASCAR no longer pays the town a visit, that is.

At Wilkes Community College, there's MerleFest. According to the brochure, it is an "annual tribute to the lives and music of Doc and Merle Watson."

Lowe's Home Improvement Warehouse headquarters is still located just up the road, and a few of the hotels and eating establishments still get along well enough to survive.

But the colorful haulers that transport men and machines to the racetracks no longer stop at North Wilkesboro. The facility sits silent, grass growing up through patches of cracked asphalt.

"We could convert it into a farm. Maybe that would reduce our (property) taxes," Smith says today. "We could do that. A lot of times that is done in different states: you change what a piece of property does.

"But there was a storm up there about four or five years ago, and [it did] a tremendous amount of damage. The track is worn out. You'd have to repave it; you'd have to rebuild it. They have a sewer problem there that would have to be solved [in order to reopen the track].

"There are so many things. You'd have to spend a few million [dollars] to get it going again."

Sadly, that won't happen. Those millions, whether they belong to Smith, Bahre, or eventually someone else, will continue to be spent elsewhere. Even the possibility of an event from NASCAR's lower-tier series is an all-but-forgotten proposal these days.

The track that wrapped up NASCAR's inaugural season, so many decades ago—and was an integral part of so many that followed—sits in lonely silence today.

History doesn't stop there anymore.

THE LEGACY OF THE NUMBER TWENTY-EIGHT

Amidst a proud tradition of success, Robert Yates has also endured an inordinate amount of tragedy with his famous—and, yet, infamous—Ford stock cars.

By Jeff Owens

R obert Yates was born to race.

From the time he built his first soapbox derby car as a kid, all he wanted to do was race. From the time he borrowed his daddy's car to run his paper route at age 12, all he wanted to do was race.

From the time he and his twin brother Richard bought their first car—a 1957 Chevy—at age 15 and raced it all over the streets of Charlotte, all he wanted to do was race.

"We grew up at a good time, when cars were a lot of fun," Robert said. "I was fascinated with wheels and cars, and that has never stopped."

From the time he landed his first NASCAR job as an engine builder at the legendary Holman-Moody Ford factory, all Robert Yates wanted to do was race. He was living a dream, building strong engines and fast cars for such legendary team owners as the Wood Brothers and Junior Johnson.

"I always felt like I was born to be a mechanic," Yates said. "The most fun thing to me was working on things and making them work, and race cars were ideal."

By age 40, Yates was one of the most successful engine builders in NASCAR Winston Cup history, having built power plants that powered drivers like Richard Petty, Cale Yarborough, Bobby Allison, and Richard Petty to victory. His engines carried Allison to the 1983 championship and Petty to his legendary 200th victory in front of President Ronald Reagan.

He was realizing his dream, because all he ever wanted to do was race.

By the time NASCAR exploded onto the national landscape, becoming a household name and a fixture on national TV, Yates was one of its most successful car owners, winning more than 50 Winston Cup races, more than $51 million in race earnings, and the 1999 Winston Cup championship.

As he built his dynasty around such drivers as Davey Allison, Ernie Irvan, Dale Jarrett, and Ricky Rudd, Yates poured most of his fortune back into his race team. Unlike most team owners, NASCAR wasn't just a business, not to a man who was born to race.

"I never set out to accumulate things or position myself in the sport," Yates says. "I just wanted to win races. That's what it's all about. It's not about how many toys you have. It's not about big boats and airplanes and helicopters. It's just fun racing. That's the American dream."

There is only one thing that has ever made Robert Yates want to stop racing. Only death has ever stopped Yates's race cars from going fast.

Yates's No. 28 Ford is one of the most popular cars in racing. With its familiar red star gracing the hood, it became synonymous with both Texaco and NASCAR, winning 25 races through 2001 and almost always running near the front.

Yet the famous No. 28 also has one of the most tragic histories in sports. Sadly, it is remembered as much for tragedy as triumph.

In 1993, just as Davey Allison was reaching his prime and making Yates's Ford one of the most dominant machines in NASCAR, Allison was killed in a helicopter crash at Talladega Superspeedway, losing his life just five years into a marvelous career.

Just 13 months later, as Yates's powerful Ford was at the front again, on its way to a possible championship with a new driver, tragedy struck again when Ernie Irvan slammed into the wall at Michigan International Speedway, fracturing his skull and suffering life-threatening injuries.

Though Irvan made one of the most remarkable recoveries in sports, he was never quite the same. He won races again, but never regained the consistency to be a championship contender, eventually forcing Yates to release him.

Two years later, Irvan retired, ending a brilliant career after suffering complications from the crash that nearly killed him in the No. 28 Ford.

Ironically, the driver who replaced Irvan, Kenny Irwin, would also lose his life in a race car, though not the No. 28. Eight months after leaving Yates's team, Irwin slammed into the wall at New Hampshire International Speedway, dying in the No. 42 Chevrolet owned by Felix Sabates's Team Sabco.

At the urging of Ford, Yates and his team had tabbed Irwin as NASCAR's next young star, hoping he could develop into a talent capable of challenging Chevy's Jeff Gordon. More important, his hiring mimicked the arrival of Allison, another young driver Yates had put all his stock in.

Unfortunately, Irwin never got to flash that potential. He was released by Yates after two struggling seasons, then lost his life while driving for Sabates. Once again, a young driver who had once wheeled the No. 28 was dead, again saddling Yates and his team with tragedy.

Irony is a common theme in sports. Its unique, intriguing plot twists tend to reveal themselves at the most inopportune times.

There are two arenas in which irony typically rears its ugly head—in tragedy and in sports. And when it manages to encapsulate both, the results are often shocking and sometimes devastating.

Robert Yates knows a thing or two about irony, bitter irony. So do the Allisons.

Yates shared some of his most glorious days with Bobby Allison, Davey's legendary father. In 1972, with Yates building the engines for Junior Johnson's fast Chevrolets, Allison won 10 of 31 races and finished second 12 times, which still stands as one of the most remarkable seasons in NASCAR's modern era.

Ten years later, Yates and Allison were reunited, winning eight races, including the Daytona 500, for DiGard Racing. A year later, they teamed to score Allison's only Winston Cup championship.

Fittingly, when Yates finally purchased his own team, his first driver was an Allison, not Bobby but his son Davey.

Yates had practically watched Davey Allison grow up, watching him follow in his father's footsteps as he tore up the Alabama short tracks. When Davey began running the ARCA Series, Yates was there to lend a hand.

And when it was time for him to pick a driver to replace Cale

Yarborough, Yates convinced team owners Harry Ranier and J. T. Lundy to hire young Davey.

"It was easy to jump in with Davey," Yates said. "I had seen him get in our car at Charlotte and run quicker than anybody there. I knew this kid was good."

The kid wasted no time following in his father's footsteps, putting a Yates-powered Ford on the front row for his first Daytona 500. The following week, he won his first career pole at Rockingham. In all he made eight front-row starts in 1987 and became the first rookie to win two Winston Cup races in his first year.

A year later, Davey would follow his father across the finish line at Daytona, giving the Allisons a one-two finish in one of the most memorable and emotional Daytona 500s in NASCAR history. Ironically, the elder Allison was nearly killed later that year, suffering a critical head injury in a crash at Pocono that left him in a coma for several weeks. Just as Davey's career was taking off, his father's was suddenly over, leaving young Davey to carry on the family name and the mantle of the famous Alabama Gang.

But before he could establish himself as a consistent winner, Davey's career hit a stumbling block. Despite their instant success together, financial troubles nearly tore the Yates–Allison tandem apart. Ranier and Lundy parted ways in 1987, and with Ranier in deep financial trouble, Yates had to pour his own money into the team just to keep it afloat.

When Ranier started to fold the team in 1988, it was Davey who convinced Yates to buy it. He had seen his father's career take a dip each time he and Yates parted company, and he wasn't about to let it happen to him.

In October 1988 Yates sold his house and nearly everything he owned to buy the team from Ranier. Thanks to young Davey, Yates had finally realized his dream of owning his own race team.

"Davey was the biggest reason," Yates recalled. "He kept saying, 'Come on, Robert, you can do it.' He encouraged me, or demanded that I buy it. And he demanded that I not take on any partners. I had a lot of guys who wanted to buy into it, but he said, 'No, you own it. You do it.'

"If he had just said, 'Whatever,' I wouldn't have done it. But he insisted I do it. He believed I could do it. I told him how much money I had, but he said, 'Come on. We can do it. I'll drive for you forever.'"

After all the Allisons had been through, watching their patriarch struggle for his life, Davey felt a kindred spirit in Yates. And he wasn't

Car owner Robert Yates (left) joins Davey Allison in victory lane at Talladega after the 1989 Winston 500. DMP Archives Photos

about to walk away from the man who served as his strength and inspiration.

"When Dad was injured, he gave me the strength to keep going," Allison said in a 1989 interview. "The team had matured together. We had all become a big family, and we wanted to stay together. We were afraid if someone else took over, it would disrupt everything."

For the next four years, Yates and Allison formed one of the most formidable combinations on the Winston Cup circuit. They won two races in both 1989 and 1990 before becoming a championship contender.

In 1991 Allison won five races, finished second four times, and finished just 199 points behind champion Dale Earnhardt. A year later, he won five races again and carried the point lead into the season finale.

With a 30-point lead over Alan Kulwicki, Allison seemed destined to win the Winston Cup title nine years after his father had won it. But on lap 253, Allison was running sixth—good enough to clinch the title—when Ernie Irvan, the man who would later replace him, spun in front of him, causing a crash that took out Allison and handed Kulwicki the title.

Sadly, Kulwicki would never finish his reign as champion, while Allison would never get another title shot. After squaring off in the greatest championship battle ever, neither Kulwicki nor Allison would survive the next season. Kulwicki was killed in a plane crash on April 1, 1993, and Allison would suffer a similar fate three months later.

Though he slumped to third in points after his season-ending crash, Allison enjoyed the greatest season of his career, winning five races and scoring 12 top-five finishes. It did not come without tragedy, however. That summer, as his father continued to recover from head injuries that had taken much of his memory, Davey's younger brother,

Clifford, was killed in a crash at Michigan during a Busch Series race. It was perhaps a sign that tragedy would continue to haunt the Allison family and the famed Alabama Gang.

Allison and Yates got off to a slow start in 1993, winning at Richmond but struggling to find the consistency that had nearly carried them to the pinnacle the year before. Allison began to rally by summer, however, finishing third on July 12 at New Hampshire.

The next day Allison was flying his helicopter to Talladega Superspeedway to see David Bonnett, the son of Neil, test a stock car. While attempting to land, Allison lost control of his chopper and crashed, suffering a critical head injury. He died the next day, one year after his brother's death and five years after his father's crippling crash, devastating a family that suddenly became the poster child for tragedy.

"How often does lightning strike?" asked family friend Eddie Gossage, who served as Bobby Allison's spokesman at the time of his career-ending crash. "It never strikes twice. And it certainly doesn't strike three times. It just doesn't happen. I can't imagine losing a child, much less two, in separate incidents, 11 months apart."

"I've known Bobby for a long time, and I've seen him hurt so bad we didn't know if he was going to make it," said former driver and family friend Neil Bonnett. "The worst I've ever seen him hurt was at Clifford's funeral. Now we've got to do it again."

Davey's death brought an end to the racing Allisons and left just one remaining member of the famed Alabama Gang that once featured Bobby and Donnie Allison, Neil Bonnett, then Clifford and Davey.

Clifford and Davey were both gone while Bobby, Donnie, and Bonnett had all been sidelined by injuries.

Ironically, Bonnett attempted a comeback, beginning with the Talladega race two weeks after Davey's death. As if receiving a frightening warning sign, his race ended when his car got airborne and slammed into the catch fence. Seven months later, Bonnett was killed in a crash while practicing for the Daytona 500.

"To think that the end of a whole legacy—a whole dynasty—of Allisons were either killed or had to retire because of a head injury, it makes you think," Charlotte Motor Speedway President H. A. "Humpy" Wheeler said after Davey's death.

"It's hard to see that for the first time in 30 years, there's no Allison in stock car racing," Gossage said. "That's an empty feeling."

The day after Allison's death, Yates stood outside his shop in Charlotte, in front of a shiny black transporter bearing a picture of Allison's race car and the famous No. 28. Wearing shades to hide his tears, he choked back his emotions long enough to announce that his team would skip that week's race at Pocono.

"There's something very big missing in our race team," Yates said, struggling to contain himself. "When our race team goes to race, we go to win, and we don't think we can win this race. We can't race with tears in our eyes."

It was the first race the No. 28 team had missed. It was the first time Yates didn't want to race.

Two months after Allison's death, the NASCAR world was abuzz over rumors about who might replace Allison in the car that had suddenly become the most famous in racing.

Young Indy car star Robby Gordon drove the No. 28 at Talladega, charging to the front, then spinning out on Allison's home track. Then veteran Lake Speed took over, giving the team a lift with two respectable finishes.

But Allison and Ford fans expected more, and they waited anxiously for Yates to name a permanent replacement. The name that emerged at the top of the list was Ernie Irvan, another hard-charging driver and, ironically, the man whose wreck cost Allison the 1992 championship.

After a messy divorce from his Morgan-McClure Motorsports team, where he had won seven races, including the 1991 Daytona 500, Irvan joined the Yates team in September. Three races later, he won at Martinsville Speedway, returning the No. 28 team to victory lane, where he ripped off his driver's uniform to reveal a Davey Allison T-shirt underneath.

Though not a popular choice at first—he had alienated many fans and fellow drivers for what was once perceived as a reckless driving style—Irvan soon won fans over with his lead foot.

He capped the 1993 season by thoroughly dominating the October race at Charlotte, leading all but a handful of laps and giving his new team a bit of comfort at the end of a troubling year.

The following year, Irvan got off to a torrid start, winning three races early in the season and climbing to the top of the points race. For 17 weeks, he led six-time champion Dale Earnhardt, returning the No. 28 team to the form it flashed with Allison in 1992.

Ironically, that all came to a screeching halt on August 24, when Yates and his team were slapped with another tragedy. Suffering an apparent tire problem, Irvan slammed into the wall during practice at Michigan, suffering severe head injuries that left him in a coma and on life support for a week.

Irvan was given only a 20 percent chance to live, and Yates and his team believed they had lost another driver and teammate.

"It's hard to believe we're going through this again," a stunned Yates said. "We are still struggling with the loss of Davey, but we were focused on racing again. We've been caught up in the chase for points, points, points. Now it's time to pull together and be a family again."

A day after Irvan's crash, Yates and his team pulled out of the Michigan event, skipping a race for the second time in a year because of a tragedy. For a week, they were by Irvan's side, praying for him to pull through. When his condition improved, they prayed he would recover enough to walk again, much less race.

But this time, the No. 28 team and all of NASCAR were witnesses to a miracle. Irvan not only recovered, but he returned to racing 14 months later, driving a Yates-owned No. 88 to a sixth-place finish at North Wilkesboro Speedway in his first race since the near-fatal crash.

The following season, Irvan returned to the Winston Cup circuit full time, winning two races, the first one at New Hampshire, the site of Allison's last race. A year later, Irvan scored one of the most memorable victories in Winston Cup history, winning at Michigan, the track that nearly took his life. When he took the checkered flag, his eyes were flooded with tears.

But despite his miraculous recovery, Irvan never regained the consistency that had marked the No. 28 team. While he struggled, Dale Jarrett, the veteran who had replaced him in the No. 28, emerged as the new star at Robert Yates Racing. He won the Daytona 500 in his first race with the new No. 88 team, winning 11 races in his first two years.

After two inconsistent years, Irvan was released following the 1997 season. He joined MB2 Motorsports in 1998, running the full season before suffering another serious concussion during a crash at Talladega late in the year.

The following year, after another hard crash at Michigan, Irvan decided to retire, calling it quits during an emotional press conference at Darlington Raceway.

"I feel very fortunate to be able to sit here and tell everybody that it's probably good for me to retire," Irvan said as he held his six-year-old daughter. "The doctors have told me it's a miracle that I've been able to do what I've been able to do, being able to survive some of the accidents that I've had."

Then he paused, choking back tears as he said, "It brings tears to my eyes, knowing I'll never drive a Winston Cup car again."

As Irvan made his emotional announcement, Yates sat in the back of the room, wondering what might have been had Allison not been killed, had Irvan not been injured.

A year later, he would stand on the top of his team transporter, watching paramedics and safety crews rush to the aid of Kenny Irwin, another young driver who had driven his famous No. 28, only to lose his life in a crash similar to Irvan's.

"I wish this didn't happen to our sport," a beleaguered Yates said the day Irwin died. "I wish it didn't happen for his family and his friends. I'm just sad. It's just a sad day."

They say death and tragedy come in cycles. It's a cycle that seems never to end with Yates and his No. 28. A year after Irwin's death, Bobby Burrell, a crewman for the No. 28 and new driver Ricky Rudd, was hit by a car on pit road at Homestead-Miami Speedway. The collision knocked him onto the pit road concrete and sent him rolling into the pit wall, causing a severe concussion that nearly cost him his life.

Though Burrell recovered and returned to his duties as a tire changer, it was yet another reminder of the tragedy that has haunted the No. 28 team.

"With all the team has been through with Davey, I don't know if they could have stood it if I had died," Burrell said. "We're all like a big family, but it's really hard to deal with things like that."

Especially when they keep happening over and over.

All Yates ever wanted to do was race. Yet he has seen too many sad times in his days as a racer, missed too many races because of tragedy.

As he reflected on those times following the retirement of Irvan, then the death of Irwin, Yates vowed he would skip many more races to have his three former drivers back again.

"This is a great sport, and we all love it. It's all we've ever wanted to do," he said. "But you wonder sometimes if it's all worth it."

SKIRTING NASCAR'S RULE BOOK

From the bygone days of the shade-tree mechanics to the modern age of multimillion-dollar teams, skilled mechanics have always played fast and loose with NASCAR's rules.

By Kenny Bruce

O n June 19, 1949, two important events occurred involving NASCAR competition. The very first Strictly Stock event was contested, taking place in Charlotte, North Carolina, and shortly afterward, the sport's very first race winner was disqualified.

Glenn Dunnaway, of Gastonia, North Carolina, was flagged the winner in NASCAR's initial race. But a postrace inspection uncovered illegal, modified springs underneath the rear of his car. Not quite Strictly Stock, in other words. It was an old bootlegger's trick, one that no doubt many in the field that day were not only aware of but taking part in as well.

By day's end, Dunnaway had been stripped of the victory. The first-place trophy, as well as $2,000 in first-place prize money, was awarded to runner-up Jim Roper.

Fifty-three years later, the rules may have changed, but attempts to get around NASCAR's ever-growing list of regulations, or at least take advantage of them, have not.

In the 2001 season alone, at least three crew chiefs were fined when their entries didn't meet NASCAR's specified height requirement of 51 inches. Nearly half a dozen more were punished for fuel-cell violations. And at least one suffered a monetary setback when the lug nuts on his team's entry were found to be "too light."

That didn't include a long list of "unapproved parts" confiscated by officials in recent years, a list that would fill a volume or two by itself.

Engineers, aerodynamicists, car chiefs, crew chiefs, shock specialists . . . the list of personnel who provide input and massage each and every car today is astounding. And all these people are looking for an edge, an advantage, something that could determine the difference in winning and losing. It isn't just enough to build a car as good as the competition; today it has to be better. And better often means different.

It is a situation that, despite the influx of learned men, hasn't changed all that much over the years.

During the 1970s, three-time Winston Cup champion Darrell Waltrip said, "There were two things you could monkey around with and probably not get caught. One was the weight because they would not weigh the cars after the race was over with. They wouldn't do it. It was almost like, 'If you can get some weight out of the car, well, have at it.' They almost invited you to do that.

"And the other thing was in the bias (ply) tire era, you could change the numbers on the side of the tires. So, at some tracks, you could run some left-side tires on the right with the right numbers on them, or just pick another tire that you liked that would work there, just by changing the numbers.

"So tires and weight were two things that you could—I won't say it was carte blanche—but those were two things that you could monkey around with a little bit."

Since it is much easier for an engine to pull a lighter car than a heavy one, teams often went to extremes to lighten the load during a race and thus lighten the front end of the car as well. Some went as far as putting buckshot, such as the kind found in shotgun shells, in the car's frame rails.

"Instead of using lead in the frame rails, they would use lead shot," said Waltrip, noting that "occasionally, some of it would leak out onto the track.

"Big chunks of lead were harder to handle than little bags of shot."

And likely harder to discard.

"You could dump those in the frame rail. They didn't cost near as much, and like I said, occasionally, accidentally, sometimes some of them would leak out."

Thereby lightening the load and making the car faster.

As for the tires?

"That [running left-side tires on the right side of the car] didn't make the car handle better. Back then, you only had three or four compounds. You had a short-track compound, an intermediate-track, and Talladega compound. That's pretty much it. So, sometimes you could take the short-track tires and run them at Charlotte [now Lowe's Motor Speedway] or somewhere and pick up a lot of speed. But only for a short period of time."

Waltrip, whose 84 career victories is tied for third-best on NASCAR's all-time win list, was involved in at least one incident in which a team used left-side tires on the right side of the car to nail down a victory. In the 1983 fall race at LMS, Waltrip saw a healthy lead evaporate in the latter stages of the race as he was caught and passed by Richard Petty.

Not only did Petty's entry have the tires mounted illegally, but a postrace inspection showed that the engine in the winning car was well over the legal limit of 358 cubic inches, measuring 381.983.

"They had the big motor all along. They had it for several weeks," Waltrip contended. "I think Richard had run it, I think Kyle ran it at Dover, and Richard had run it at Martinsville. They had it for several weeks there.

"But what made the difference at Charlotte was we almost had him lapped at one time. Then it comes down to the end of the race, and there was a caution. [Petty] came in and put left-side tires on the right side, and with that big motor and left-side tires, that's when he took off.

"In that case, it was like, 'Let's think of all the things we can do to get this thing in the winner's circle.' They were trying desperately to win 200 races, and sometimes when you get to the point where desperation kind of drives you, that's what you're being led by; you'll try a lot of things. They had the deck stacked, but, then, they overdid it when they went with the left-side tires. It was obvious they had them, they were caught with them, and then [the officials] found out about the motor.

"Yeah, we knew something was up because I had outrun him all day, and with about 25 laps to go, he came from about a straightaway behind me, caught me, passed me, and beat me by a straightaway. So we knew something was up."

Petty was fined what was at the time a record $35,000 and docked 104 points. But, as would be the case in the coming years, the win was allowed to stand.

NASCAR may have discovered Petty's illegal motor, but there is little doubt that over the seasons, drivers and teams have won their share of the technical battles, getting illegal or unapproved pieces past the prying eyes of the inspectors.

"Oh, yeah, and they still do," said Junior Johnson, a winner of 50 races from 1953 through 1966, followed by a successful career as a car owner. Johnson's entries won six championships, three with Waltrip behind the wheel, and 140 races.

"There's so much going on at that racetrack, there ain't no way they can keep up with 1,000 people or more," Johnson said. "How the heck are you going to watch that many people?"

The search for speed, he said, even as early as the 1960s, meant "everyone was offsetting (moving the chassis) and running them as light as possible.

"Then NASCAR came with the weight deal for everybody to make them equal. You had to run the same height and stuff like that," Johnson said. "As they went along, if one car dominated the sport for three or four races, then they would go after him to see what he had, how he was dominating. I was quite involved in that kind of stuff anyway. Most of the time, probably 99 percent of the time, it was me they'd get after.

"It was an engineering situation: If you could figure out the best puzzle, you had the advantage on everybody."

That he was able to outsmart engineers and even entire auto companies, despite his limited education, wasn't that big of a deal, according to Johnson.

"Once you kind of trigger that thought of what it takes to make an automobile run," he said, "then it was pretty common that you would go test [and] go in a particular direction. Basically, you were looking for low or narrow bodies and left-side weight. It wasn't a big problem for somebody to figure out. It was later on, when it got to where you almost had to be a genius to outsmart the other guys, because everybody picked it up and started doing it."

There wasn't, he said, anything that escaped his notice.

"If somebody outran me, it wasn't very long until I had their secret. If it was something I hadn't thought of, I'd just add to it, come back and take care of things."

After all, there were ways to deceive officials, Johnson said, just as there were ways to bend the rules without actually breaking them.

"Actually, he cheated less than anybody," noted Waltrip of his former employer.

"There were all kinds of variables, options, and things that you could play with," said Johnson. "You go through inspection and the car is the right height and then as quick as you hit the first bump (on the track), it would trigger some mechanism that you'd hooked up to lower (the car) down. Stuff like that.

"Like the cambered rear ends. When we came with them at Daytona with Bill Elliott and Sterling Marlin, we sat on the pole and outside pole. Our car didn't look any different and check any different than anyone else's. Except they didn't check the rear end at that particular time to see if it had any camber in one side or the other."

Camber is the amount, measured in degrees, a tire is tilted in or out from vertical. While it wasn't an area specifically addressed in the NASCAR rule book, its omission didn't automatically mean it was legal, a fact of which Johnson was already aware.

"When they went hunting for how and why we had an advantage on everybody, they found it," he said. "Once they found it, they threw us out. But the very next race everybody could run cambered rear ends.

"So your advantage . . . sometimes you don't even keep it one race . . . sometimes you don't even get by with it one race. But if you work in the gray areas where NASCAR doesn't have a rule against it, you go to the limit on everything else. If you go over, you're caught, and if you go under, you're beat. So you're damned if you do and you're damned if you don't."

Johnson, however, wasn't always at odds with the sanctioning body. In 1968 he got several breaks that left the competition fuming.

At Atlanta Motor Speedway, Johnson arrived with a Ford entry unlike any seen on the circuit. Painted yellow, the car was quickly dubbed "The Banana." It featured a lowered roof line, sloped front end, and raised rear. None of which resembled the factory production model cleared for competition by NASCAR.

Despite his competitors' protests, Johnson's entry passed tech inspection. Driver Fred Lorenzen led 23 laps before crashing with little more than 100 laps remaining.

The car, Johnson said, was an attempt to bring the automaker back into the sport. Ford had pulled its backing earlier that year because of the weight restrictions placed on its new OHC (overhead-cam) engine.

"It was an effort to try to get Ford back into the sport through making their car competitive," he said. "It's like now, if they [NASCAR] have a problem with one [make of] car being a little slower than the others, then they adjust that car. And that's basically what that was.

"Chrysler, through the efforts of myself, Ray Fox, Richard Petty and a bunch of people that had worked on their products through the hemi engine, had left the Fords behind. And Chevrolet wasn't involved at that particular time. It was between Ford and Chrysler, and Chrysler just dominated every race you went to, basically.

"In an effort to try and make Ford more competitive, it was agreed to try [to] fix the car. They also gave [Ford] some relief on the motor to where they could kind of catch up."

It was one of the first instances where automakers began to streamline their vehicles and get away from the boxy shapes that had been so prevalent previously.

"It had a different shape, more of an aerodynamic look, like some of the things you see today," Johnson said. "This thing had a very high top on it. Basically, what we were trying to do was get the air to flow over the top of it and out the back. To not have so much drag on it and get it more streamlined. The Chryslers had those winged cars and all that stuff. That was probably part of the beginning of the aerodynamic program coming into play at a lot of races."

Johnson wasn't the only owner to have his entry breeze through the inspection process. Veteran car owner Smokey Yunick's slightly scaled-down version of a 1966 Chevelle did likewise. But the Ford of Ned Jarrett was deemed illegal, while two other drivers, Lee Roy Yarbrough and David Pearson, failed to make the starting grid when their entries failed prerace inspection, as well.

Officials found blocks of wood in the springs on the Yarbrough entry, items that could drop out during the event and lower the front end of the car. Cotton Owens created a device while at the track that would allow Pearson, the points leader, to tug on a cable and lower the front end of the car during the race.

Today, said Larry McReynolds, teams not only look for innovative ways to get their cars lower to the ground, but continue to search for ways to integrate lighter materials into the package.

A commentator for Fox during that network's race coverage, McReynolds is a former Winston Cup crew chief.

The rule book "states a lot about what material certain things have to be made out of, whether it be steel or something of that nature," he said. "If there is a lighter material that a team thinks it can get by with, and looks the same, whether it's 'chrome moly' or aluminum or titanium, for that matter, that's probably one area that a lot of teams try to work within. If they think they can get by with it and they think it can be an advantage.

"Anything you can do to lighten the car, that's just going to allow you to put more lead or ballast where you want it. Anything you can do to lighten wheels—what we call unsprung weight—especially in the form of what's rotating. Anything in the transmission or the gear area, the motor. That's one of the reasons [NASCAR] has mandated these weight minimums [for engine pieces]. Especially where you're talking about restrictor-plate racing, any time you can relieve that motor from having to turn something that's heavier, it's going to help it."

McReynolds said he is still amazed at some of the bodywork he sees on entries in the garage area. Bodywork that may appear to be aerodynamically superior, although perhaps not quite within the specified guidelines. Such attempts at gaining even the slightest speed over the past few years haven't changed.

"You'd look at somebody's back window, or you'd look at somebody's quarterpanel shape or spoiler shape, especially at Daytona or Talladega," he said. "The way somebody's fender was shaped or the way somebody's roof or greenhouse area was mounted. And you'd go, 'My gosh, look at that.' And I still do that today. I'll walk by somebody's car, and I'll go, 'Man, you've got quite a fender on that thing, don't you? Have you been through inspection with that thing yet?'

"To me, that's the more obvious thing, anything to do with the body. And, of course, that area is getting squeezed tighter and tighter because there's such a gamut of templates being used today. But still, you'll see things on cars and go, 'Lord have mercy, how are they getting by with that?'"

From illegal rear deck lids to oversized gas tanks and shocks filled with questionable fluids, teams continue to push the envelope as they search for that elusive edge, throwing NASCAR a bone from time to time, it seems, in an attempt to divert its attention.

"If you did something to the front of the car that you didn't want to get caught with, you'd make something real obvious on the back of the car so they would focus on that and not something you'd done to the front. That's old school," explained Waltrip.

"The other theory is, 'If I do 100 things wrong and I get by with 25 of them, then I'm that much ahead.' But those are always little things."

With winners' purses fattened to hundreds of thousands of dollars in many cases, and over $1 million for a race such as the Daytona 500, it's easy to see why a team might feel a bit of creative engineering today is worth the risk. Rules violations seldom exceed $25,000 to $30,000, and it's nearly a given that NASCAR won't strip away the win.

"I'm sure there's a mentality out there like that," said Jimmy Makar, crew chief for 2000 Winston Cup champion Bobby Labonte. "I feel certain people will look at what you've got to gain versus what you've got to pay for."

But in the end, according to Waltrip, "You've got to remember something," he said. "The guys that win get checked the most. It's not the guys who win that cheat. It's the guys who don't win, the guys that you might say occasionally, 'Where'd that come from?'

"Those are the guys you've got to look at. The guys who win all the time, everything on their cars gets checked every week: qualifying, racing. The guys who win are usually not the guys doing the cheating. It's the guys trying to catch up with them."

AT HOME WITH THE YARBOROUGHS

"Around here, he's just Cale."

By Jim McLaurin

etty Jo Yarborough talks like a hummingbird flies, dancing from flower to flower, one thought interrupted briefly by another that strikes her fancy. But instead of collecting nectar, she dispenses it.

"We did have a stormy wedding. He came to get me the night we were supposed to get married—for the second time—and this time my mother and daddy said, 'We're not planning a wedding. We're not going to do anything.' We were just going down and getting married at the parsonage. Something happened, and we broke up that night before we even got to the church.

"Cale took off, and I was real sad, and I thought, 'Oh, I wish I had just gone on now,' and I guess that's when I realized that I really loved him. It took almost up to the night that we were supposed to get married to realize I did love him.

"He rode down the road a couple of miles, turned around and came back, and I was still sitting in my yard, sitting on my little suitcase. He picked me up, and we went on and got married.

"It was kind of like a movie," she said. "It would make a cute movie."

That it would. That it would.

Duane Hobbs is the third-generation proprietor of the country store that sits not in the center of the Sardis, South Carolina, community proper, but about a quarter of a mile or so down from it, at the intersection.

Over the phone earlier in the week, Cale Yarborough told the visitor seeking directions to his house how to get off at exit 150 on I-95, follow South Carolina 403 until it curved around, missing Sardis, then go on down a little bit until you get to Hobbs's Grocery. When you get there, he was told, stop and ask Duane. There are five roads that meet there, and if you don't get the right one, you'll never find us.

Hobbs's Grocery is caught in a time warp. The white framed store was built in 1938, and, but for the few concessions to modernity like the racks of rental movie tapes and the microwave oven, it could still be sitting on the trailing edge of the Great Depression.

The shelves are lined with staples that folks would otherwise have to drive to Timmonsville or Olanta to get, within easy reach. A little harder to get to, on the top shelves nearly all the way around the store, is an accumulation of racing, wrestling, and baseball memorabilia that would set a collector's heart aflutter. You'll find a six-pack of Sun Drops, one for each of Dale Earnhardt's first six Winston Cup championships, and dusty Pepsi bottles commemorating various racing accomplishments—some of Yarborough's, some of others'—interspersed with action figures of this or that hero of the World Wrestling Organization

(WWO) or World Wrestling Federation (WWF), and baseball treasures enough for the most discriminating fan.

On the picture board on the front wall of the store is a photo of a young, crewcut Roger Maris, cigarette dangling from his lips, signing an autograph for a young fan.

"That's my brother, Ira," Hobbs said. "My uncle took us up to see the Yankees play the week Roger was going for 60. He didn't get to 60, but he got to 59, and we got to see that."

The visitor is early, and it's about lunchtime—pardon, dinnertime; in Sardis, it's dinnertime—so he collects a can of Vienna sausages, and beanie weenies, a pack of Nabs (peanut butter–filled crackers) and a Pepsi, and settles in to pick up a few pointers on the life and times of Cale Yarborough.

"I can tell you all you want to know about Cale," Hobbs said. "We've known each other since we were little fellows. But the only thing you really need to know about him is that, around here, he's just Cale.

"I've got pictures of Cale with just about every car he ever drove," Hobbs said, pointing to the wall with dozens of photos, not just of Yarborough, but an eclectic mix that includes everything from a big portrait-sized one of the Las Vegas Elvis, with sequined, high-collared jumpsuit, to a small snapshot of "Grandpa" Jones of "Hee Haw" fame, taken right in the store, with Grandpa, Cale, and a much younger Hobbs, each holding a bottle of Red Rock Cola and smiling to beat the band.

"I don't usually do this, but when he walked in the door, I hollered, 'Hey, Grandpa, what's for supper?'—you know, the way they used to do it on "Hee Haw"—and he'd give 'em that long list? Well, when I did it, he looked at me and said, 'I hope you got it.'"

Cale Yarborough with Leonard (left) and Glen (right) Wood, the original Wood Brothers.
DMP Archives Photos

The visitor notices a box of Wheaties on a shelf, one with Yarborough's smiling mug on the front of it, autographed in his bold hand. The box appears to be shrink-wrapped.

"Oh, I just wrapped it up in Saran Wrap, so it wouldn't get dusty," Hobbs said. "Cale brought it by one time when they came out with a Legends Series. He told me, 'Heah. I'm gonna beat you to it, because I know you're gonna be asking me for one.'"

Yarborough's house—a huge, rambling brick affair big enough to raise the three girls and big enough, even now, to hold them, their husbands, and the five grandchildren, when they come to visit—sits back off the highway in the middle of his 4,000-acre farm.

"Betty Jo had to go to Timmonsville, and she apologizes, but she said she'd be right back," the neat little once-a-week cleaning lady said when she answered the door. "Just come on in and make yourself at home."

The visitor is led through a den that is likely bigger than the first house the couple could call their own, and if you didn't know it, you'd never guess a stock car racing legend lived there.

It is only when you go down the hall into a room nearly as big and see the trophy-lined walls, that you get some sense of just where you are. Once you're in there, there's no doubt.

Trophies are everywhere, from the four big ones signifying Yarborough's Daytona 500 wins to the three even-bigger ones that commemorate his three consecutive Winston Cup championships, to the unique grandfather clock trophy given to him for one of his six wins at Martinsville Speedway.

And photos. Snapshots of Cale and Betty Jo, arm-in-arm, with Jimmy Carter, Cale dapper in a bright red coat, white duck pants, and white patent leather shoes; Cale and musician Roy Clark sprawled on a rustic-looking front porch; one of the couple with George H. W. Bush, this time with Cale in a more subdued dark business suit, and an autographed one behind the bar: Cale, kneeling in front of his old buddies David Pearson, Darrell Waltrip, Dave Marcis, and Richard Petty.

There is even a poster, tucked away in a corner, featuring a knockout of a young lady lifting a racing helmet off her head, with the words inscribed: "Mrs. Cale Yarborough also drives safer with Grey Rock brake linings."

When she breezes in from Timmonsville, Betty Jo doesn't say,

"Oh, pshaw, that old thing," but she could have. It is pretty clear whose room this is.

Sitting on the sunporch that overlooks the pool and tennis court out back, it is easy enough to see why Cale turned around 40 years ago and went back to get Betty Jo. Of all the daring moves of his life, that 180-degree spin was the smartest move he ever made.

Wearing a simple black pantsuit, she is a picture of the aristocracy of Southern womanhood and looks as if she were born to pose in the handsome wicker chair, adorning a gracious room by her mere presence. But the look is deceiving. Underneath it all is a Scarlett O'Hara–like iron will, one that stood her in good stead when, like generations of her forebears, she minded the farm while her man was off fighting in the war. Make no mistake: At times, it was a war.

"I was so young, and I knew that Cale had to be gone to make a living for us," she said. "We had been married for a while that we really struggled. When we went to Charlotte, we didn't have a car and had to live in a duplex apartment that was $85 a month, and Cale didn't make much more than that a week.

"Our outing was to go to the movie with our three-year-old daughter and eat pizza. I can remember going to the discount store to buy clothes."

Oddly, since the couple grew up only a few miles apart, they did not meet until Betty Jo, three years younger than Cale, had graduated from high school. If she had gone to Timmonsville High, and not Hebron, she probably would have been taken with the cocky youngster, who was an All-State fullback. Since she didn't, when they did meet, she was not smitten with the brash young man who by then was claiming he was the best race car driver around, not nearly as smitten as he was with her.

"He made a date with me, and he had a race to go to," she said. "Back then, you didn't have telephones like you do now, so he had a friend come and tell me that something had come up. . . . I was so aggravated with him, but later on, he did call, and he kept coming on back to see me.

"Right after we started dating, he said, 'I'm going to marry you,' and I was, 'Uh-huh,'" she said, rolling her eyes. "Anyway, he gave me a diamond, and I threw the diamond away, he came back, we had the biggest knock-down, drag-out, and it just kind of came on gradually.

"I hope to die, he had me talked into everything. Everything was going to be peaches and cream, no matter what. We were going to go into farming, and logging, and raising turkeys. It sounded real wonderful. I was 20, and he was 23.

"I had no earthly idea he was going to be a race driver. He said 'race driver,' but I didn't know anything about racing. It didn't take me long to find out that he was serious."

The move to the big city—Charlotte—was a necessary evil. Yarborough landed a job as little more than a floor sweeper with the Holman-Moody race team, but it was a foot in the door. Once he got inside that door, he was headed for the big time. It would be a long and sometimes rough road, and it would be one that he would travel mostly alone. He wanted to get his family back where it belonged: in Sardis.

"Cale hated to be away from home. To this day, he hates to be away from home," Betty Jo said. "I think that's one reason Cale wanted to make sure that when we had our kids, they had the same feeling.

"I really don't know of anyone I know in racing that. . . . We stayed

Cale Yarborough with wife Betty Jo and six-year-old daughter Julianne in front of their South Carolina home, shortly after his 1968 Daytona 500 victory. DMP Archives Photos

out of the limelight a lot, because we weren't running up and down the road on the weekends and doing stuff like that. But our children had such a good time growing up that I wouldn't have changed it for nothing in this world."

These days, the Yarboroughs don't stray far from the farm. Since his retirement from driving in 1988, and, finally, his retirement from owning his own race team, Yarborough spends as little time as he can tending to his businesses and as much of it as he can working— "piddling in the dirt," according to Betty Jo—on his land.

His current project is clearing stumps out on the "back 40," where he plans to put in a new fishing pond. Before the visitor can leave, he is admonished to "go by and see Cale. No telling who he's got back there with him, but go on back there. He'll be glad to see you."

Yarborough is sitting in one of a half-dozen chairs pulled up around a homemade stove in one of his two huge shops with a fellow named Bill Godley, who's also dropped by. Godley is an auctioneer of some note hereabouts and, according to Cale, "probably [has] got enough money to buy and sell us both, but you'd never know it."

To look at Yarborough, you'd never know he was rich as Croesus, either. He's wearing a pair of jeans and scuffed-up cowboy boots, a well-weathered sweatshirt with the words "RCA Racing" on the front, and a ballcap.

"How about a beer?" he asked. "Usually about this time of day, we gather back here, have a couple of beers, and just tell lies."

The visitor remarked that Yarborough doesn't exactly fit the image of a retired gentleman farmer, and Yarborough said, "Well, in the first place, I don't farm anymore. I rent the place out; it just got to be too much. And in the second place, the only thing I'm retired from is racing. There's plenty around here to keep me busy."

Yarborough has pared his automobile dealerships down from a dozen to one, over in Florence, and is occupied with getting the new TRAC racing series off the ground in 2003. His latest venture, though, is coal mining. He and a group of friends have bought mineral rights on several thousand acres of coal-mining land, and he points with pride to a couple of freezer-sized bags filled with coal. The visitor notes that he doesn't believe that it's enough to keep the heater going for very long.

"The good thing about the heater is that it burns wood," Yarborough said, "and if you haven't noticed it, one thing we've got a lot of around here is wood."

Wood, and contentment. For a fellow who rode to fame and fortune in the wild and dangerous world of racing and dined with kings and presidents, it is hard to imagine a man more at peace with himself as Yarborough is at that moment, sipping on a beer, feet propped up, and resting from the labors of the day.

A little later, after the good-byes, the visitor wonders at that dichotomy. How could a guy who has been everywhere and done everything in racing be as content out of the limelight as he was in it?

Then he remembers something Hobbs said earlier that day, down at the grocery store: "Some of these people who go out and make a lot of money and get famous can't wait to get away from home," Hobbs said. "Cale never left it."

FAN FRIENDLY

Racing has changed down through the years, but the fans remain loyal, struggling to keep up with changing times.

By Thomas Pope

I n the dark of a February morning, 1968, Jack Smith climbed from his homemade camper—a plywood shell affixed to a pickup truck bed, with bunks for four—and began preparing breakfast in the salt-filled air of Daytona Beach, Florida.

Smith was a singular sentinel in the midst of a culinary juggling act, but not for long. As he tended to a pair of gas cookstoves, the aroma of frying bacon and country ham filled the morning air. The coffee was perking, eggs were waiting to take their turn on the griddle, and "Southern ice cream"—grits—was bubbling as it thickened.

"All of a sudden, you could see lights and lanterns coming on all over the place," Smith said. "You could hear folks talking: 'Lord have mercy, that smells good!'"

Jack Smith smiled. His stomach was still empty, but he was filled with the campground spirit. It wasn't the first time he had savored that particular moment, nor would it be the last. The once-lone man standing watch over breakfast soon found others taking their cue from him as the campground woke from its slumber.

Virtually everything has changed in more than a half-century of NASCAR racing, but the joy the fans find in the fellowship of camping burns steady.

It's a scene repeated thousands of times on any NASCAR race weekend, from Daytona Beach to Sonoma, California. Overnight, a small town sprouts among the acres of infield grass or the campground areas adjacent to a track. For the folks who assemble these temporary communities, life doesn't get any better than sitting around a roaring fire with friends old and new.

That's why Jack Smith and his good buddy, Martin Roberts, don't fret about motel reservations when they pull out of Fayetteville, North Carolina, and head to the races. Camping, cooking, and fellowship have provided them with decades of priceless memories.

Make no mistake: To these two longtime friends, a race is much more than an excuse to have a party. They don't spend their hard-earned money on grandstand seats for the purpose of napping in them after a hard day's night. But the exploits of the Gordons, Labontes, and Wallaces wouldn't be half as much fun without the campground experience.

Over the years, Smith and Roberts have swapped thousands of stories and risqué jokes with friends old and new. They've sung hundreds of songs around a campfire, and danced when so moved by a tune. Not just any music will do: "There's only two kinds," Roberts insists, "country and western."

Roberts and Smith have been friends for more than a quarter-century. Roberts was once co-owner of a Sportsman car driven by

Left to right, Martin Roberts, former Busch Grand National champion Sam Ard, and Jack Smith. Martin Roberts

Smith at tracks near Fayetteville, the home to two military bases and North Carolina's fourth-largest metropolitan area.

There wasn't a track in southeastern North Carolina that Smith didn't tackle between 1954 and 1973, when he finally stopped racing on a regular basis. Ned Jarrett, Hoss Ellington, Glen Wood, Ralph Earnhardt . . . pick a driver from that era, and odds are he rubbed fenders with the man known as "Jack the Ripper."

Smith's first race car was a 1934 Ford coupe and was fitted with a roll cage made of iron pipes that were screwed together.

"A fellow had given me the car and another fellow gave me the engine," said Smith, retired from jobs as a maintenance technician from Fort Bragg and the U.S. Postal Service. "I had $100 of my own money in that race car, and most of that was the pipes."

Get Jack Smith talking about his early racing years and the stories flow. Like the one about Ellington, whose car once landed upside down in a tree at a track near Bladenboro, North Carolina.

"We got over there to him," Smith recounted, "and he was hanging upside down in his seat belt, talking about, 'If ya'll boys can get this thing turned over, I believe I can win this race.'"

Roberts never raced but has loved motorsports since his days as a boy growing up in Danville, Virginia. When he couldn't afford the price of admission, he'd peek through gaps in the pine-wood fencing.

Sometimes, he got caught.

An Army tour of duty sent him to Germany, where he toured Europe on a motorcycle and took in races at Le Mans, the Nurburgring, and Hockenheim. They were nothing like the stock cars back home in old Virginia, but it filled the racing void until he could return home.

When Roberts's military service ended in 1962 at Fort Bragg, he decided to make neighboring Fayetteville his home. He spent $2,000 to get a used car business rolling, and hub caps decorated the walls of his first office. To this day, Roberts Used Cars remains a no-frills place off the main drag that runs from Fort Bragg to Fayetteville.

"I've never had a tow truck, no computers, no secretary," says Roberts. "Most used car dealers, they have to have a briefcase, a big ol' diamond ring, and don't want to get their hands dirty. I like to get up under something I'm buying and check it out myself.

"I always carry a dealer plate and a check with me everywhere I go, and a tow bar and dolly. I'll buy something that's for sale on the side of the road if I like it and can get a good deal."

Smith and Roberts met in 1963, and Roberts became one of the biggest supporters of Smith's racing efforts. After Smith retired as a driver, his family and Roberts's would travel together to NASCAR races in pull-along campers.

The campers were sold after Roberts's wife, Pat, the center of his life for 33 years, died of cancer in 1990. In the early days of their marriage, when money was tight, Martin would pack Pat in the trunk of the car and sneak her into the races.

"Boy, I'm tellin' you, she loved the races," he said. "She would call me up at work and say, 'You said we were leaving at 12 o'clock. Well, it's past 12,'" he recalled. "I said, 'Honey, I'm kinda busy here at the lot,' and she'd say, 'Well, the camper's packed and I'm ready to go.'"

Races at Martinsville Speedway were special occasions for the Roberts clan: Martin and Pat, their son Jay, and daughter Kelly. Martinsville was a chance to return to their southern Virginia roots, and they shared experiences that, while seemingly trivial, are as fresh in Martin Roberts's mind as if it were yesterday.

The Roberts children loved to balance pennies on the railroad track that runs along the backstretch, wait for the train to pass, then race over to pluck the warm, wafer-thin mementoes from between the cross-ties. The Canadian national anthem was often played before the race in addition to the "Star Spangled Banner," and the Confederate battle flag flapped alongside those of the United States and Virginia.

"One time it rained up there, and we stayed over an extra day because we had so much fun watching those guys with four-wheel drive trying to get unstuck from that old red Virginia clay, and the tow trucks would get stuck trying to pull them out," Martin Roberts said. "We just laughed and laughed."

Given the closeness of the family, Martin Roberts fell into a lengthy funk after Pat Roberts died of malignant melanoma. Jack Smith refused to let his friend waste away, and he used the remembrance of the good times spent at the racetrack as a way to get Roberts back on his feet.

In 1994 Roberts ran across a 10-year-old, 28-foot Chevrolet motorhome. The RV belonged to an Army officer who had parked it under trees, and the effects of the elements had left the motorhome black with mildew. Roberts paid $10,500 for the motorhome, then had to scrub it twice with Clorox to get it presentable enough for his taste.

It's nothing fancy, but it is quite a home away from home. It is equipped with a TV, CD player, shower, and sleeping quarters. It has seen a lot of good times and happy days since Roberts became its proud owner, and a big step up from the plywood-covered, bunk-laden pickup he and Smith used to use as their mobile home.

"The atmosphere, the carrying on and talking . . . that's the fun of it," Roberts said. "We've got a good buddy, Delbert McCoy, who meets us a lot, and we really look forward to the whole thing. We'll go someplace like Sam's Club and load up on drinks and chips and whatever else, and we'll chip in to buy a pig—$20 apiece or whatever—to cook for Saturday night. Sometimes Delbert will call me a month ahead of time and ask, 'What do you want me to bring?'

"We always bring horseshoes with us. We'll pitch horseshoes if we've got a place that's got room for it. If it's raining, we'll stay inside and play cards or arm wrestle. We'll sit around a campfire and tell stories and jokes—nothing out of line, just good, clean fun."

Aside from the pork—chopped or sliced, your choice—there's

always a big pot of slow-cooked beans and other trimmings. If pork doesn't suit your fancy, well, grab a piece of chicken or venison off the portable cooker. They've even had clams as the main course. No matter what is prepared, it seems, it's of a quality that makes a man lift his eyes to the heavens and praise God for taste buds.

"I don't know why, but everything tastes better when it's cooked outside," Roberts said.

The scrumptious scent has a hypnotic effect on all who wander by when Smith or Roberts are tending the grill. The more, the merrier is the motto when court is held in their campground, and drivers Kenny Wallace, Sterling Marlin, and Jimmy Spencer have been among the number lured to dine by the aroma. Old-timers such as Hall of Fame Busch Series champ Sam Ard and "Big" John Sears supped with Roberts and Smith, as have relative newcomers such as Buckshot Jones.

To hear Spencer tell it, turning down an invitation to break bread with Roberts, Smith et al., wasn't an option.

"My dad's good friend had a motorhome down in the infield at Rockingham one time," Spencer said, "and we went down there to see it. Martin and Jack and their friends saw us and said, 'Hey, man, how 'bout some barbecue?' I said, 'As good as that stuff smells, you bet.'"

Spencer didn't simply take, he also gave back in the spirit of fellowship.

"One night there was a fellow from Fredericksburg, Virginia, who had stopped by and had cancer," Roberts said. "Spencer give him a real nice racing jacket."

Wallace, accompanied by his mother and his wife, couldn't resist the temptation. Roberts remembers the young driver plopping down on the ground and digging into a plate of pork barbecue and chicken. "Man, this is like heaven," he muttered between bites.

From left, Delbert McCoy, driver Kenny Wallace, and Martin Roberts as Kenny chows down on some home cooking in the infield at Rockingham. Martin Roberts

After dinner, the entertainment consists of singing, and sometimes dancing, to familiar tunes. There's always a guitar or banjo waiting to be plucked, and they don't stay idle for long.

That wasn't, of course, the extent of the entertainment. Roberts can't begin to guess how many amateur wet T-shirt contests he's stumbled across while walking the campgrounds and speedway infields he's visited. And there's the tattooed man with a python around his neck, and streakers, male and female.

It's not exactly a freak show, but it can be quite a shock to the uninitiated. Roberts's girlfriend of close to a decade, Jenny Klosner, is a native of Queens, New York. She was as green as green gets the first time she accompanied Roberts to a race.

"They cranked up a car, and I almost had to catch her, she jumped so bad. But she got into it real good," he said.

"I told her once, 'I'll be back after a while.' She had something to read there in the camper and the TV, so I knew she had something to entertain herself with. Well, I got carried away talking to folks, you know, and when I finally got back she was fussing, 'I didn't come over here to be by myself.' I opened the door and told her, 'Hell, you ain't alone—there's thousands of people out here.' And that made her madder."

Most of the time, Roberts is on everyone's good side. He's a soft touch for a struggling racer who needs a helping hand from time to time. Many is the time he's reached into his pocket for $500 to buy a local driver a set of new tires. Sometimes the cost is much, much steeper.

In 1990 former Busch champion Tommy Ellis was sponsorless and needed a trailer to haul his race car. Roberts spent $13,000 and bought him one. Months later, Ellis won the first NASCAR Busch Series race at New Hampshire International Speedway, and soon after he eventually sold his equipment to another team owner, a check for $13,500 showed up in Roberts's mailbox.

Roberts has gradually cut back on his trips to Winston Cup races because of skyrocketing ticket prices. He'll still make his annual trip to SpeedWeeks in Daytona each February, but now he watches the qualifying races and goes home, unwilling to fork over $150 for seats at the Daytona 500.

"That's just one thing I'd like to see change about NASCAR:

ticket prices," he said, climbing aboard his soapbox. "I don't think there ought to be provisionals [starting positions]. If you're not fast enough to make the field, you ought to go home; I don't care who you are or how many championships you've won. I don't think a man ought to get credit for winning if it turns out his car's illegal. If you cheat, you ain't won. I don't like these multicar teams, either; they just make it too hard on the little guys like Dave Marcis and Brett Bodine and folks like that. And I think the NASCAR banquet ought to be in Charlotte, not New York, and the fans ought to be able to go to it."

As NASCAR grows, it is, Roberts and Smith fear, losing its most loyal, long-term fans. Fans have frequently mixed with the drivers and crews after races, but that's almost impossible in the 21st century. Speedways such as North Wilkesboro have vanished from the NASCAR schedule, and the three short tracks that remain—Bristol, Richmond, and Martinsville—all accommodate between 75,000 and 160,000 fans.

Richard Petty, David Pearson, Bobby Allison—the stars of the late 1960s and early '70s when Martin Roberts and Jack Smith started traveling together—would gladly take the time to sign autographs for hundreds of fans after races in those days. The drivers and fans used to stay in the same motels, eat in the same restaurants, and build relationships that few other sports offered.

Now, with six-figure crowds easily the average, drivers can't, and don't, mingle with the fans. The drivers take refuge in six- and seven-figure motorhomes during race weekend, and when the race is over, they make a mad dash for helicopters and jets to spirit them home before the fans have hit the highway.

Spencer, for one, hates the ever-widening gap between drivers and fans, but that's in no small part because he is one who has taken time to get acquainted with the folks who have helped make him a wealthy man.

"I've gone to a lot of race tracks and met a lot of fans, but not like Martin and Jack and guys like that," Spencer said. "It's people like them who've been coming to Winston Cup races for 25 and 30 years that made this sport. We have a lot of new fans all over the United States, but these kind of people watched David Pearson, Richard Petty, Cale Yarborough, Junior Johnson, and those guys in the prime of their careers, and that's important. They know that when this sport was started a long, long time ago, there'd be maybe 10,000 people watching a race at a place like Rockingham, and now there are 70,000.

"They were happy I stopped over and I enjoyed it, too, because I got a chance to get closer to some really good guys."

That's a sentiment shared by Martin Roberts and Jack Smith about their racing version of the Welcome Wagon. Given a choice of having riches or friends, "friends" is their immediate response. They've helped each other through some bad times, and built a lifetime of happy memories around a crackling campfire.

"If you've got one true friend, and I mean true friend," Smith said, "you're lucky."

"My daddy used to say you'll have three good friends in your lifetime," Roberts said. "I've got a lot more than that."

INDEX

ABOUT THE EDITOR

Monte Dutton is the motorsports writer at the *Gaston Gazette* in Gastonia, North Carolina. His work regularly appears in the weekly trade papers *FasTrack*, of Gastonia, North Carolina, and *Area Auto Racing News*, of Trenton, New Jersey, and on the Go-Carolinas and RacingOne web sites. Dutton's stories have also appeared in a wide variety of publications, including *TV Guide, Details, Heartland USA, Racing Milestones, Auto Racing Digest, Winston Cup Illustrated*, and *Inside NASCAR*. He was the winner of the Eastern Motorsports Press Association's Writer of the Year award for 1999. Monte Dutton is a graduate of Furman University (class of 1980) and lives in Clinton, South Carolina.